Cats Are People, Too

A Collection of Cat Cartoons to Curl up With

AND THEY LIVED HAPPILY EVER AFTER AND AFTER AND AFTER AND AFTER AND AFTER AND AFTER AND AFTER AND AFTER AND AFTER.
FELINE FAIRY TALES
DIST. BY CREATORS | SPEEDBUMP.COM

DAVE COVERLY

Christy Ottaviano Books

SQUARE FISH NEW YORK

SQUARE
FISH

An imprint of Macmillan Publishing Group, LLC
120 Broadway, New York, NY 10271

Library of Congress Cataloging-in-Publication Data
Names: Coverly, Dave, author.
Title: Cats are people, too : a collection of silly cat cartoons / Dave Coverly.
Description: First edition. | New York, NY : Square Fish, an imprint of Macmillan Publishing
Group, LLC, [2020] | "Christy Ottaviano Books."
Identifiers: LCCN 2019018050 | ISBN 9781250186287 (trade paper : alk. paper)
Subjects: LCSH: Cats—Comic books, strips, etc. | Caricatures and cartoons—United States. |
American wit and humor, Pictorial.
Classification: LCC SF445.5 .C68 2020 | DDC 636.8—dc23
LC record available at https://lccn.loc.gov/2019018050

Our books may be purchased in bulk for promotional, educational, or business use. Please
contact your local bookseller or the Macmillan Corporate and Premium Sales Department at
(800) 221-7945 ext. 5442 or by email at MacmillanSpecialMarkets@macmillan.com.

First edition, 2020

Square Fish logo designed by Filomena Tuosto

Printed in China by 1010 Printing International Limited, North Point, Hong Kong

1 3 5 7 9 10 8 6 4 2

Dedicated to the Humane Society and all its local branches, especially
the Humane Society of Huron Valley and the Kalamazoo Humane Society,
as well as all rescue organizations and clinics that devote themselves
to the welfare of our furry family members.

Many thanks to Pete Kaminski for his assistance coloring many
of these cartoons, and to Christy Ottaviano for literally
everything else in this book.

"Way down deep, we're all motivated by the same urges. Cats just have the courage to live by them."

—Jim Davis

CONTENTS

INTRODUCTION

Okay, about the book title: I know cats aren't actually people, too. But I think for many of us, a cat is the animal we aspire to be most like: graceful, independent, languid but quick, elegant, purposeful. Cats are cool, cats are hep, as the jazz moniker goes. And who hasn't had a moment when retractable claws would have come in handy?

I grew up with dogs and have pretty much always had a dog in my house, so I guess that makes me a "dog person." Yet I love cats and, to be honest, they're probably more interesting to observe (no offense to my fellow dog lovers). They keep their cards closer to their chest, making them seem more mysterious, as though plans are being plotted, distances are being measured, scenarios are being formulated. A mad dash into another room for no apparent reason feels like a reaction to stimuli invisible to everyone but the cat. It confirms its quiet, private evaluation. What did it see? Should you be worried? If your cat could talk, would it scream "RUN!" every time it did that? I doubt it—it's too cool for screaming.

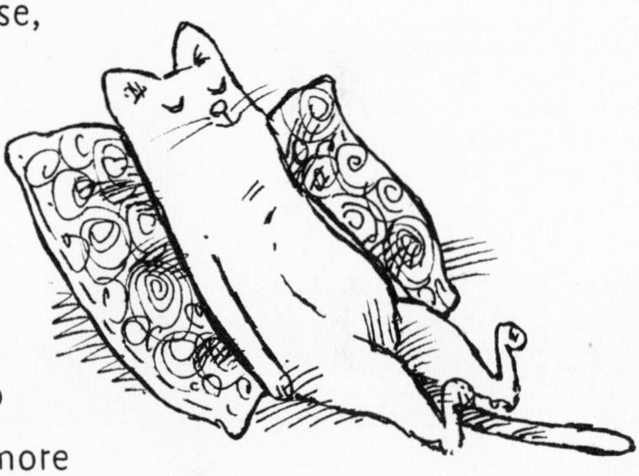

In any case, I, for one, am thankful cats can't scream at us. That would freak me right out.

It's also true that cats are generally confident creatures, and if you want to get close to one, you have to earn the privilege. I can respect that. Cats carry their autonomy well.

I did live with a cat, very briefly, in an apartment during my senior year of college. It was my roommate's cat, which he never did get around to naming. Halfway through the school year, my roommate moved out due to personal issues, but the cat stayed. It was a very sweet cat, but still fairly feral, having been adopted off the streets of Ypsilanti, Michigan, and was always looking to run away. It eventually succeeded, but during our time together, it would often curl up next to me on the couch in the morning, when I would eat Pop-Tarts and watch *Inspector Gadget* before heading off to work at the school bookstore.

All cats can jump, of course, but this cat was the Dick Fosbury* of felines. The first night after my roommate moved out, I was asleep on the top bunk of our bed, with my feet hanging off the end of the mattress. You can guess the rest. I woke up to the sound of screaming. It was a movie scream, a primal shriek that I didn't even realize was coming from me. The cat had jumped nearly six feet and was dangling by its claws from my big toe. Just imagine the worst possible "Hang in There, Baby" motivational poster and you'll get the picture.

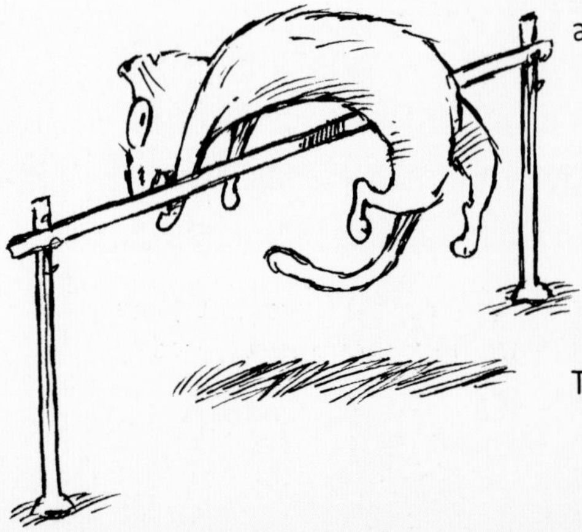

The next night, my bandaged toe

and I moved to the bottom bunk, where the cat slept with me for the rest of the year.

The cartoons in this book are my own mad dashes into the minds of cats and cat people. And because some of my greatest friends happen to be not only artistic geniuses but also cat people, I've asked a few of them to contribute a drawing and a few words about their felines. Their pieces are astonishing, beautiful, and funny, and all of them reflect a deep bond that every pet lover will immediately recognize. Heartfelt thanks to Nick Galifianakis, Genevieve Godbout, Laurie Keller, Hilary Price, Jay Fosgitt, and Rick Kirkman. I'm in awe of all of them.

DAVE COVERLY

*Winner of the gold medal at the '68 Olympics in the high jump, and inventor of the famed "Fosbury flop," the back-first technique still used by high jumpers today.

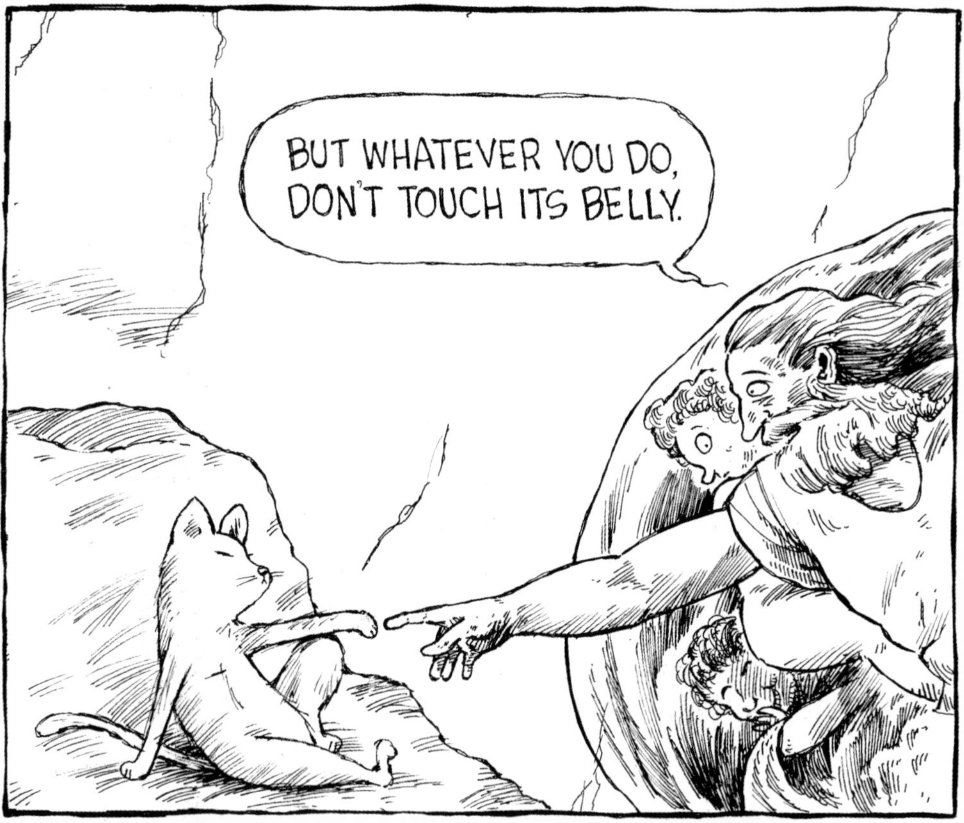
BUT WHATEVER YOU DO, DON'T TOUCH ITS BELLY.

The Creation Story of the Cat

In the beginning—Day One—God created the heavens, earth, light, and six personal assistants, because, as any good boss knows, the ability to delegate is an essential skill.

And so, on Day Two, "high energy" Kelly made the sky, land, seas, and plants. Done before nightfall, Kelly still had time to sneak in some hot yoga and a nonalcoholic margarita.

Day Three was assigned to Ines, who was often caught staring into space. Except space hadn't been created yet, so Ines struck God as perfect for the job. It was slow going, and God had to pop in often to check on progress. But just before midnight, there was a great unveiling of the sun, moon, stars, and other planets, as well as some weird black holes that felt like afterthoughts, but it was getting late, so whatever.

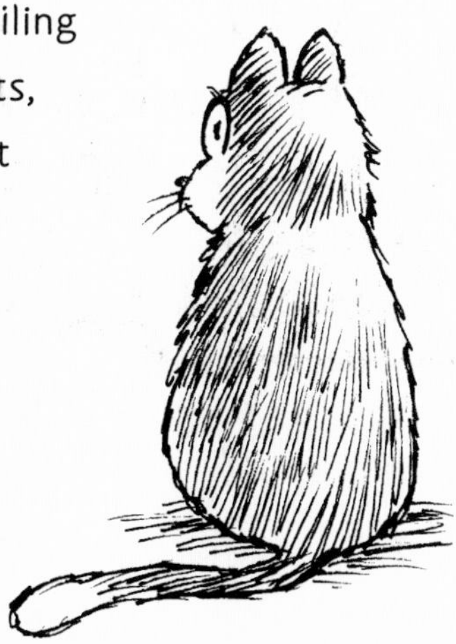

On Day Four, Otto—visibly annoyed to have been passed over for the Sky and Seas account because it would have looked great on a resume—was tasked with the fish and the birds.

In a fit of overcompensation, Otto filled the sea with every crazy design that came to mind. God told Otto to maybe dial it back a bit with the birds, but as a compromise allowed Otto to go bonkers with the color palette.

Artist Leona was given free rein with land animals on Day Five, with the caveat that maybe none of the designs should be as weird as a transparent fish with a built-in light bulb hanging over its forehead because, really, that thing was just plain nuts.

On Day Six, it was agreed that there was only one thing missing: comic relief. All eyes turned to Bob, whose hand was in an armpit making farting noises. And so humans came to be.

On Day Seven, God decreed that they all rest. At that moment, Henrik wandered in with a decaf latte, extra shot, lots of cream.

"Did I miss anything?" he yawned, adjusting a pair of sunglasses.

God's eyes rolled. "You missed literally everything. Every. Thing. Where have you been?"

Henrik set down the latte. "Sleeping. It was so weird, but you made that light beam and I just had to curl up in it and get some zzz's. Then I was wide awake all night, wandering around looking for things to do."

"Well, we already wrapped up this big shebang, but I still need to evaluate you." God put a finger on Henrik's chest for emphasis. Henrik instinctively grabbed God's finger and bit it.

"Hey, don't act like you're in charge here!"

Henrik just stared at God, unblinking. Then he turned his head and gacked up a hair ball.

"We're in a time crunch," God continued, "so why don't you just make one more animal and we'll call it a week."

"Yeah, okay, if I feel like it. Whatcha got in mind?"

"Just create what you know, something from your heart."

Henrik turned to the latte and knocked it over, then curled up on God's giant lap.

"Cool," Henrik purred as his eyes closed. "I think I have an idea."

CHAPTER 1

DOMESTI-CAT-ED

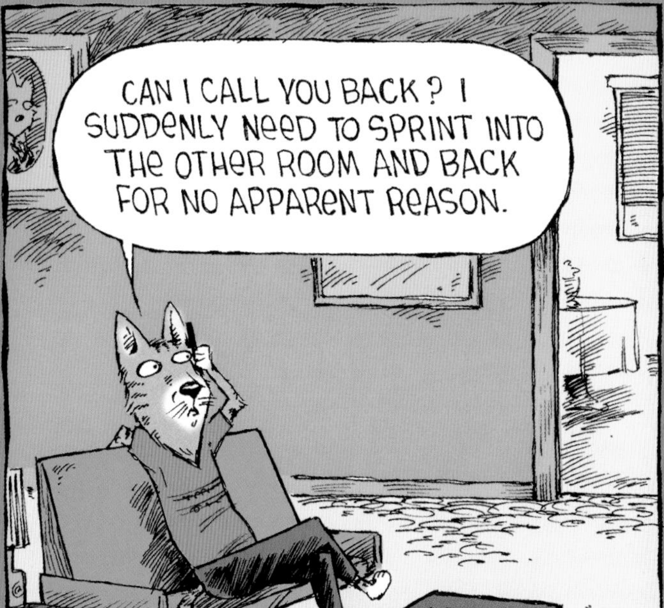
CAN I CALL YOU BACK? I SUDDENLY NEED TO SPRINT INTO THE OTHER ROOM AND BACK FOR NO APPARENT REASON.
12-28
©2017
COVERLY
SPEEDBUMP.com
DIST. BY CREATORS

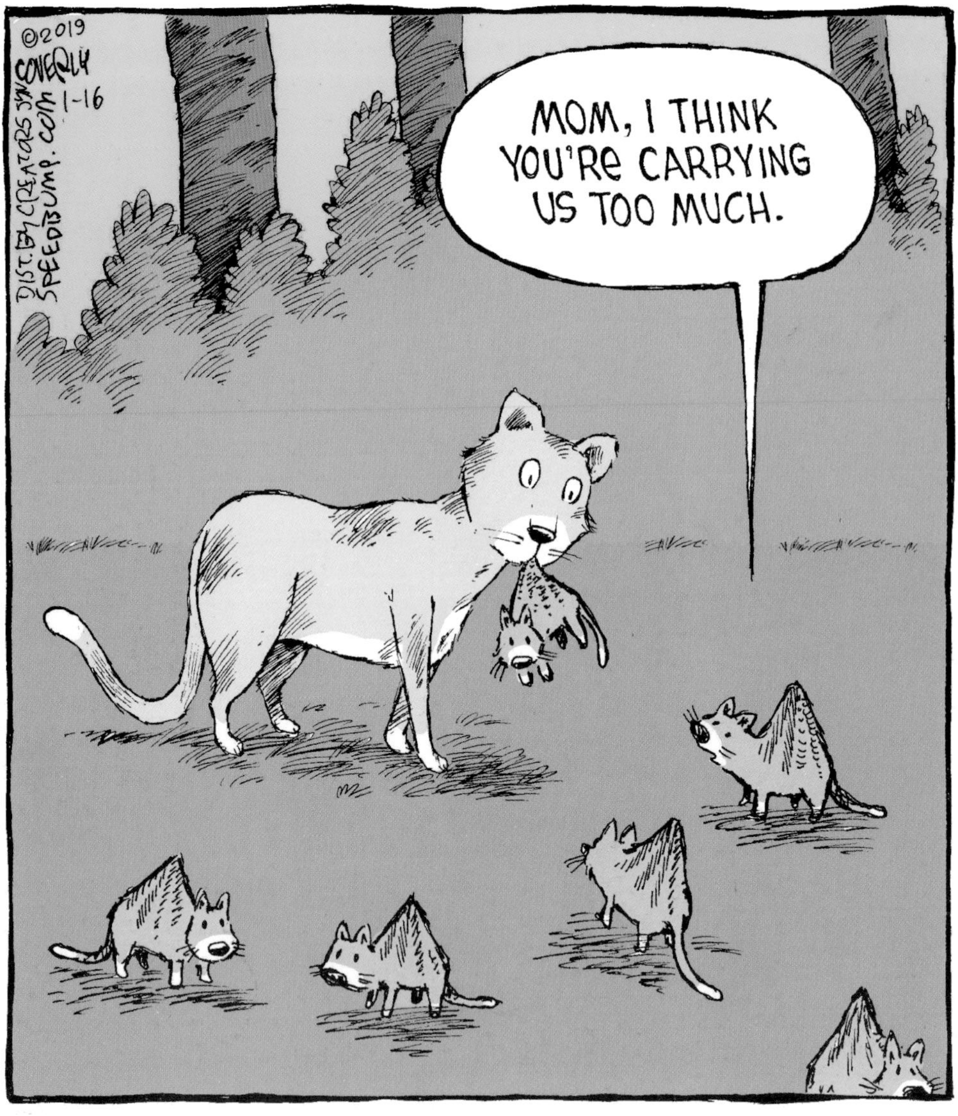
©2019
COVERLY
1-16
DIST. BY CREATORS SYN.
SPEEDBUMP.COM
MOM, I THINK YOU'RE CARRYING US TOO MUCH.

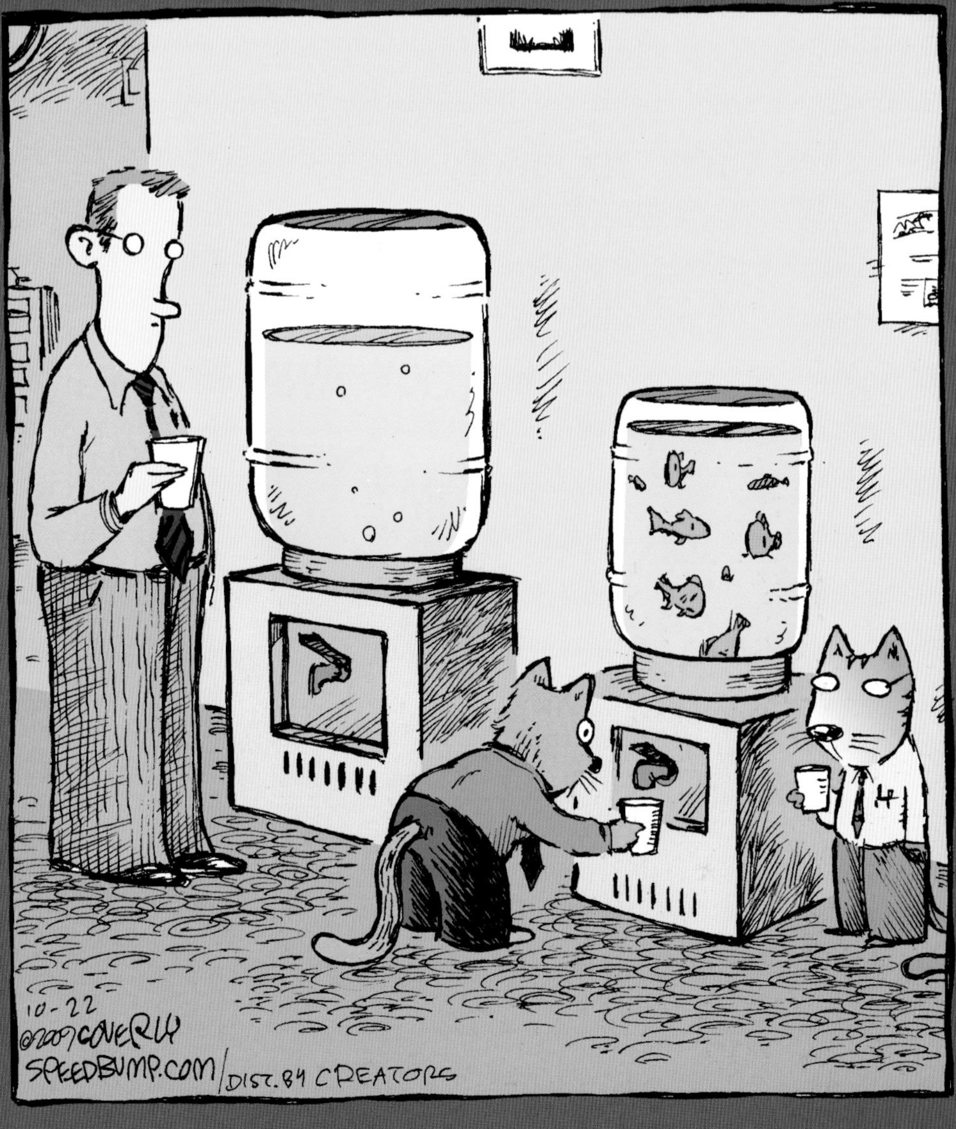
10-22
©2009 COVERLY
SPEEDBUMP.COM/DIST. BY CREATORS

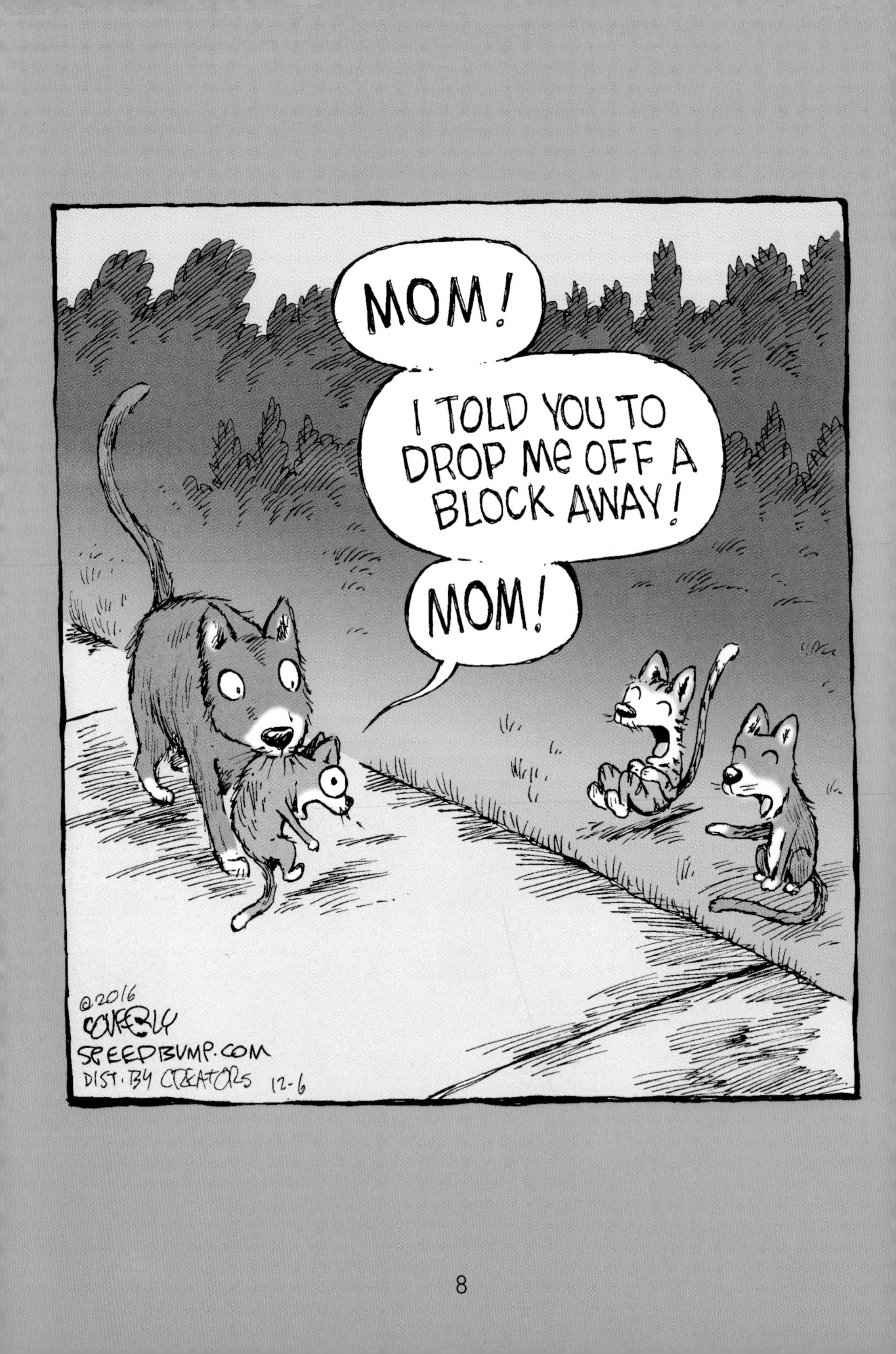
MOM!
I TOLD YOU TO DROP ME OFF A BLOCK AWAY!
MOM!
©2016 COVERLY
SPEEDBUMP.COM
DIST. BY CREATORS 12-6

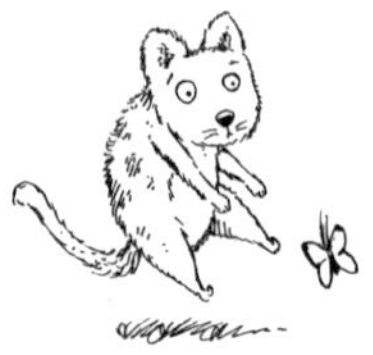

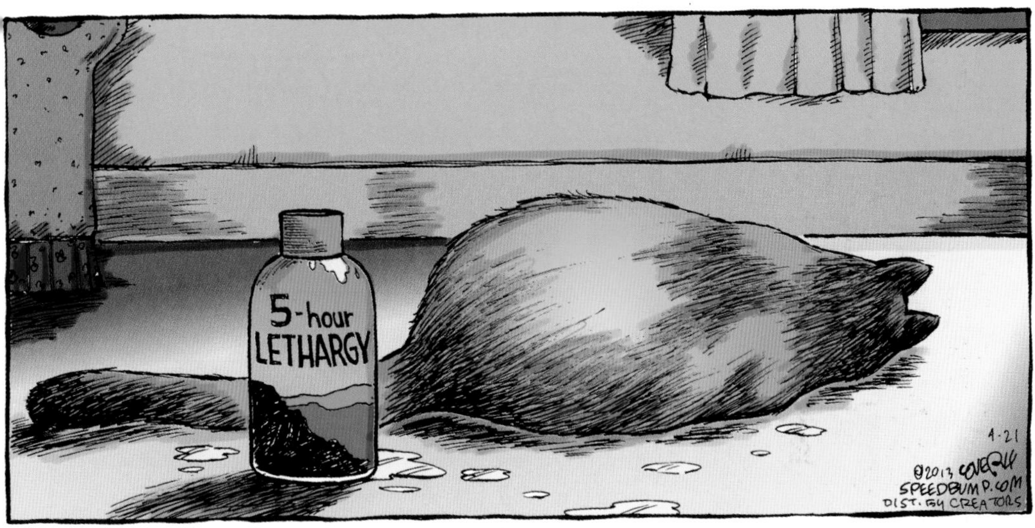
5-hour
LETHARGY
4-21
©2013 COVERLY
SPEEDBUMP.COM
DIST. BY CREATORS

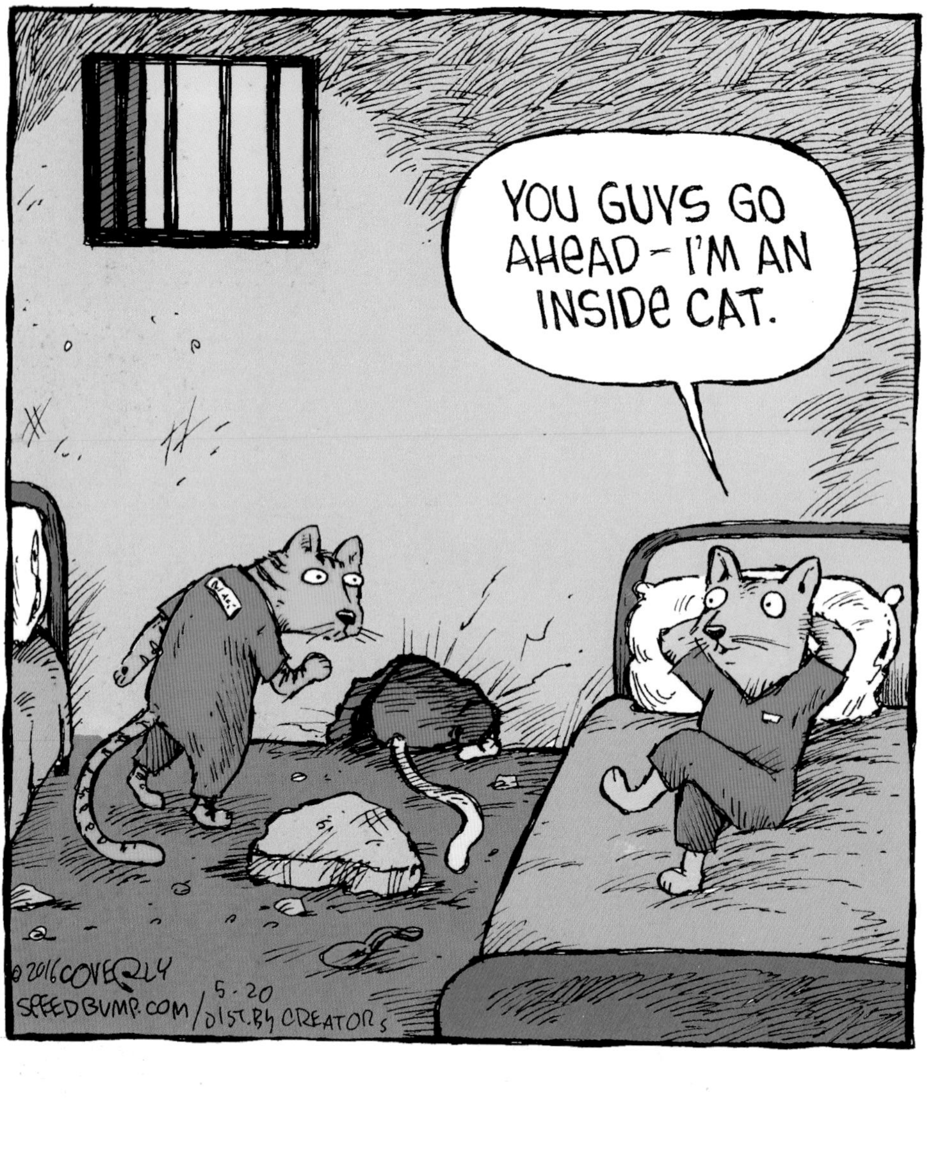
YOU GUYS GO AHEAD – I'M AN INSIDE CAT.
© 2016 COVERLY
SPEEDBUMP.COM / DIST. BY CREATORS
5-20

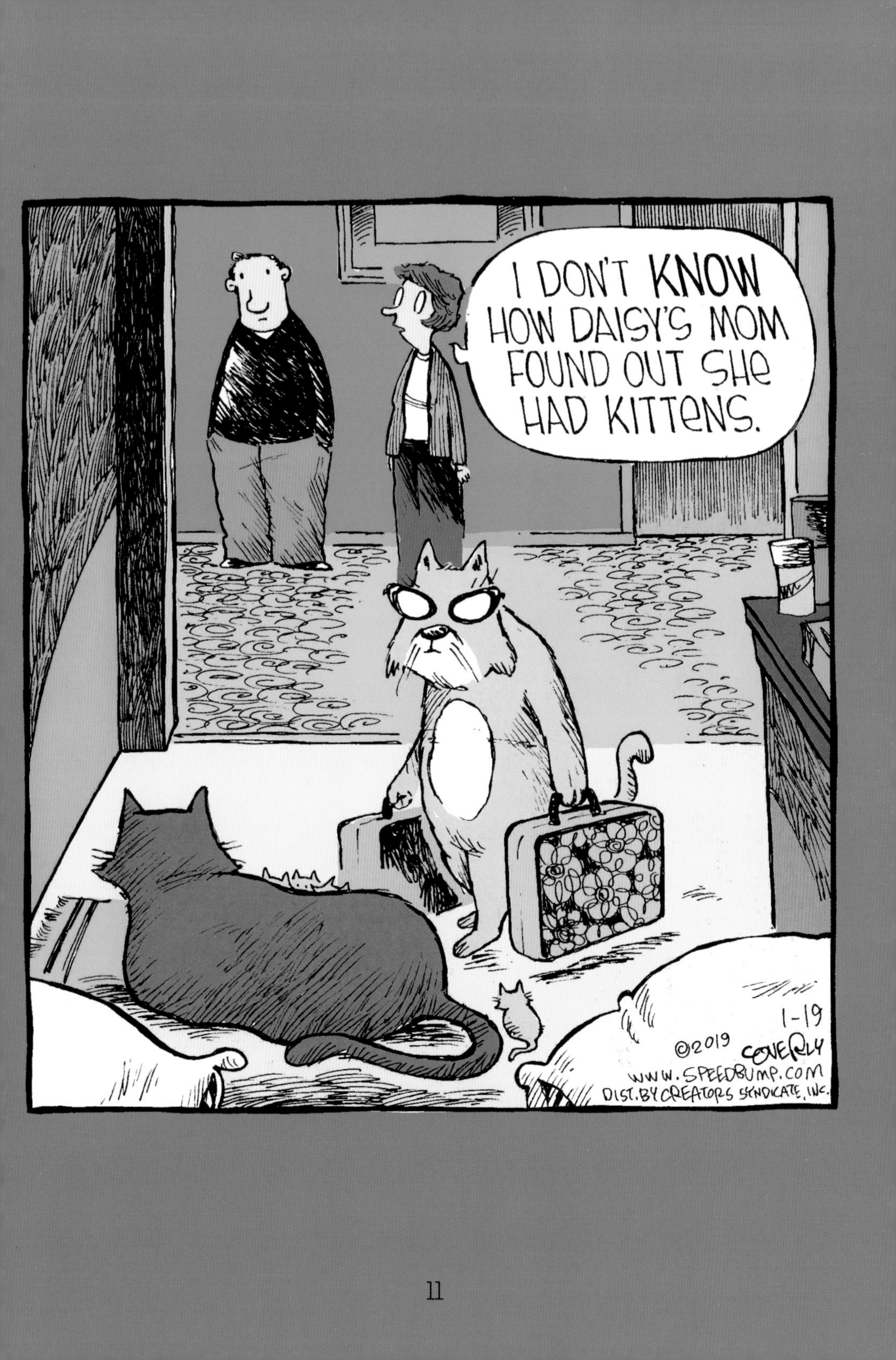
I DON'T KNOW HOW DAISY'S MOM FOUND OUT SHE HAD KITTENS.
1-19
©2019 COVERLY
WWW.SPEEDBUMP.COM
DIST. BY CREATORS SYNDICATE, INC.

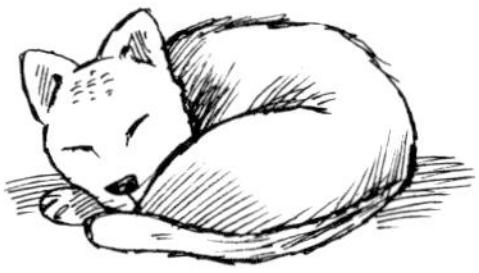

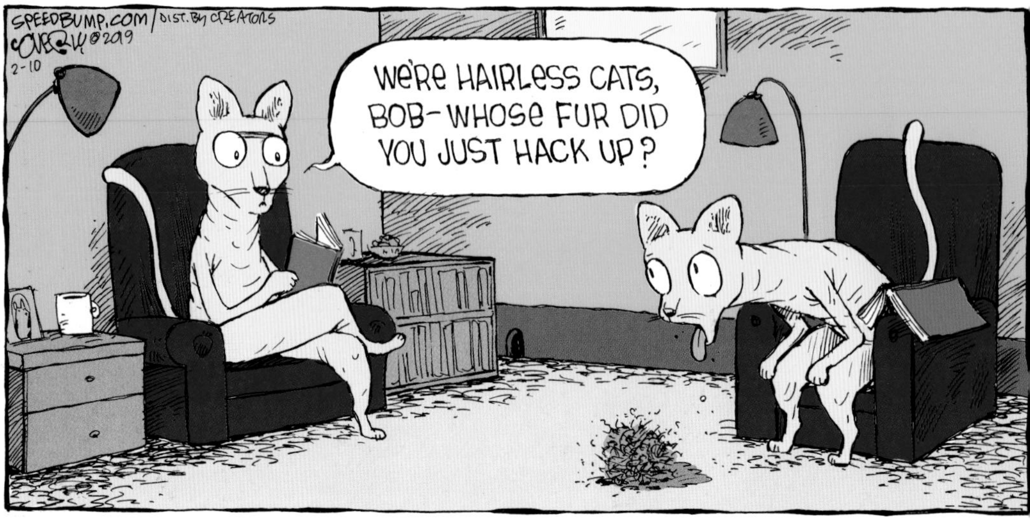
SPEEDBUMP.COM / DIST. BY CREATORS
COVERLY ©2019
2-10
WE'RE HAIRLESS CATS, BOB— WHOSE FUR DID YOU JUST HACK UP?

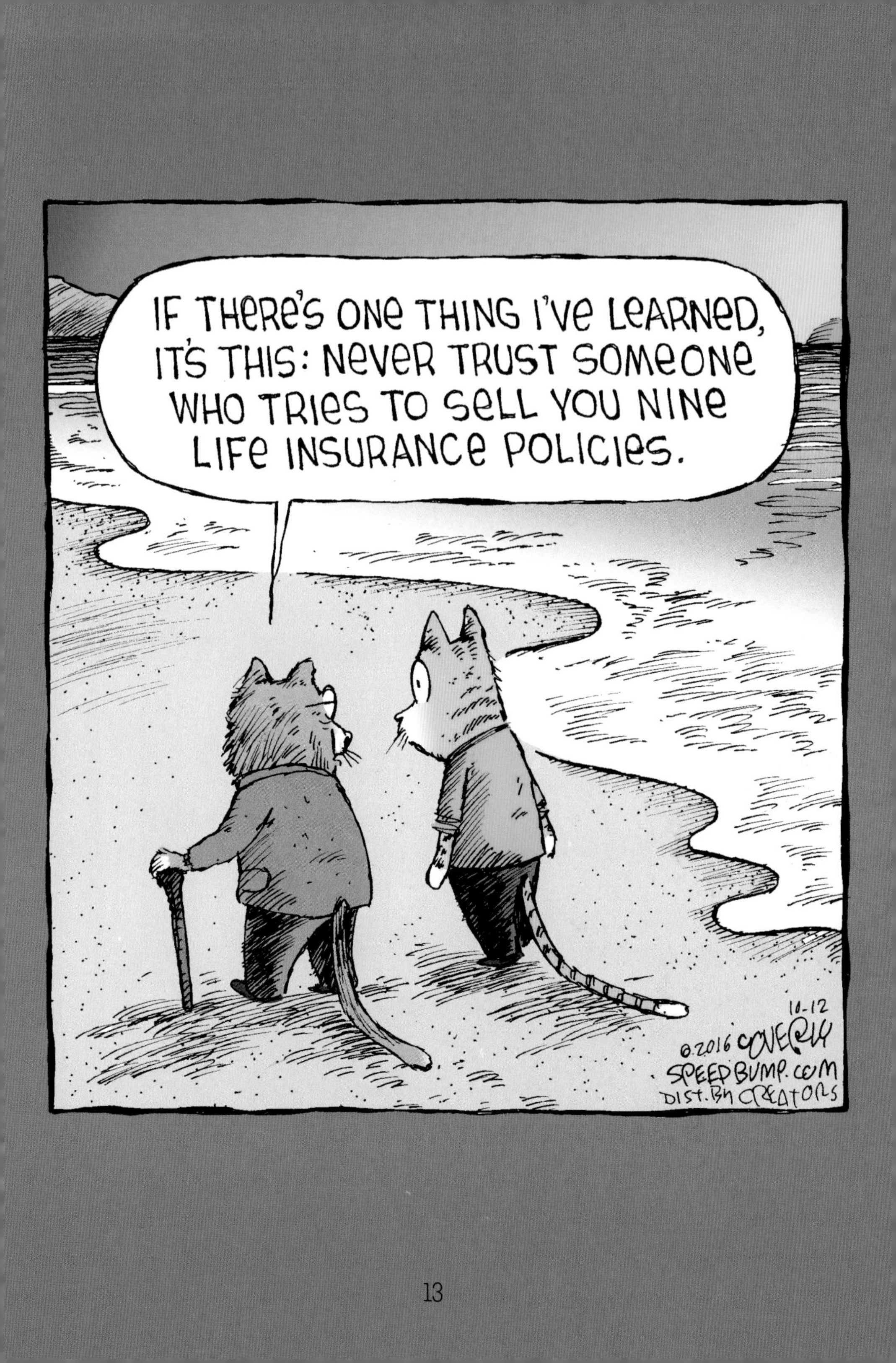
IF THERE'S ONE THING I'VE LEARNED, IT'S THIS: NEVER TRUST SOMEONE WHO TRIES TO SELL YOU NINE LIFE INSURANCE POLICIES.
10-12
©2016 COVERLY
SPEEDBUMP.COM
DIST. BY CREATORS

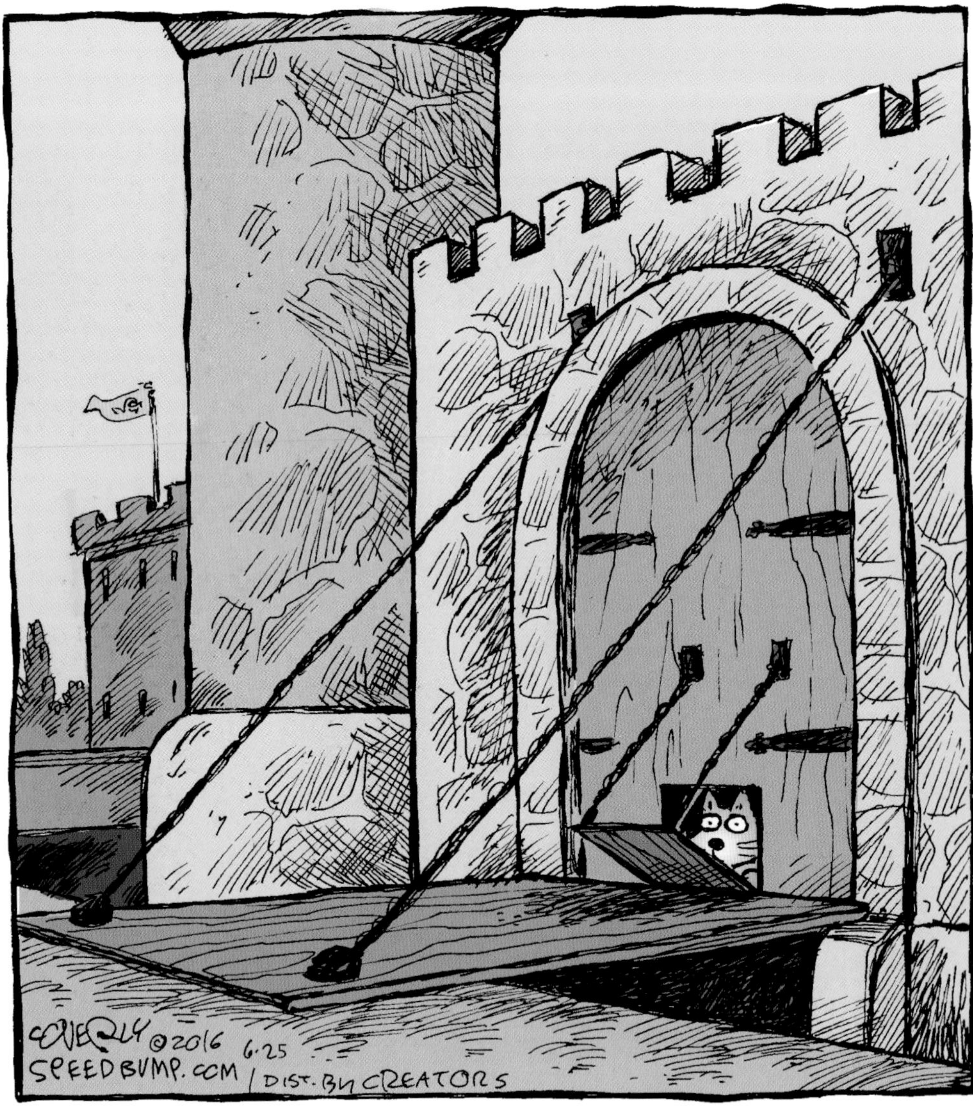
COVERLY ©2016 6.25
SPEEDBUMP.COM / DIST. BY CREATORS

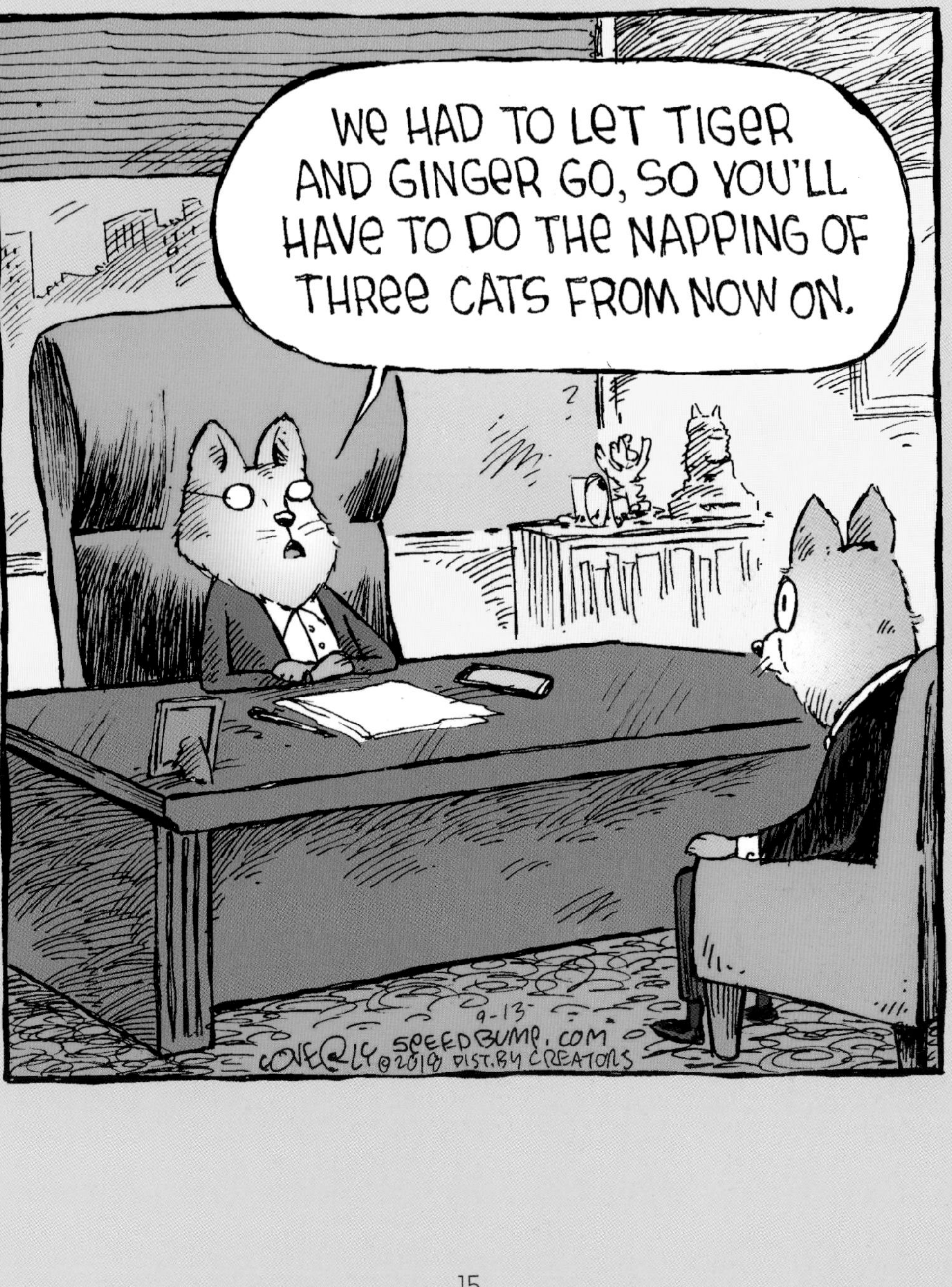
WE HAD TO LET TIGER AND GINGER GO, SO YOU'LL HAVE TO DO THE NAPPING OF THREE CATS FROM NOW ON.
9-13
COVERLY SPEEDBUMP.COM ©2018 DIST. BY CREATORS

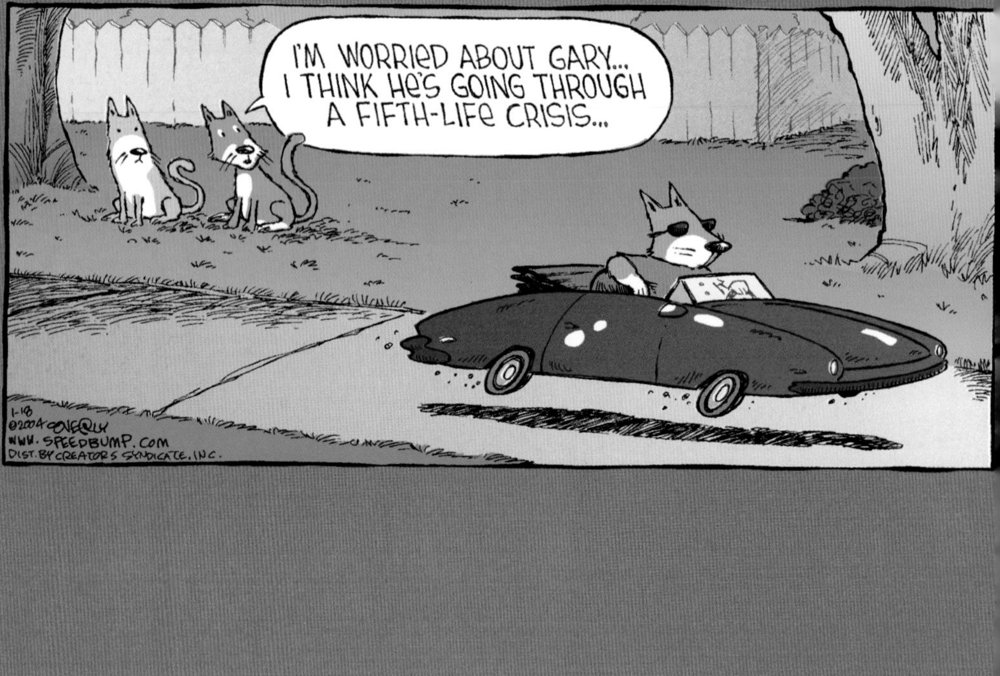
I'M WORRIED ABOUT GARY...
I THINK HE'S GOING THROUGH
A FIFTH-LIFE CRISIS...
1-18
©2004 COVERLY
WWW.SPEEDBUMP.COM
DIST. BY CREATORS SYNDICATE, INC.

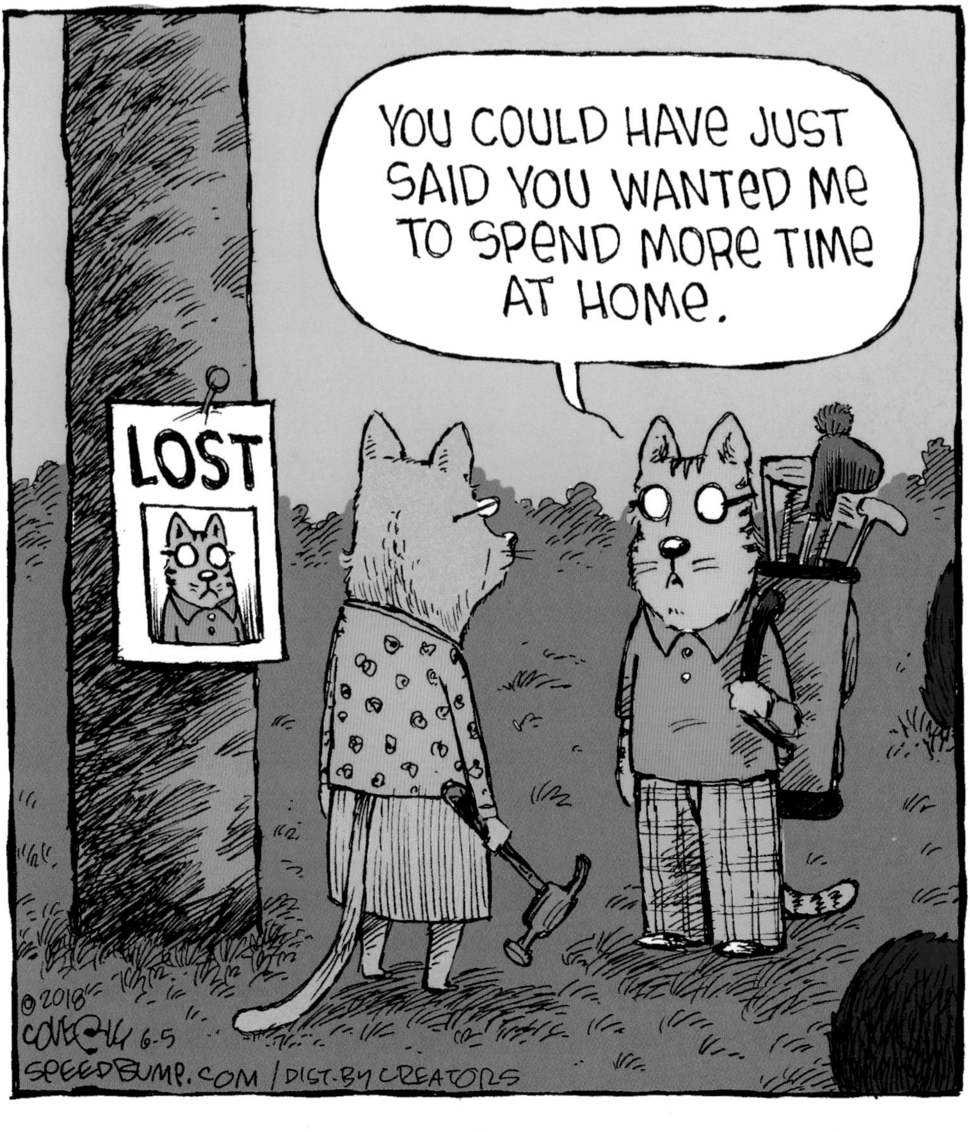
LOST
YOU COULD HAVE JUST SAID YOU WANTED ME TO SPEND MORE TIME AT HOME.
©2018 COVERLY 6-5
SPEEDBUMP.COM / DIST. BY CREATORS

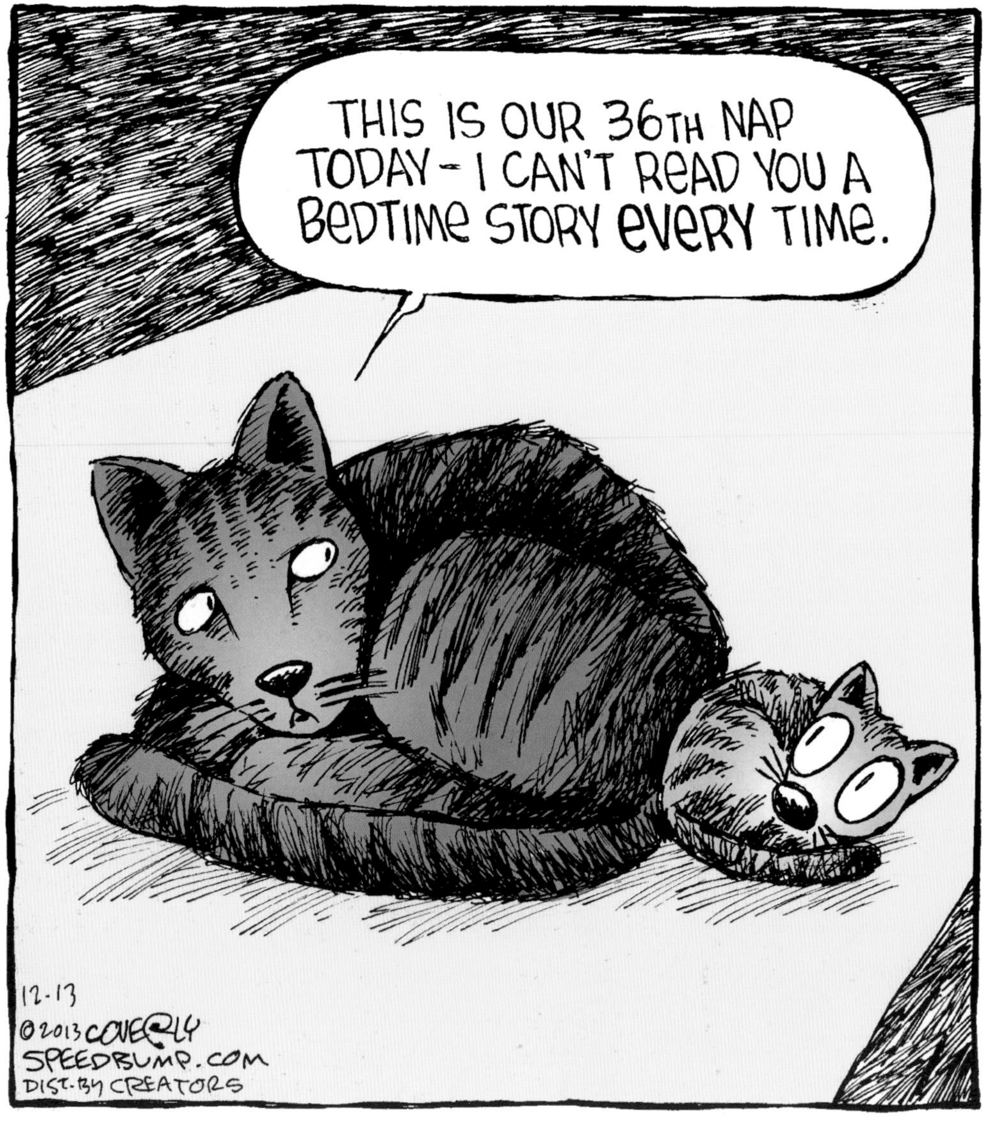
THIS IS OUR 36TH NAP TODAY - I CAN'T READ YOU A BEDTIME STORY EVERY TIME.
12-13
©2013 COVERLY
SPEEDBUMP.COM
DIST. BY CREATORS

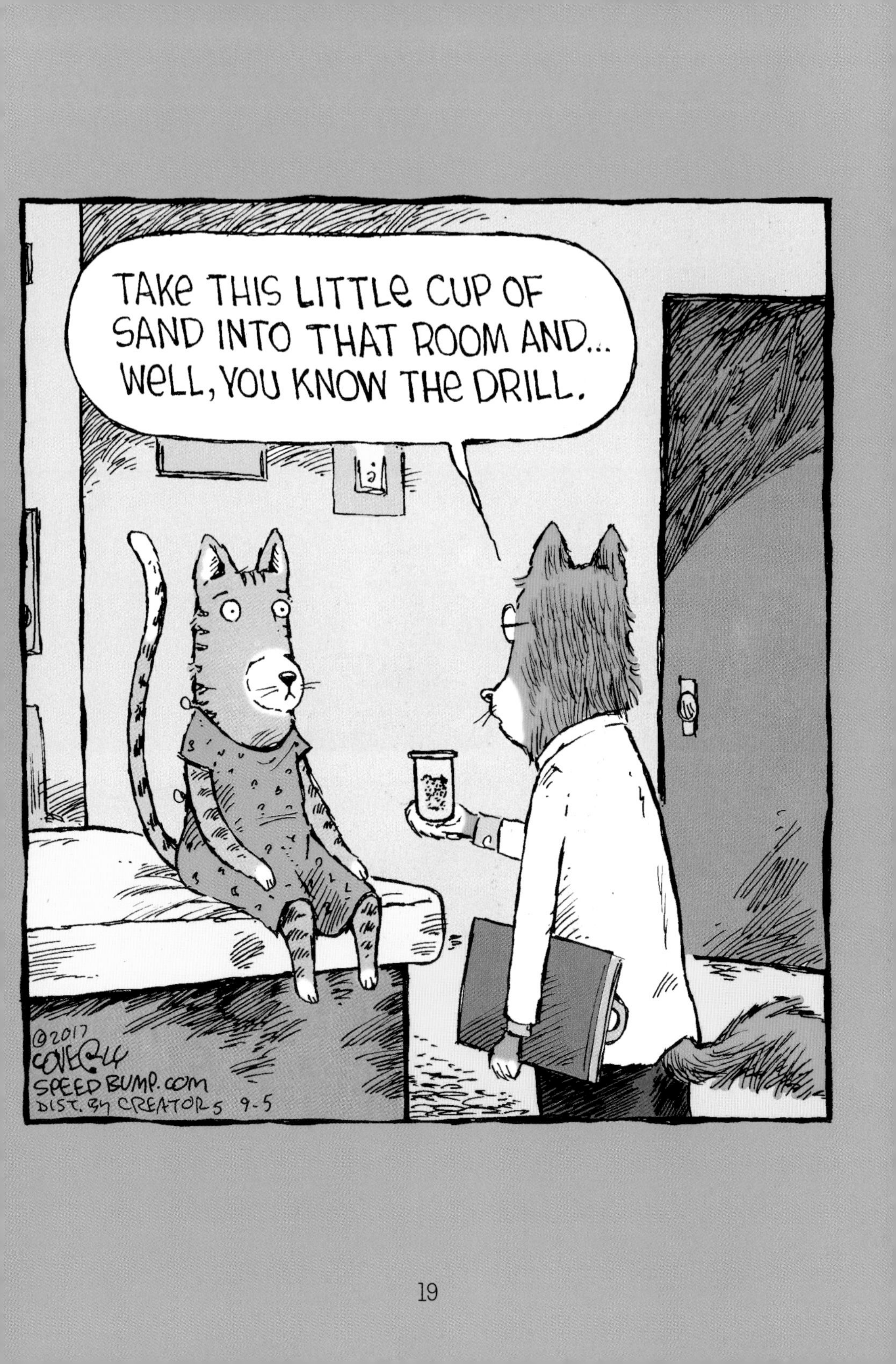
TAKE THIS LITTLE CUP OF SAND INTO THAT ROOM AND... WELL, YOU KNOW THE DRILL.
©2017 COVERLY SPEEDBUMP.COM DIST. BY CREATORS 9-5

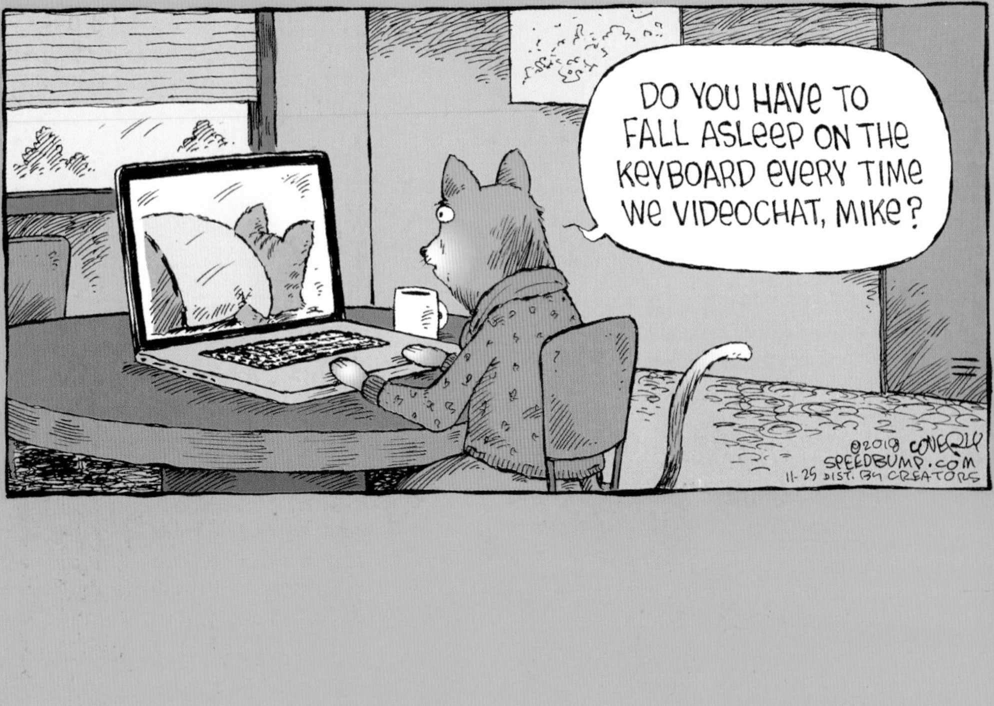
DO YOU HAVE TO FALL ASLEEP ON THE KEYBOARD EVERY TIME WE VIDEOCHAT, MIKE?
©2018 COVERLY
SPEEDBUMP.COM
11-25 DIST. BY CREATORS

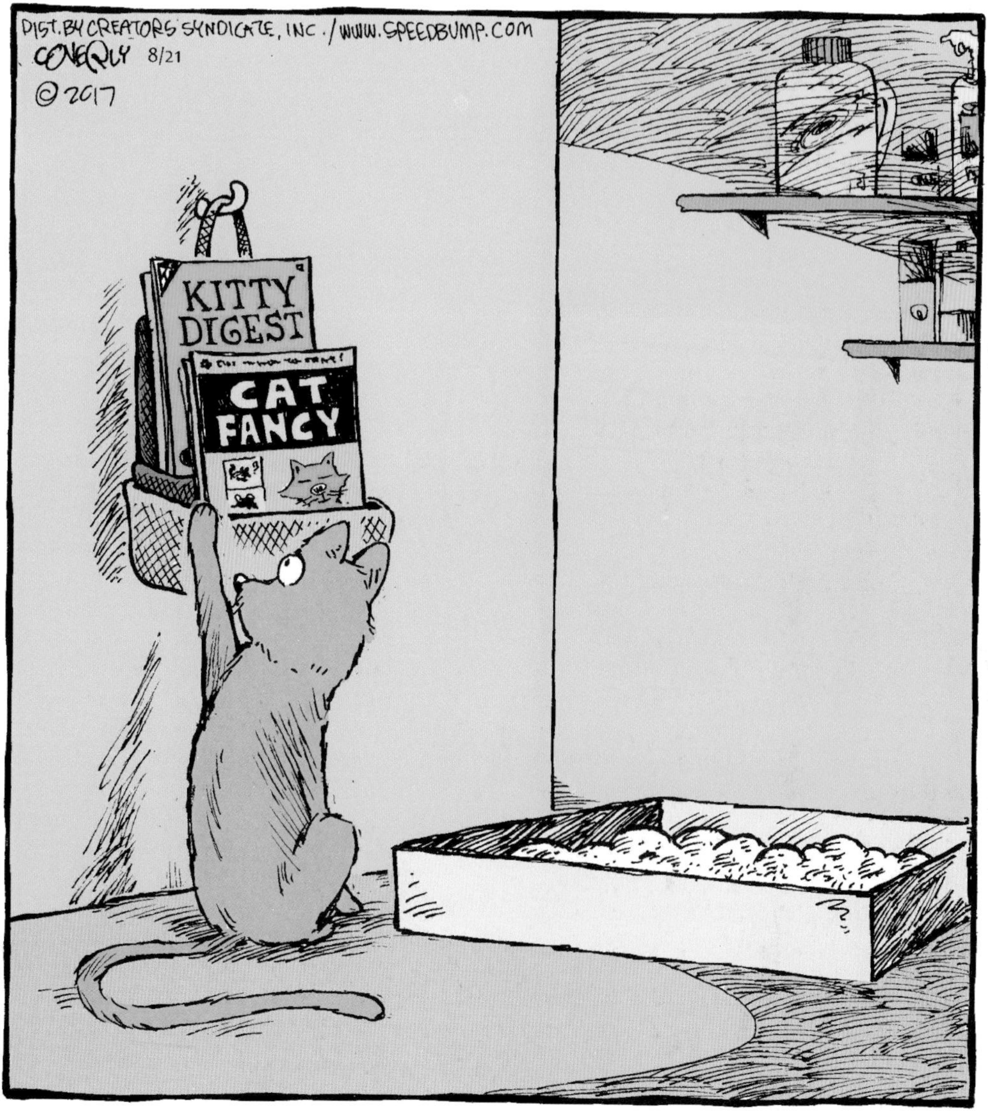
DIST. BY CREATORS SYNDICATE, INC. / WWW.SPEEDBUMP.COM
COVERLY 8/21
© 2017
KITTY DIGEST
CAT FANCY

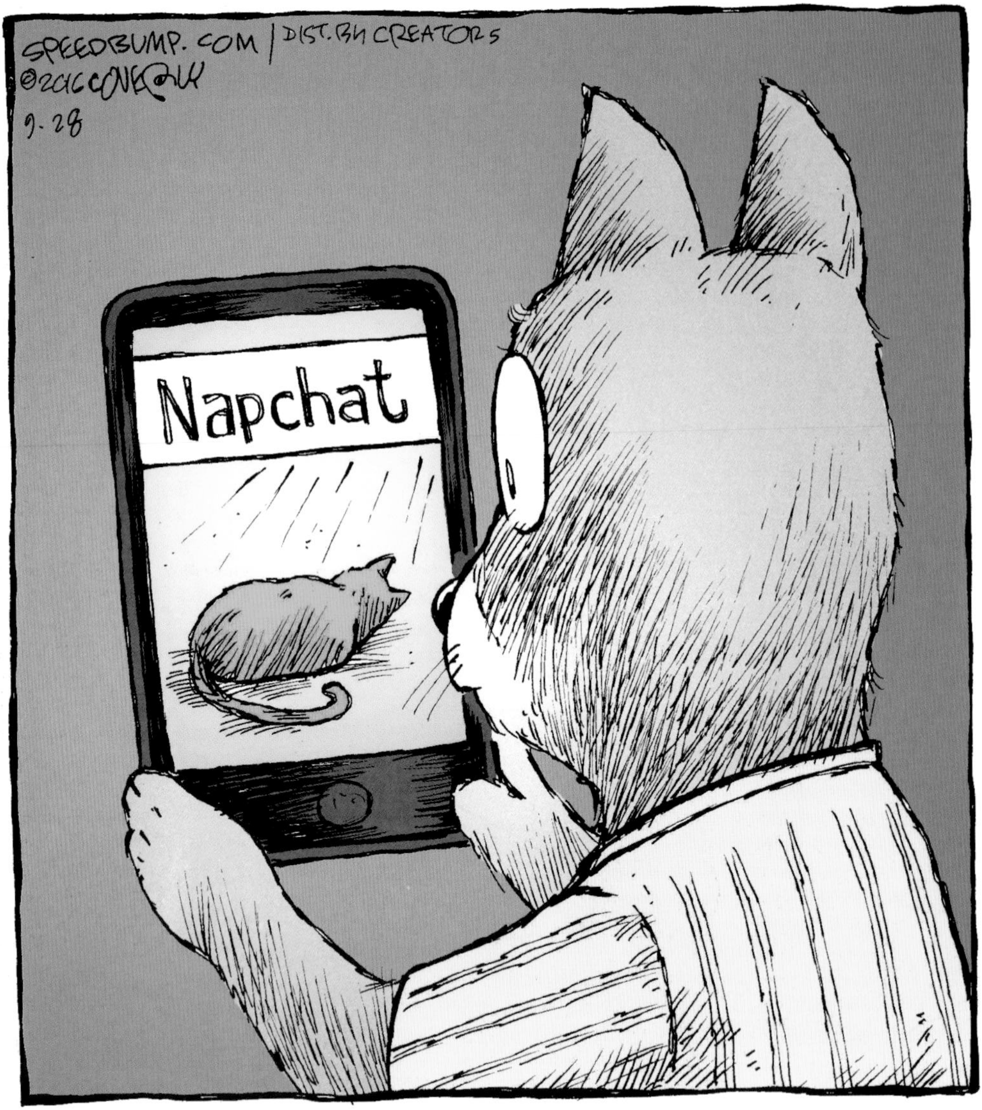
SPEEDBUMP.COM / DIST. BY CREATORS
©2016 COVERLY
9-28
Napchat

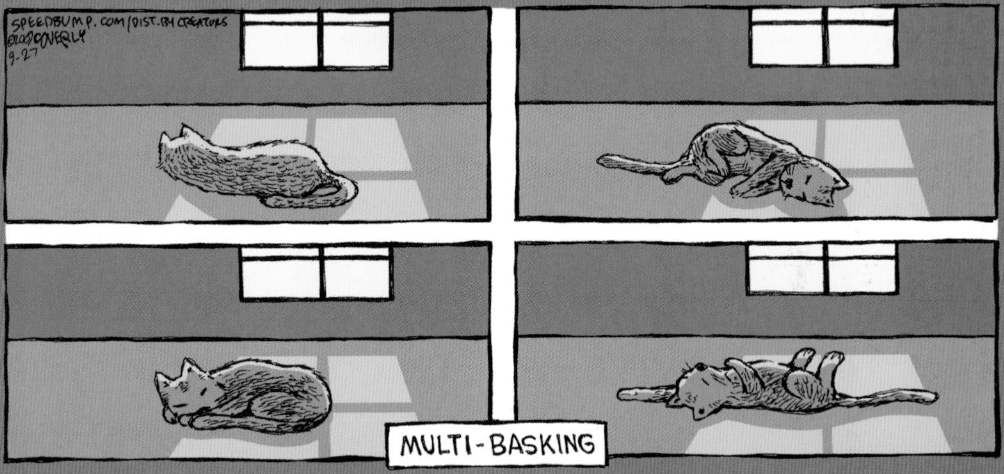
SPEEDBUMP.COM/DIST. BY CREATORS
9-27
MULTI-BASKING

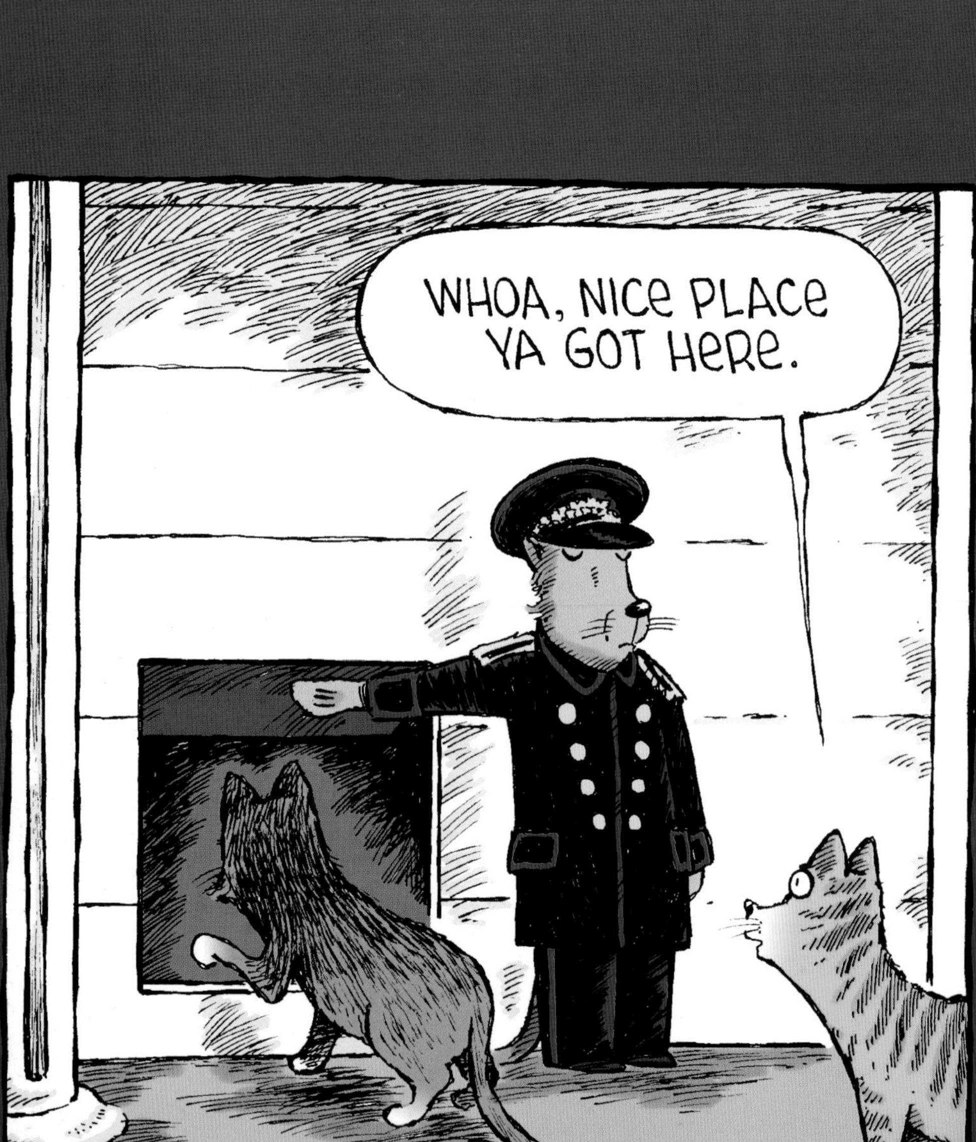
WHOA, NICE PLACE YA GOT HERE.
©2014 COVERLY 5-29
SPEEDBUMP.COM / DIST. BY CREATORS

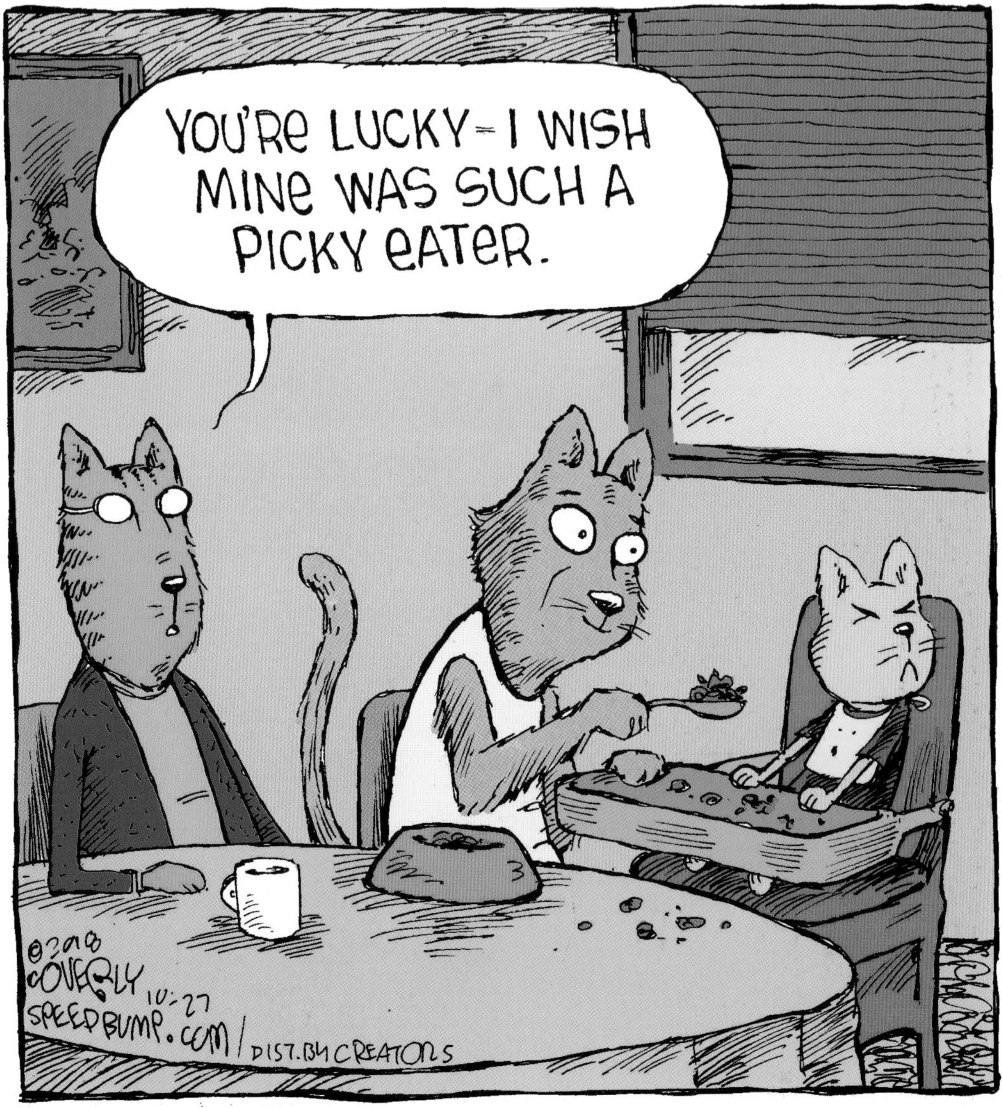
YOU'Re LUCKY- I WISH MINe WAS SUCH A PICKY eATeR.
©2018 COVERLY 10-27
SPEEDBUMP.COM / DIST. BY CREATORS

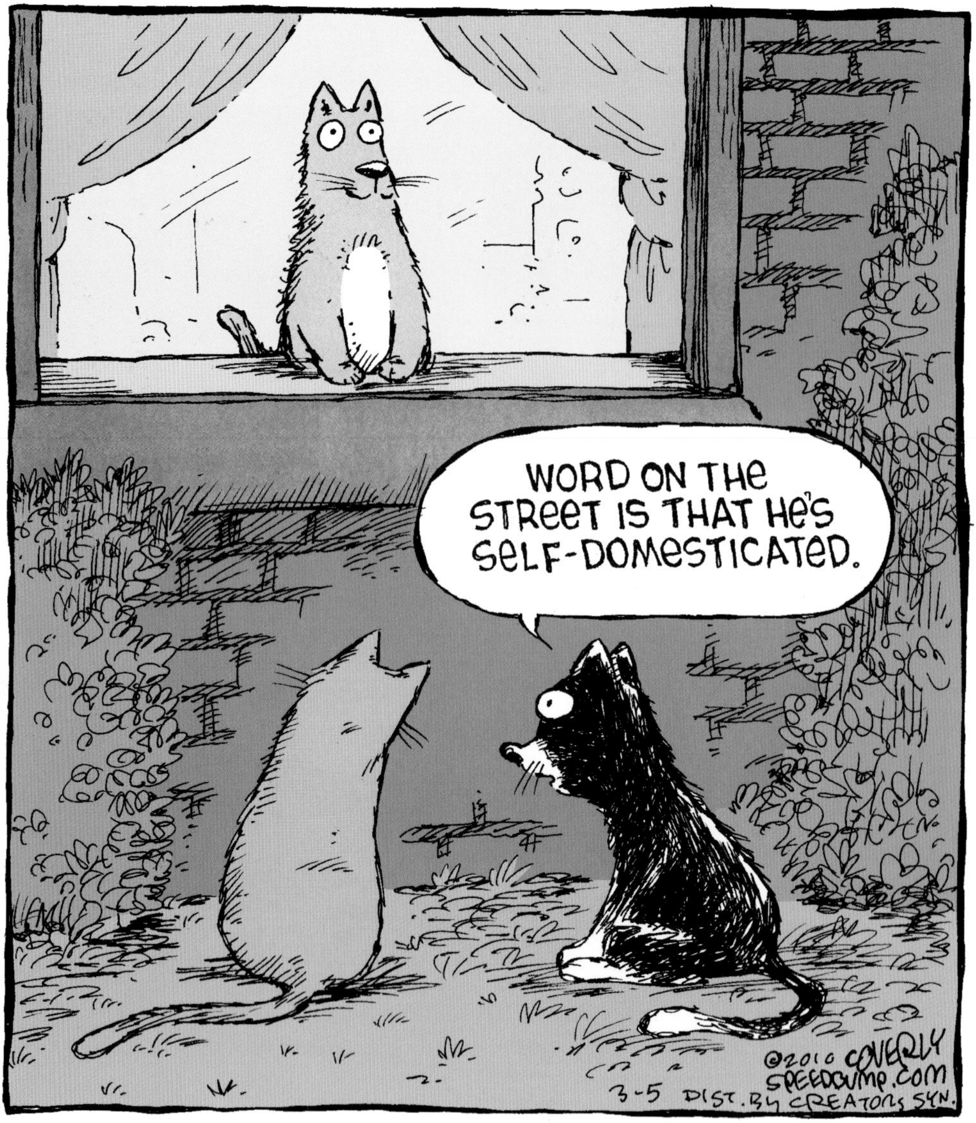
WORD ON THE STREET IS THAT HE'S SELF-DOMESTICATED.
©2010 COVERLY
SPEEDBUMP.COM
3-5 DIST. BY CREATORS SYN.

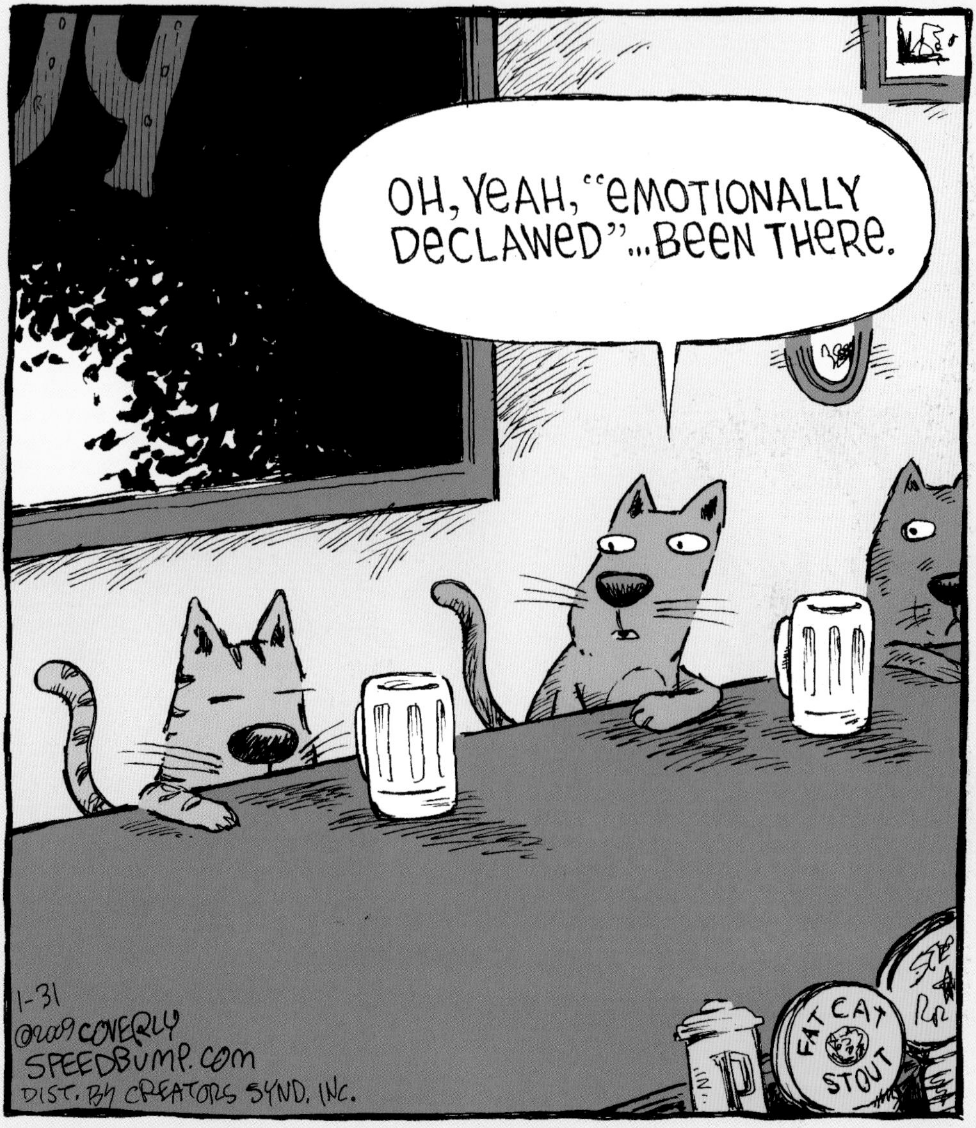
OH, YEAH, "EMOTIONALLY DECLAWED"...BEEN THERE.
1-31
©2009 COVERLY
SPEEDBUMP.COM
DIST. BY CREATORS SYND. INC.
FAT CAT STOUT

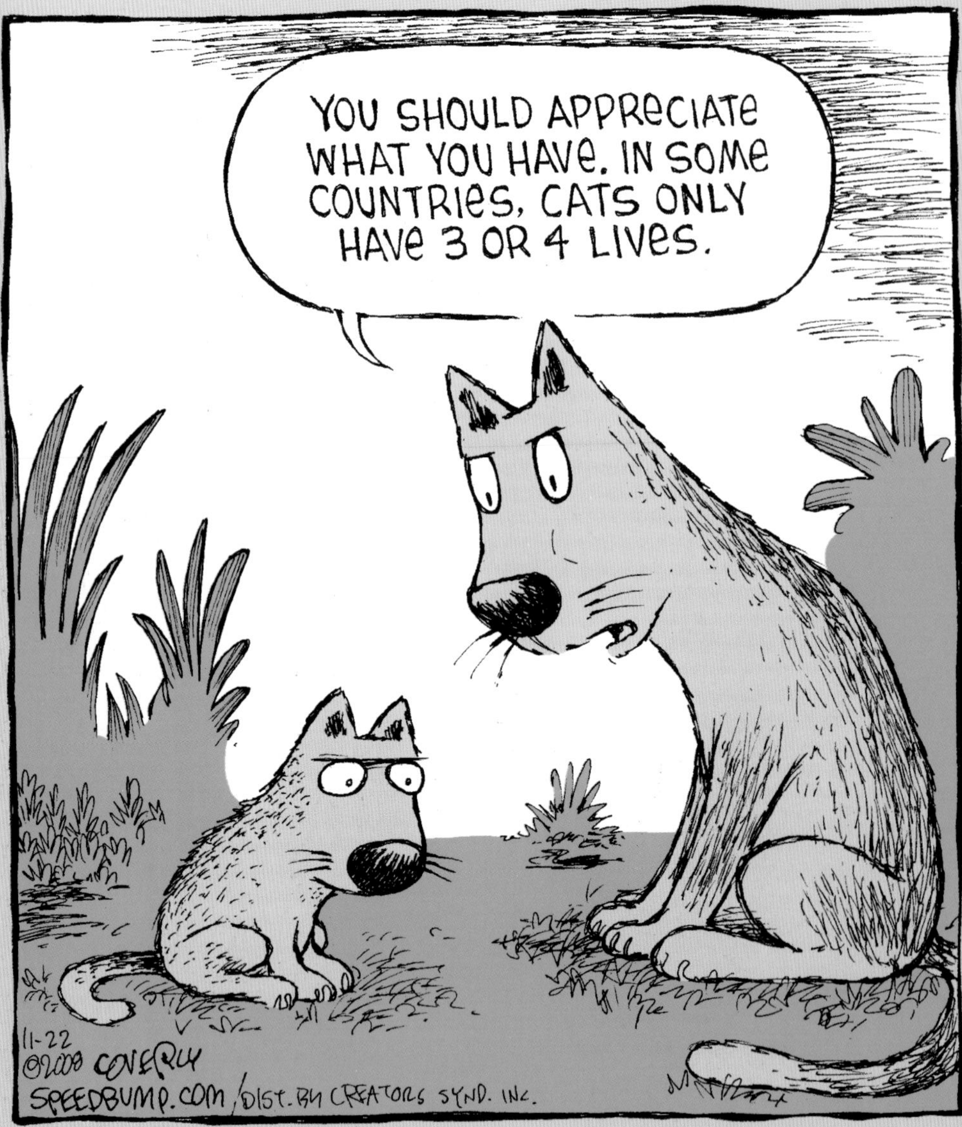
YOU SHOULD APPRECIATE WHAT YOU HAVE. IN SOME COUNTRIES, CATS ONLY HAVE 3 OR 4 LIVES.
11-22
©2008 COVERLY
SPEEDBUMP.COM / DIST. BY CREATORS SYND. INC.

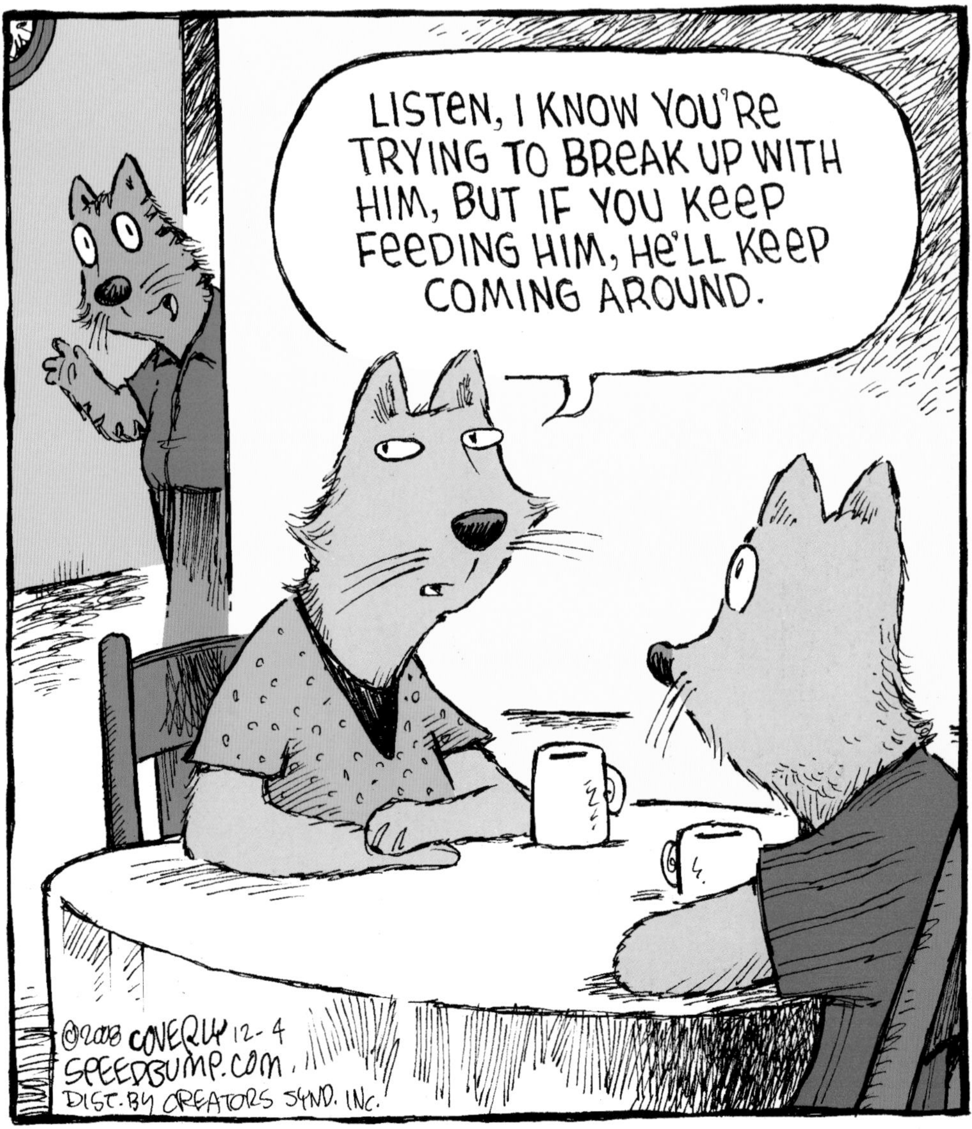
LISTEN, I KNOW YOU'RE TRYING TO BREAK UP WITH HIM, BUT IF YOU KEEP FEEDING HIM, HE'LL KEEP COMING AROUND.
©2008 COVERLY 12-4
SPEEDBUMP.COM.
DIST. BY CREATORS SYND. INC.

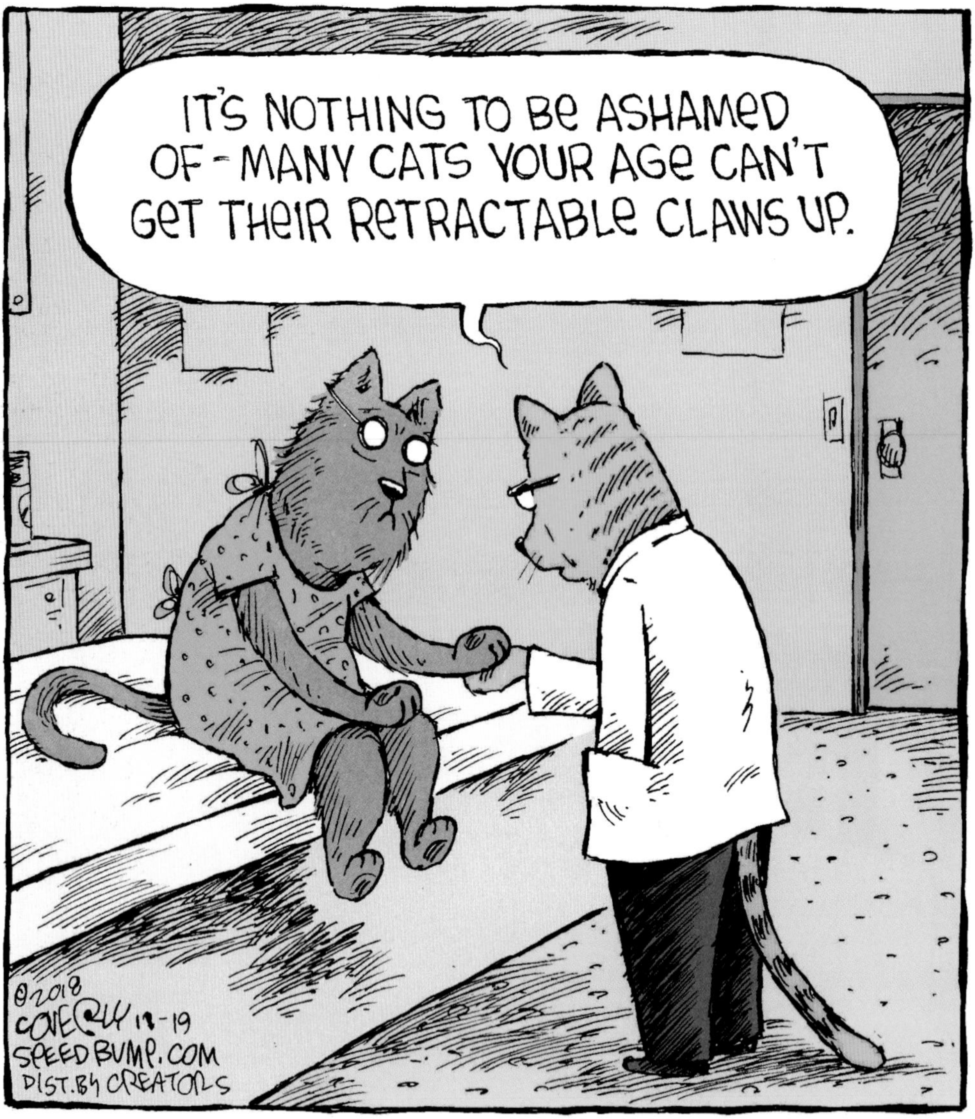
IT'S NOTHING TO BE ASHAMED OF - MANY CATS YOUR AGE CAN'T GET THEIR RETRACTABLE CLAWS UP.
©2018 COVERLY 12-19 SPEEDBUMP.COM DIST. BY CREATORS

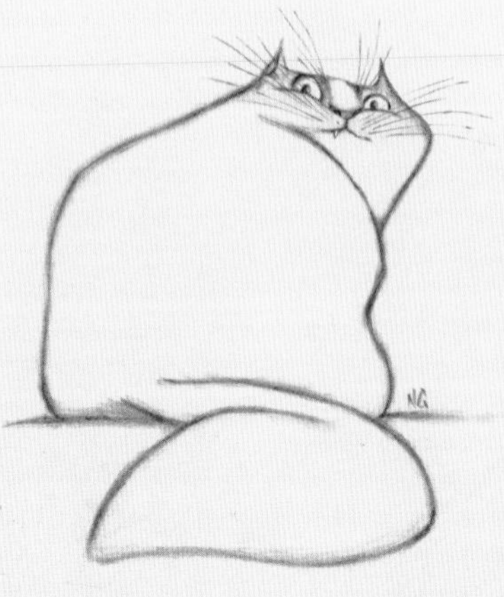
NG

NICK GALIFIANAKIS

The stay at my sister's began with delight.
We caught up and laughed in the waning daylight.

There were nieces and nephews and smiles just because,
when another joined in, a grand ambling of fuzz.

She sleuthed in from outside
   (could I be the lure?).
Immense or just fluffy,
   I couldn't be sure.

She sauntered right past me, unblinkingly calm,
part watchful and wary, part queen of the prom.

That's fine, I was new, and I hoped we'd be friends.
But then she just vanished before evening's end.

I was shown to my room, what a fine but long day.
In bed, in the dark, I let my thoughts stray.

Then sudden and quiet,
   a change in landscape.

The light 'neath my door
  was cleaved by a shape.

It sat there unmoving, affixed to the floor.
It sat there and sat there and sat there some more.

I opened the door and met unblinking eyes.
No meowing or purring, just my annoyed sighs.

She started downstairs, then shot a quick look,
and somehow she knew that was all that it took.

I followed her through to the sliding glass door,
then she stood up against it, on two legs, not four!

Does she want to go out? I suppose it's okay,
since that's where she'd been at the start of my stay.

Tap tap tapping she tapped, and I smiled just a tad,
'cause the sound that fat paws make is "pad pad pad pad
  pad."

I had just cracked the door when she squeezed herself
  through.
But she didn't go far, just a foot, maybe two.
Then spun 'round to face me, a great pyramid of hair,
her shadow behind her, she just sat there and stared.

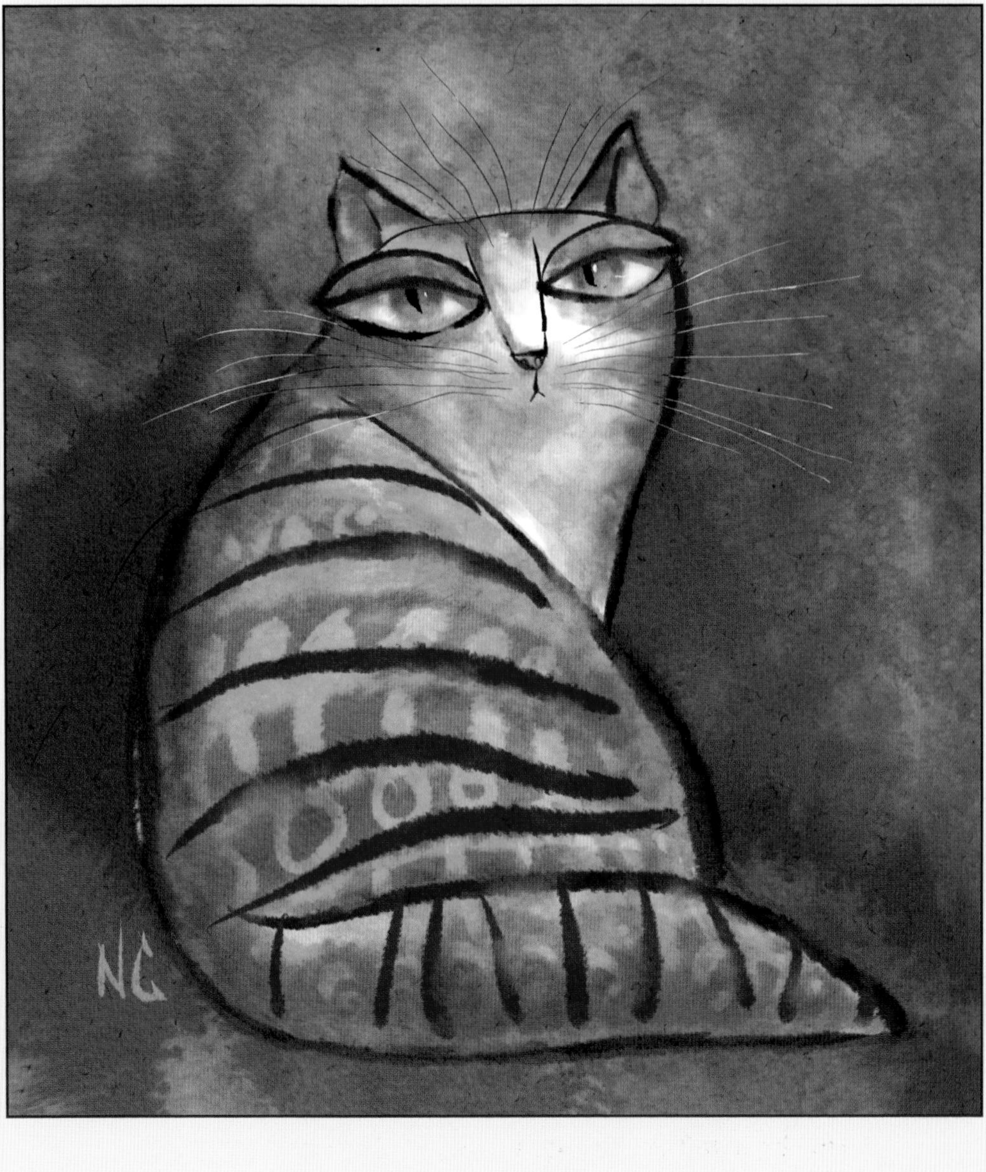
NC

I wondered awhile, confused, I admit.
Till I looked down between us . . .
  and then I saw *it.*

Its eyes were still open, a fixed moment of dread,
and a mouth locked in shock,
  on the small severed head.

They say these are gifts, and that may well be true.
But her unblinking eyes said, "I'm coming for you."

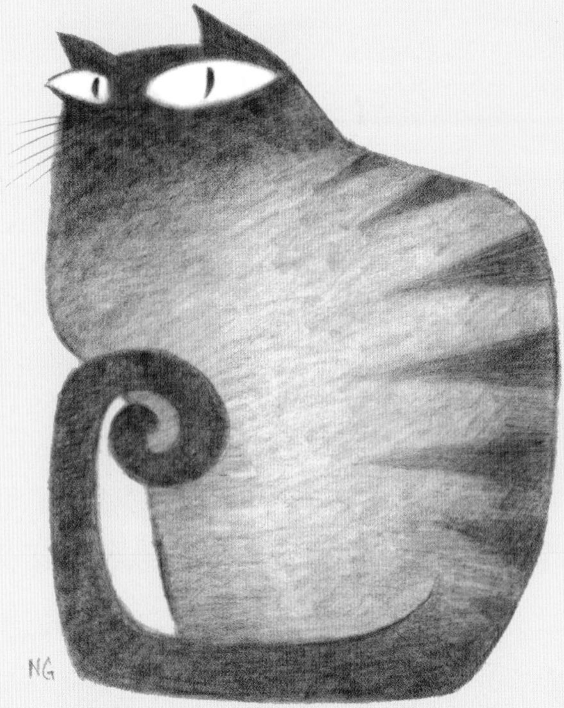
NG

About Nick Galifianakis

Nick Galifianakis is a character designer and award-winning syndicated cartoonist with the *Washington Post,* and the author of *If You Loved Me, You'd Think This Was Cute: Uncomfortable True Cartoons About You.*

He is also the coauthor of *The Art of Richard Thompson,* along with illustration historian David Apatoff and *Calvin and Hobbes* creator Bill Watterson.

His syndicated cartoons can be found at: instagram.com /nickgalifianakisart.

nickgalifianakis.blogspot.com

CHAPTER 2

CAT AND MOUSE GAMES

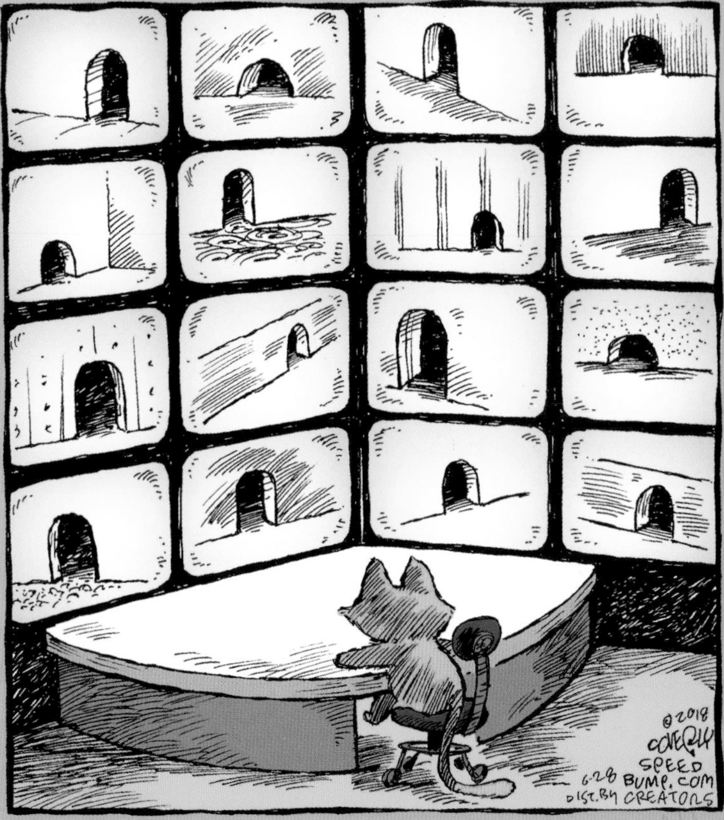

©2018
COVERLY
SPEED
6-28 BUMP.COM
DIST. BY CREATORS

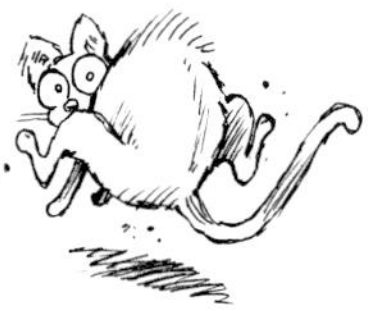

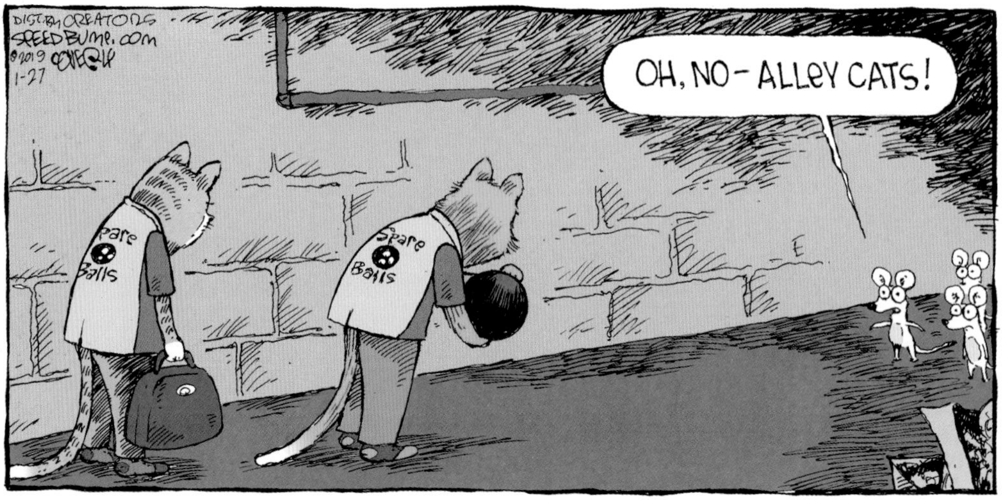
DIST. BY CREATORS
SPEEDBUMP.COM
©2019
1-27
OH, NO - ALLEY CATS!
Spare Balls
Spare Balls

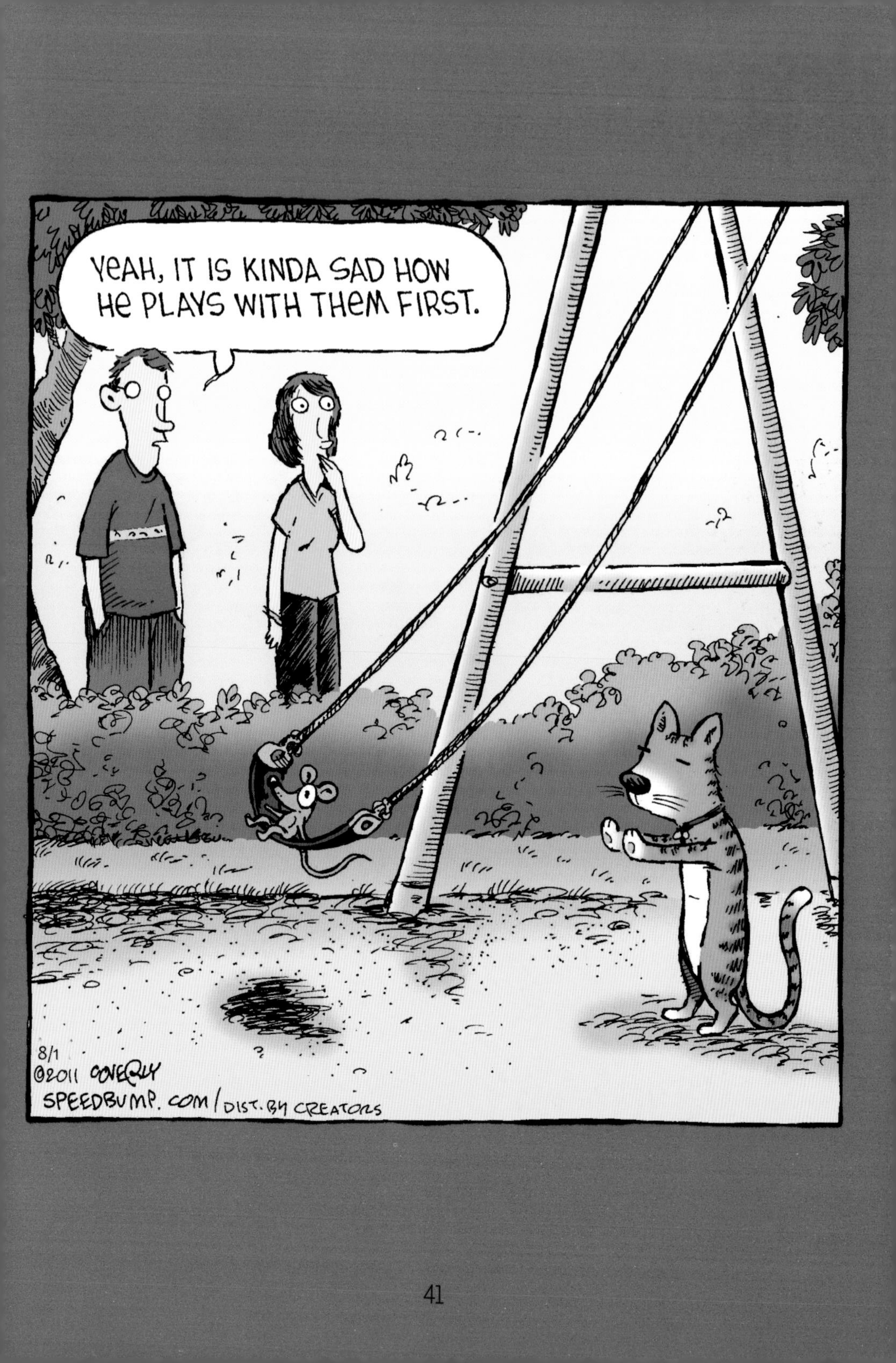
YEAH, IT IS KINDA SAD HOW HE PLAYS WITH THEM FIRST.
8/1
©2011 COVERLY
SPEEDBUMP.COM / DIST. BY CREATORS

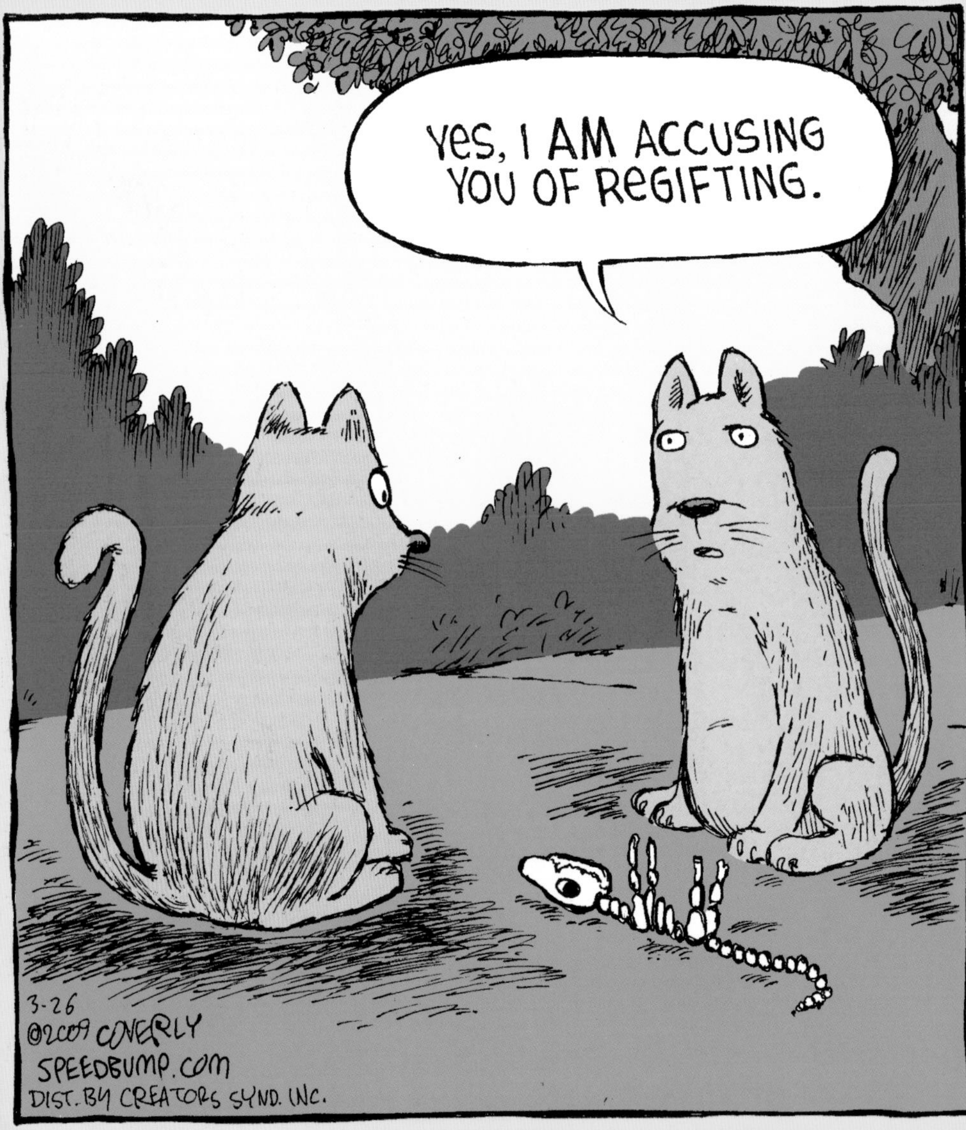
YES, I AM ACCUSING YOU OF REGIFTING.
3-26
©2009 COVERLY
SPEEDBUMP.COM
DIST. BY CREATORS SYND. INC.

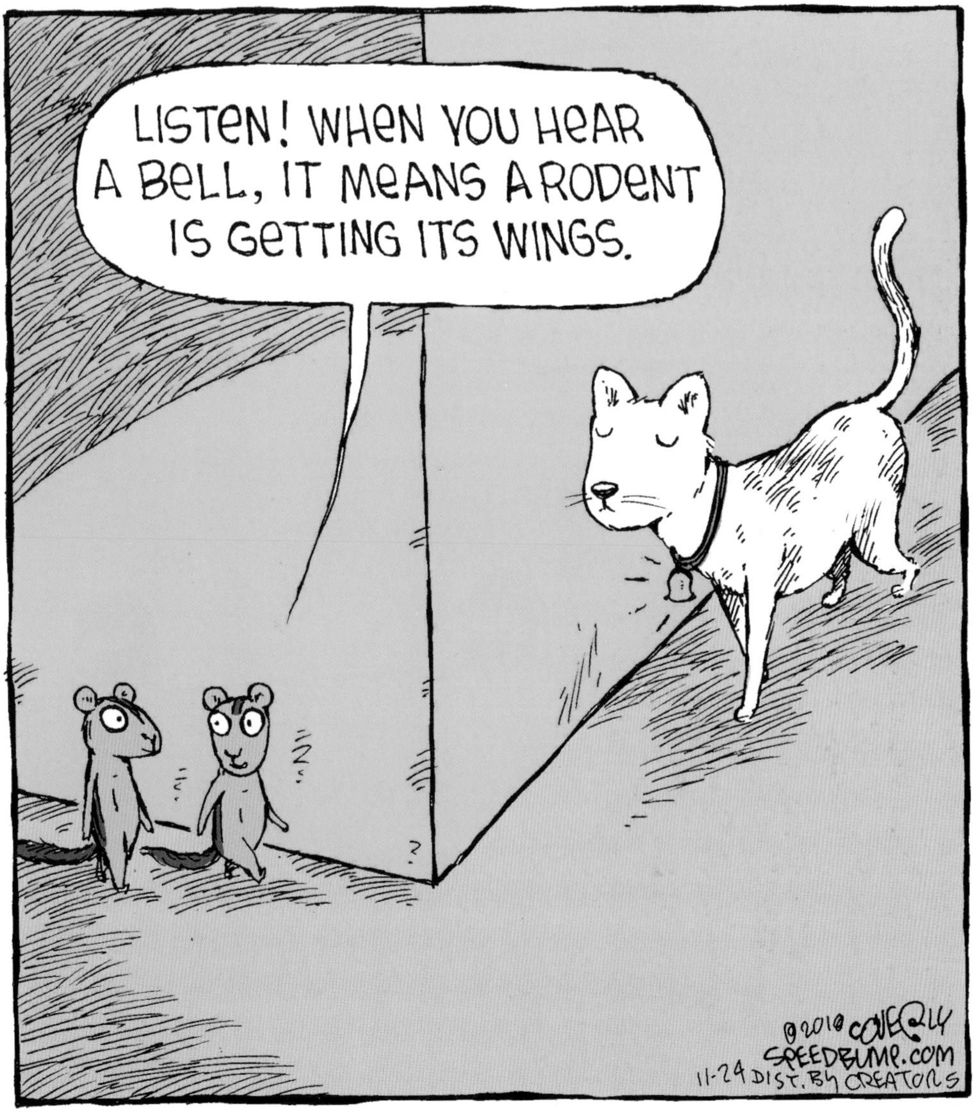
LISTEN! WHEN YOU HEAR A BELL, IT MEANS A RODENT IS GETTING ITS WINGS.
©2010 COVERLY
SPEEDBUMP.COM
11-24 DIST. BY CREATORS

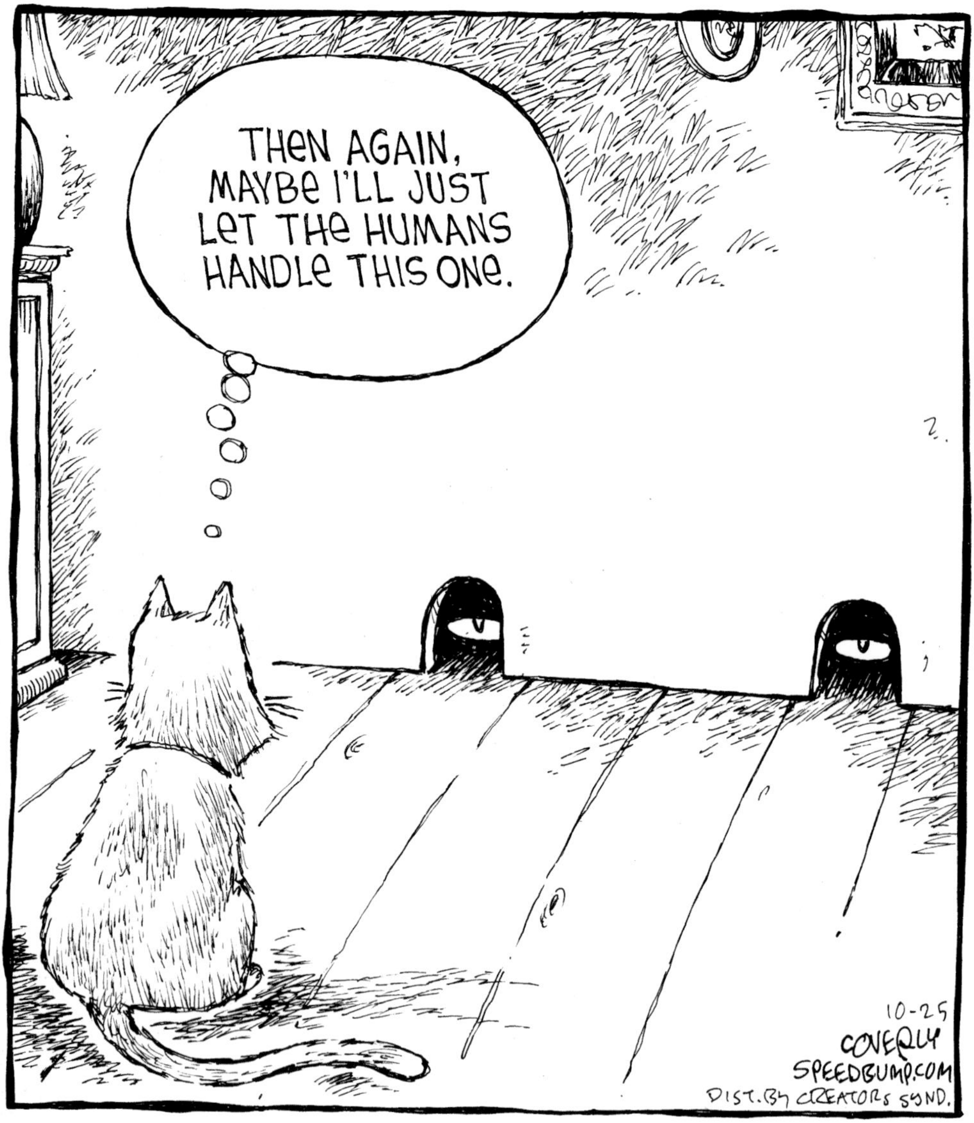
THEN AGAIN, MAYBE I'LL JUST LET THE HUMANS HANDLE THIS ONE.
10-25
COVERLY
SPEEDBUMP.COM
DIST. BY CREATORS SYND.

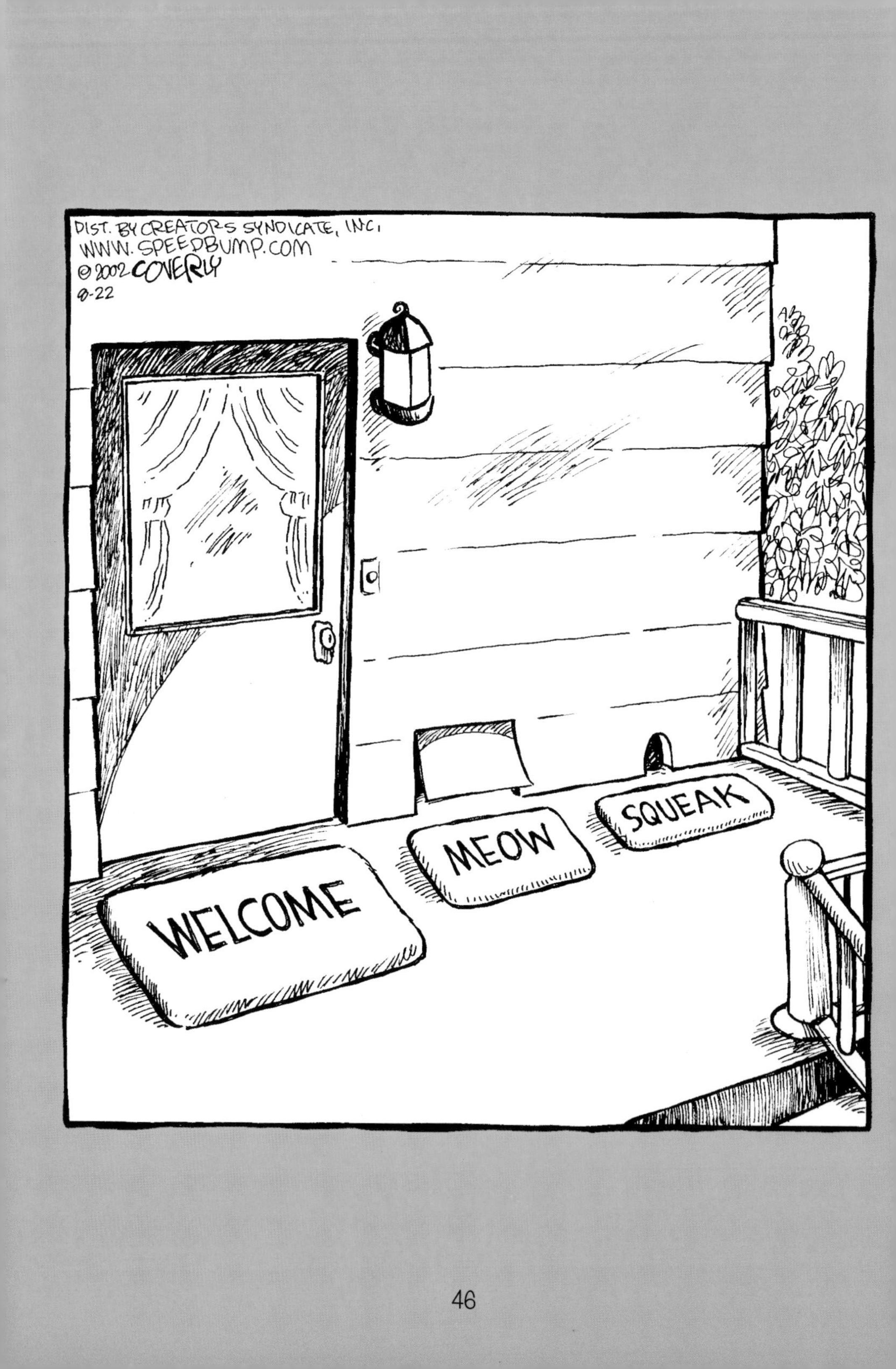
DIST. BY CREATORS SYNDICATE, INC.
WWW.SPEEDBUMP.COM
© 2002 COVERLY
WELCOME
MEOW
SQUEAK

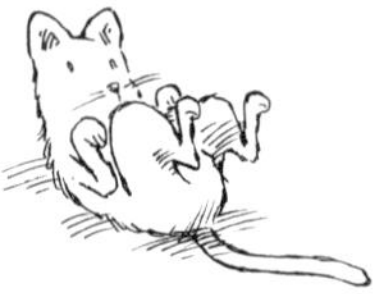

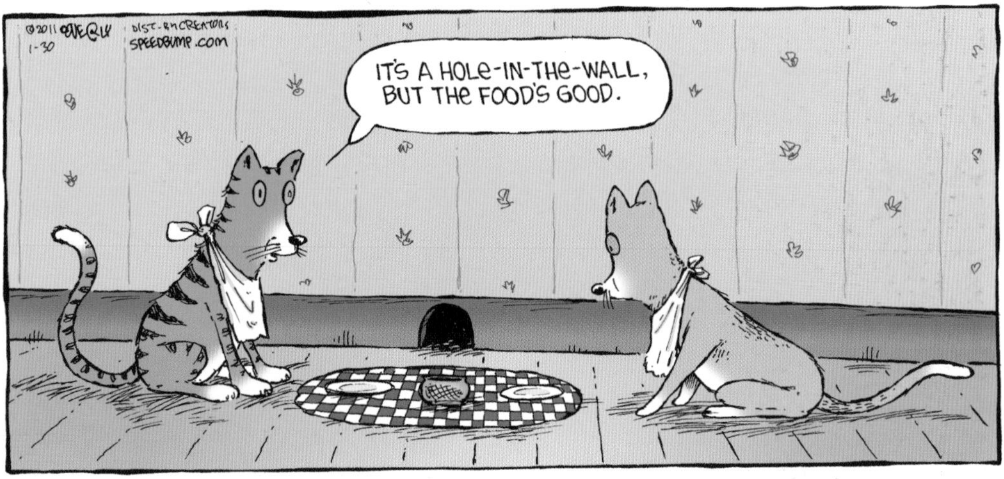
©2011
1-30
DIST-BY CREATORS
SPEEDBUMP.COM
IT'S A HOLE-IN-THE-WALL, BUT THE FOOD'S GOOD.

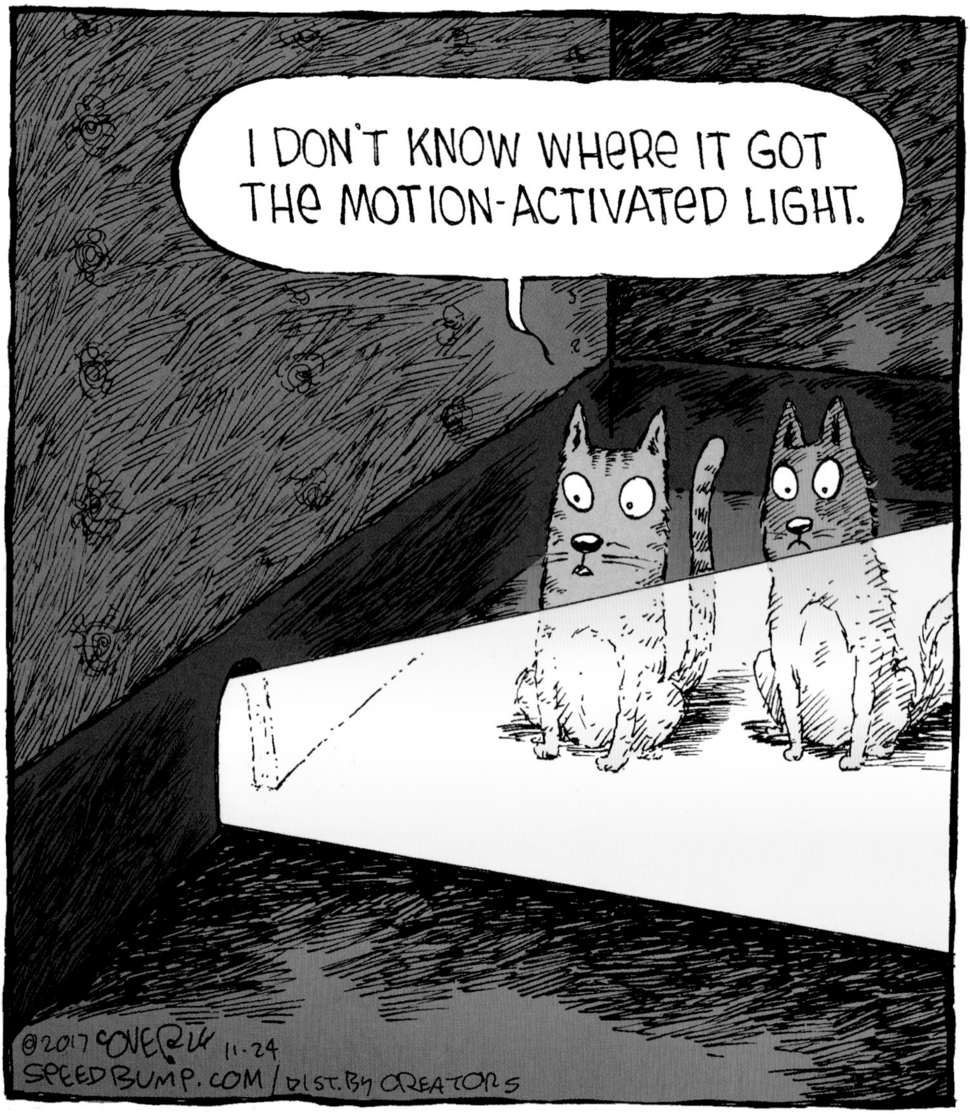
I DON'T KNOW WHERE IT GOT THE MOTION-ACTIVATED LIGHT.
©2017 COVERLY 11-24
SPEEDBUMP.COM / DIST. BY CREATORS

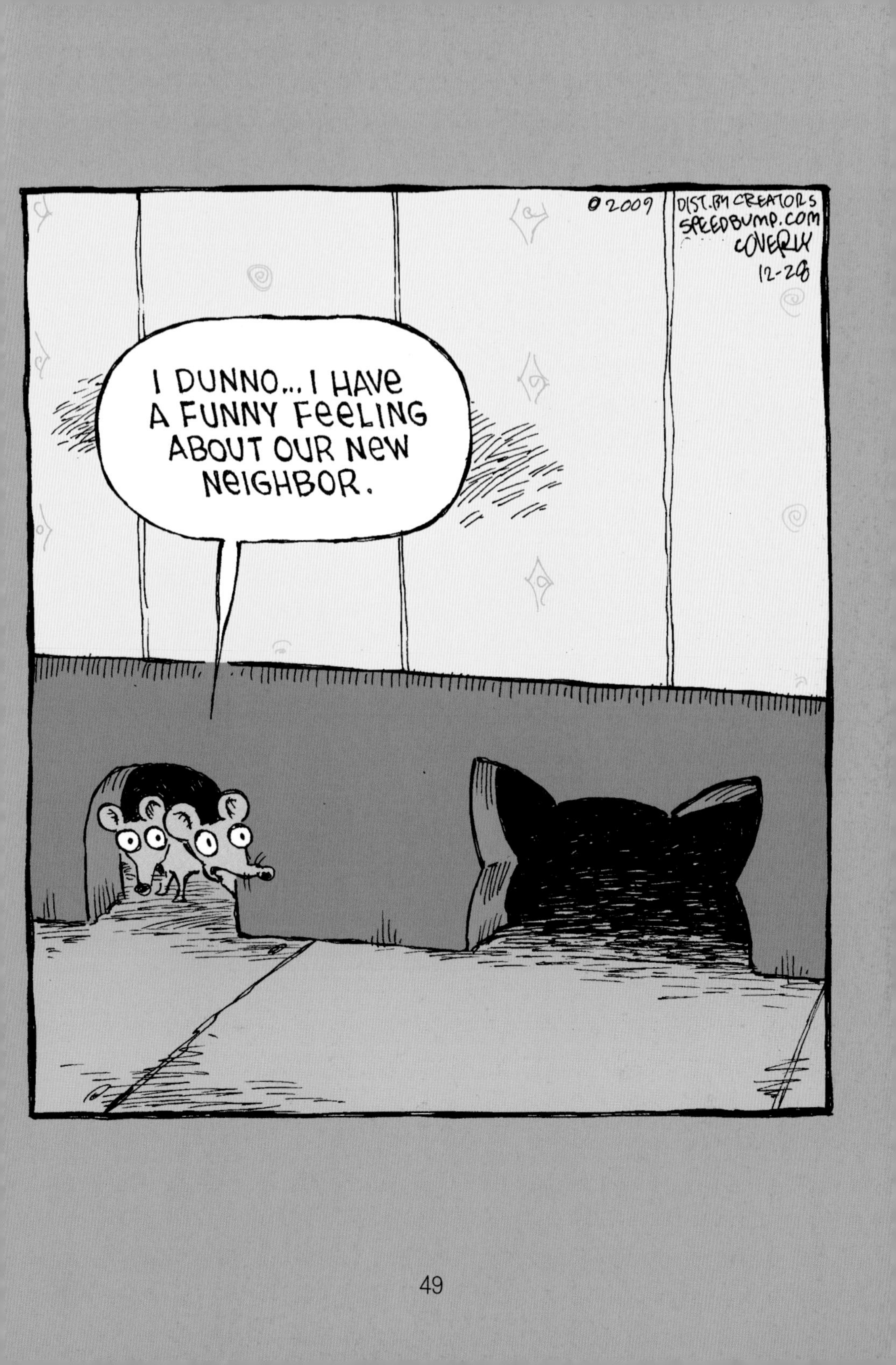
©2009
DIST. BY CREATORS
SPEEDBUMP.COM
COVERLY
12-28
I DUNNO... I HAVE A FUNNY FEELING ABOUT OUR NEW NEIGHBOR.

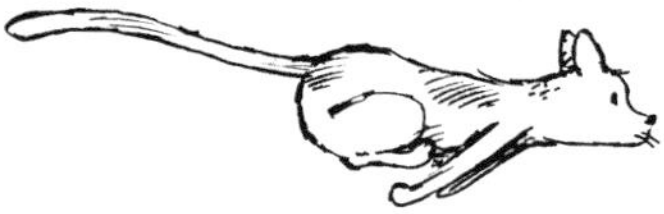

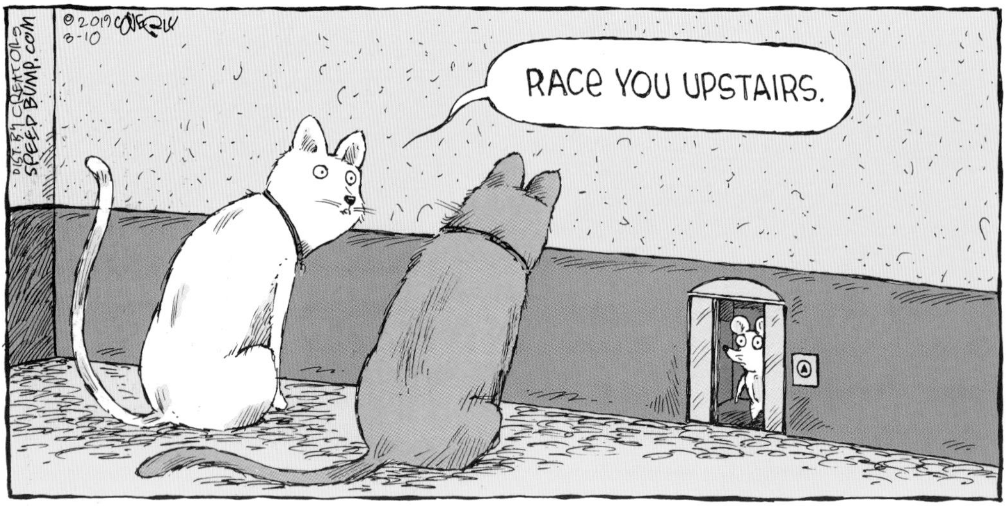
DIST. BY CREATORS
SPEEDBUMP.COM
RACE YOU UPSTAIRS.

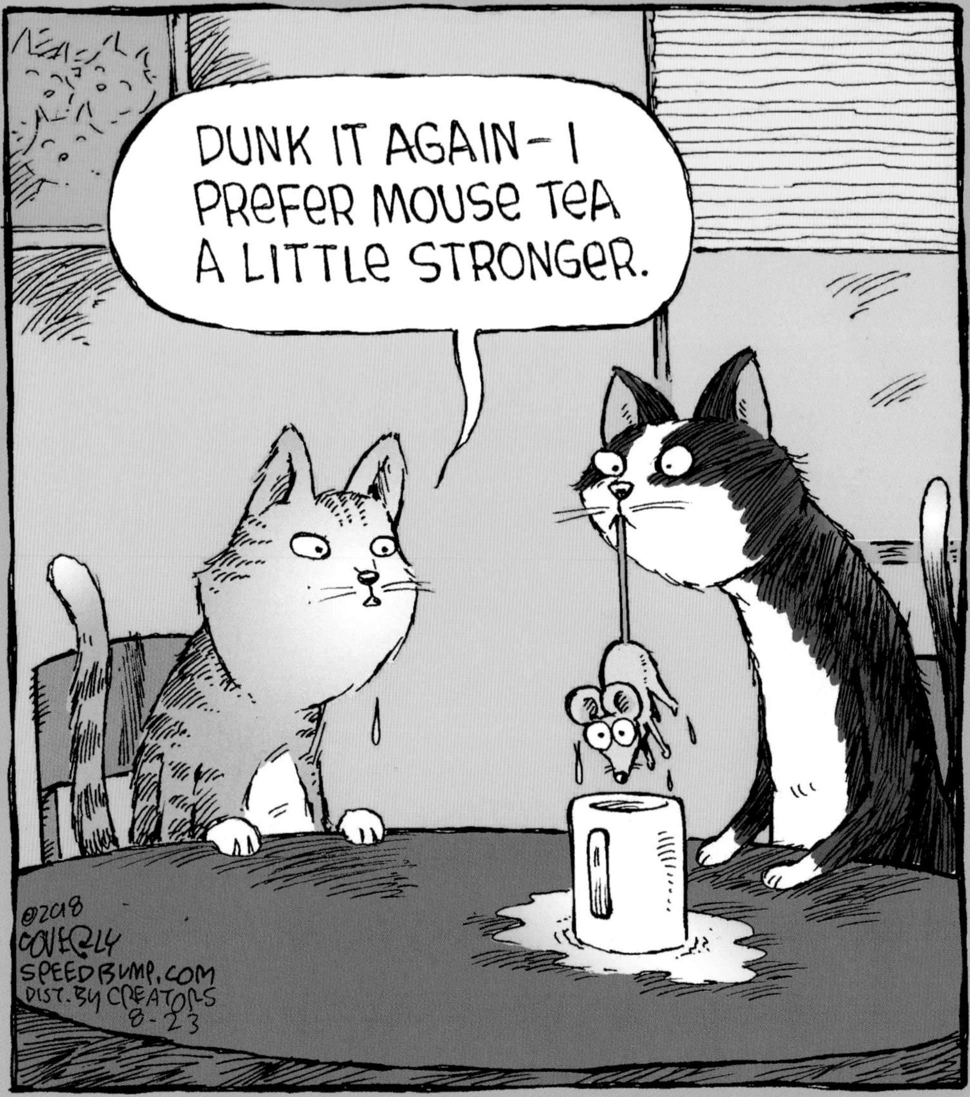
DUNK IT AGAIN– I PREFER MOUSE TEA A LITTLE STRONGER.
©2018 COVERLY SPEEDBUMP.COM DIST. BY CREATORS 8-23

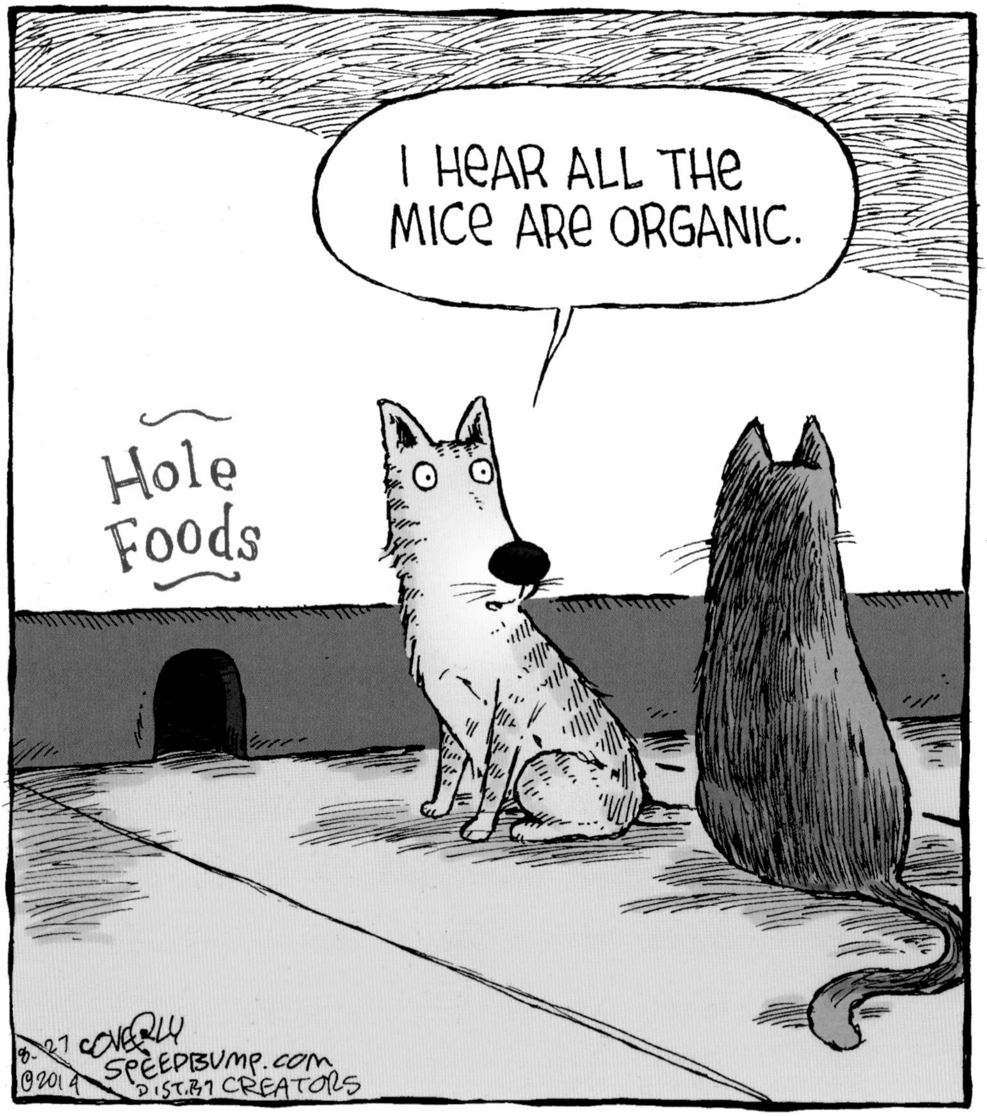
I HEAR ALL THE MICE ARE ORGANIC.
Hole Foods
8-27 COVERLY
SPEEDBUMP.COM
©2014 DIST.BY CREATORS

LOVE THE HOUSE, HATE THE LOCATION.
©2018 COVERLY 7-30
DIST. BY CREATORS/ SPEEDBUMP.COM

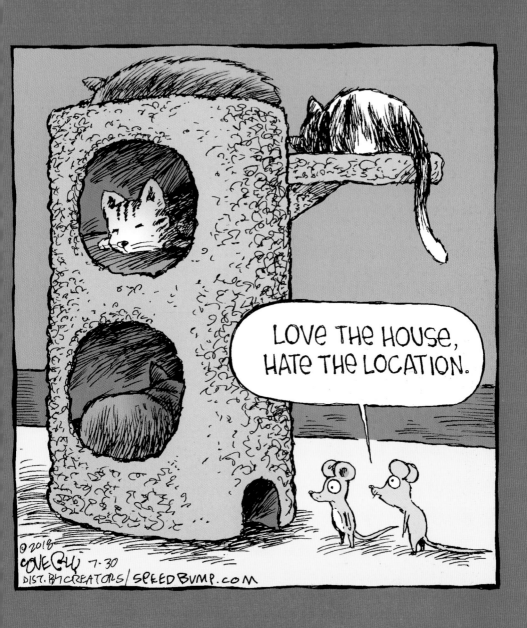

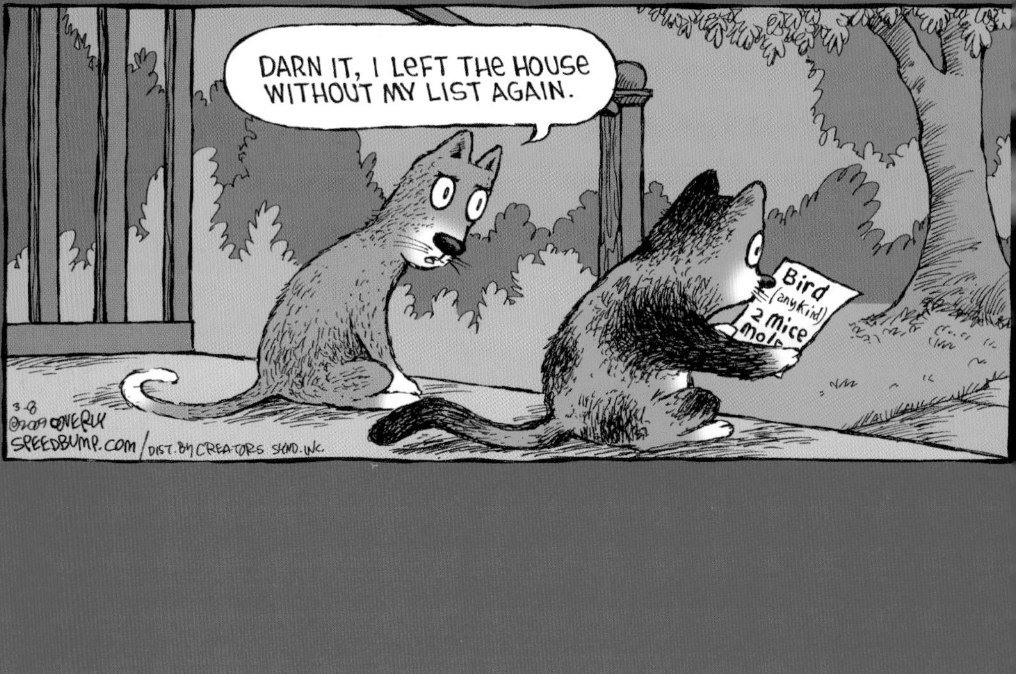
DARN IT, I LEFT THE HOUSE WITHOUT MY LIST AGAIN.
Bird (any kind)
2 mice
3-8
©2009 COVERLY
SPEEDBUMP.COM / DIST. BY CREATORS SYND. INC.

GENEVIEVE GODBOUT

The Siamese is Noah and the ginger tabby is Phoebe (she's thirteen, can you believe it?). They love to cuddle, and they never scratch (except our beautiful velvet sofa)!

About Genevieve Godbout

Genevieve Godbout was born and raised in Quebec, studied traditional animation at the Cégep du Vieux-Montréal and the school of Gobelins in Paris. She then moved to London, where she worked as a character artist at Disney Consumer Products for six years. She has since moved back to Montreal as a full-time illustrator. She has illustrated various children's books, including *When Santa Was a Baby* (Tundra Books) and an adaptation of *Mary Poppins* (Houghton Mifflin Harcourt). Her latest, *Goodnight, Anne* (Tundra Books), was selected for the Society of Illustrators Original Art Exhibit in New York. Her first book as both author and illustrator, *Malou*, is forthcoming with Tundra Books in 2020.

Genevieve hides her Siamese cat, Noah (pictured here), in most of her books and illustrations. And she's happy to have Phoebe, a miniature ginger tabby, too.

genevievegodboutillustration.com

CHAPTER 3

CATS AND THEIR HUMANS

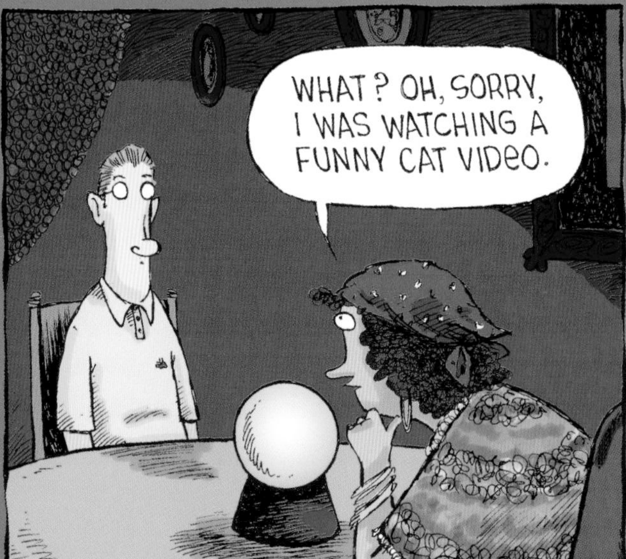

WHAT? OH, SORRY, I WAS WATCHING A FUNNY CAT VIDEO.
9-5 ©2014 COVERLY SPEEDBUMP.COM DIST. BY CREATORS

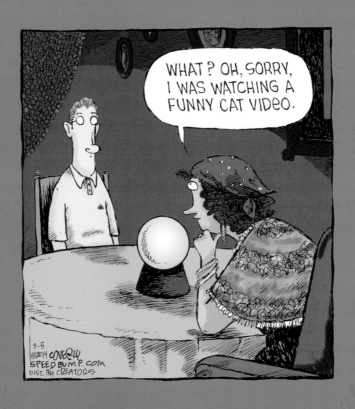

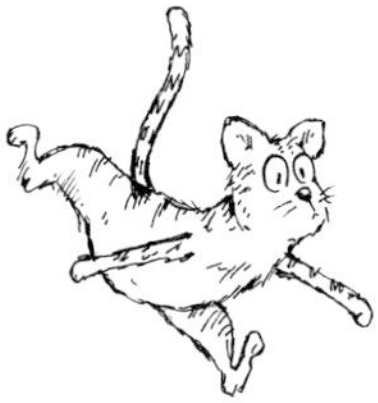

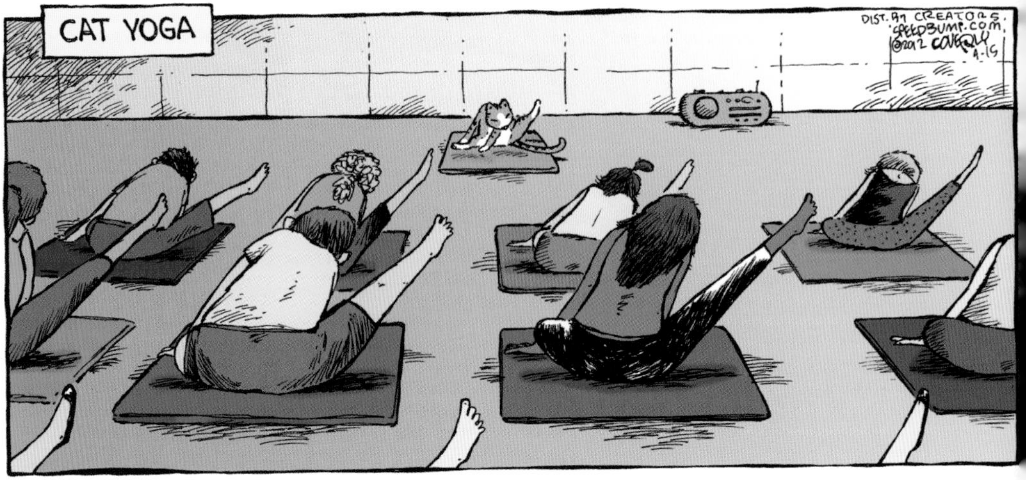
CAT YOGA
DIST. BY CREATORS.
SPEEDBUMP.COM
©2012 COVERLY

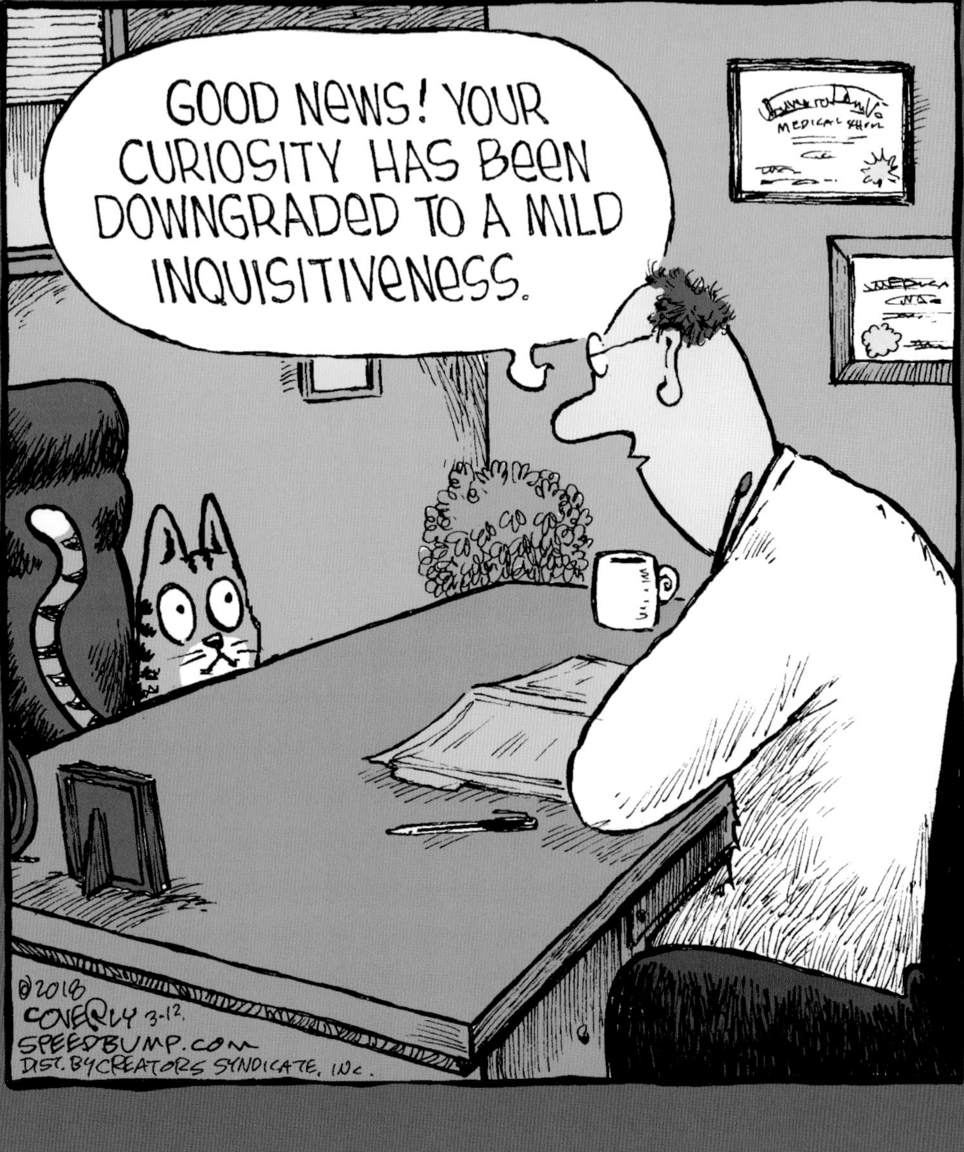
GOOD NEWS! YOUR CURIOSITY HAS BEEN DOWNGRADED TO A MILD INQUISITIVENESS.
©2018 COVERLY 3-12.
SPEEDBUMP.COM
DIST. BY CREATORS SYNDICATE, INC.

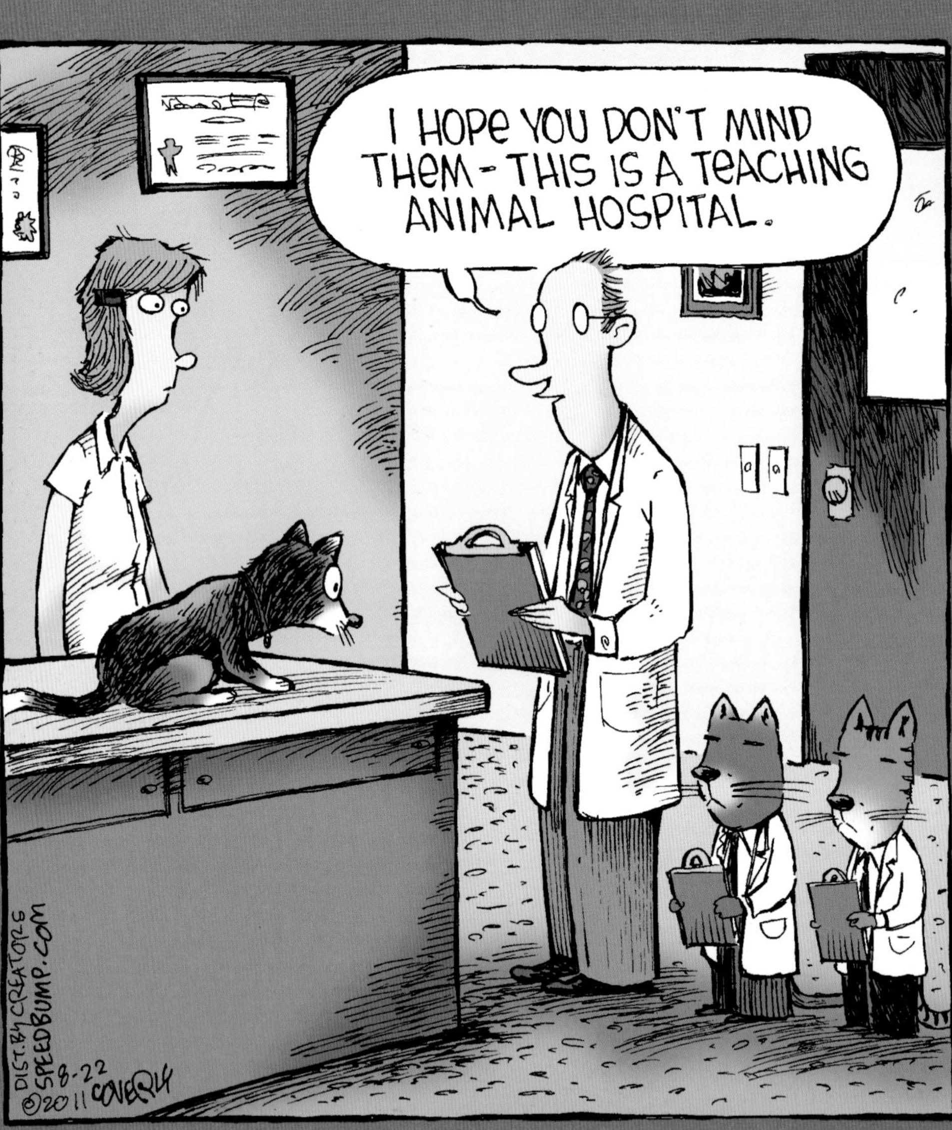
I HOPE YOU DON'T MIND THEM - THIS IS A TEACHING ANIMAL HOSPITAL.
DIST. BY CREATORS
SPEEDBUMP.COM
8-22
©2011 COVERLY

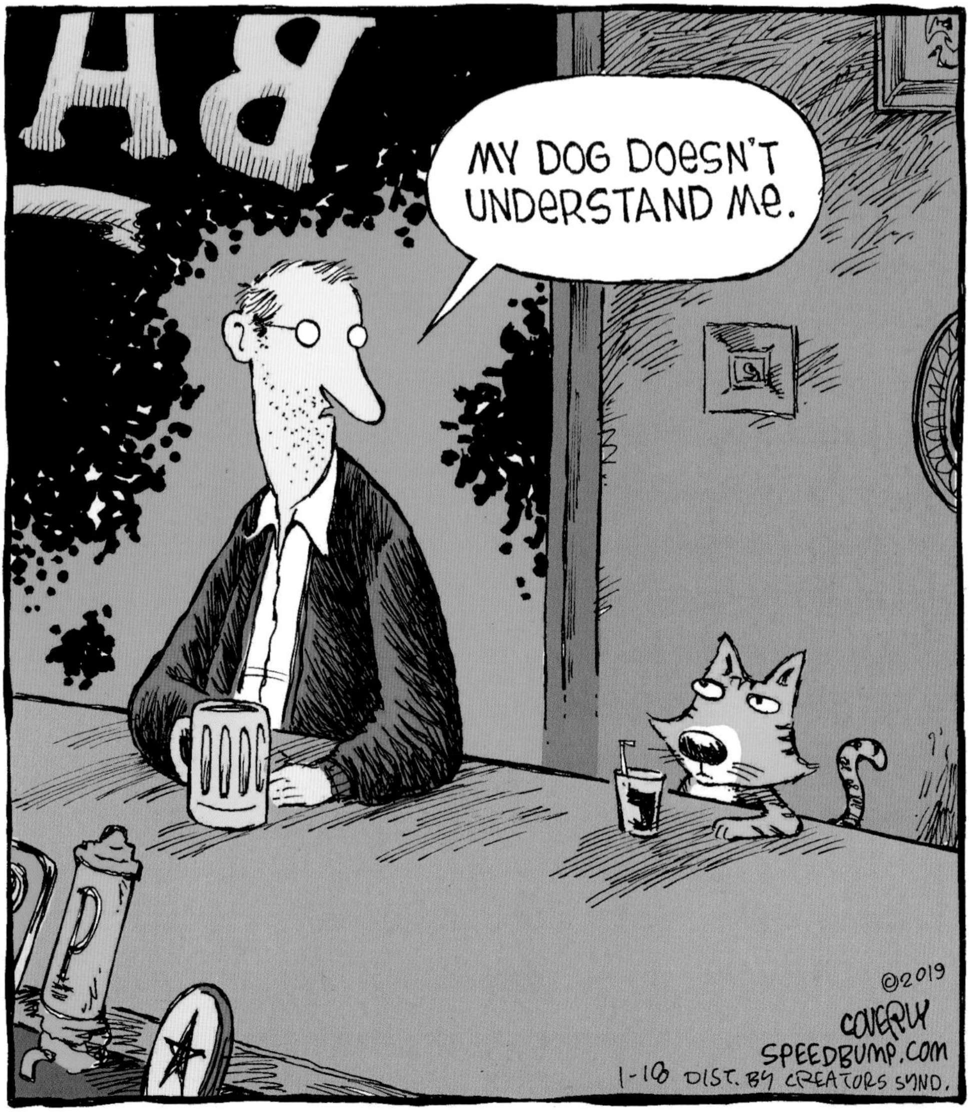
MY DOG DOESN'T UNDERSTAND ME.
©2019
COVERLY
SPEEDBUMP.COM
1-18 DIST. BY CREATORS SYND.

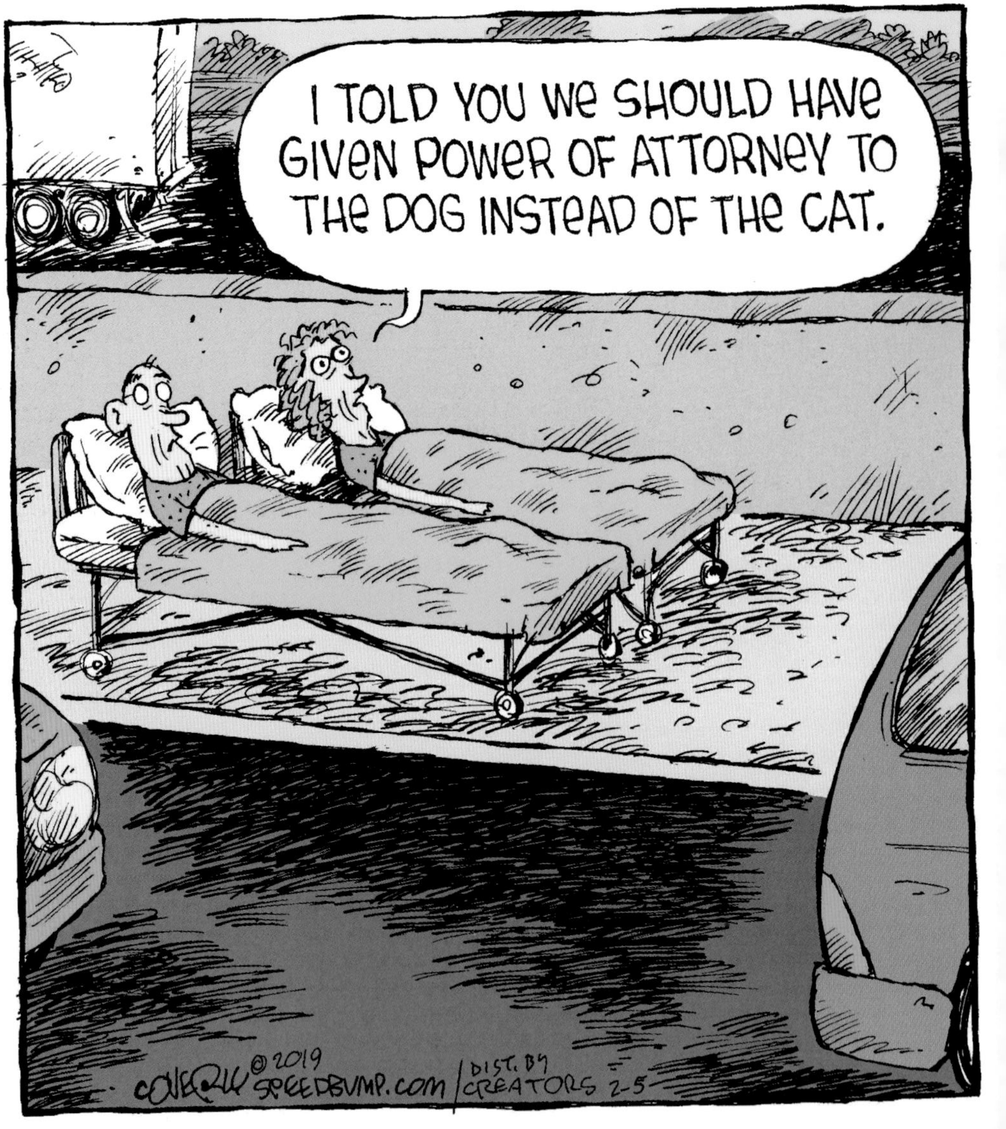
I TOLD YOU WE SHOULD HAVE GIVEN POWER OF ATTORNEY TO THE DOG INSTEAD OF THE CAT.
COVERLY © 2019 SPEEDBUMP.COM / DIST. BY CREATORS 2-5

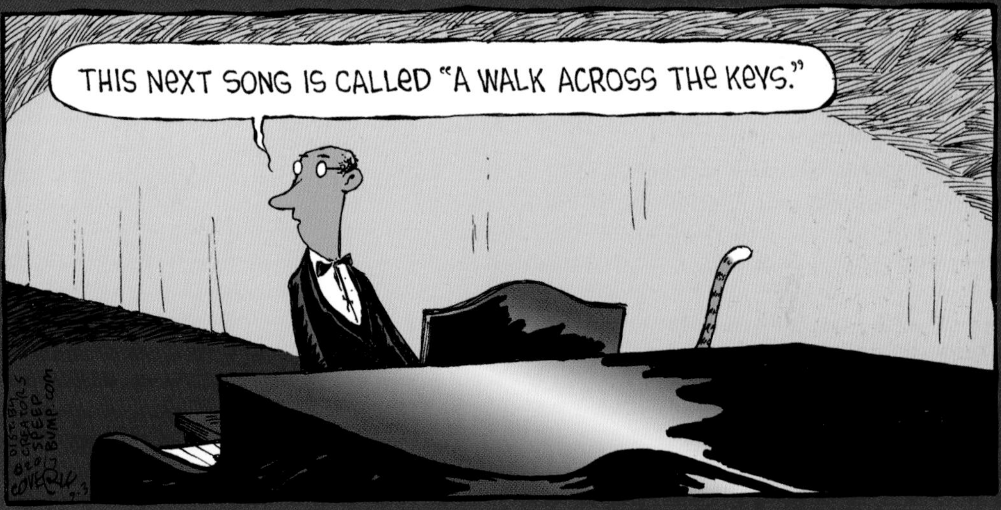
THIS NEXT SONG IS CALLED "A WALK ACROSS THE KEYS."
SPEED BUMP.com

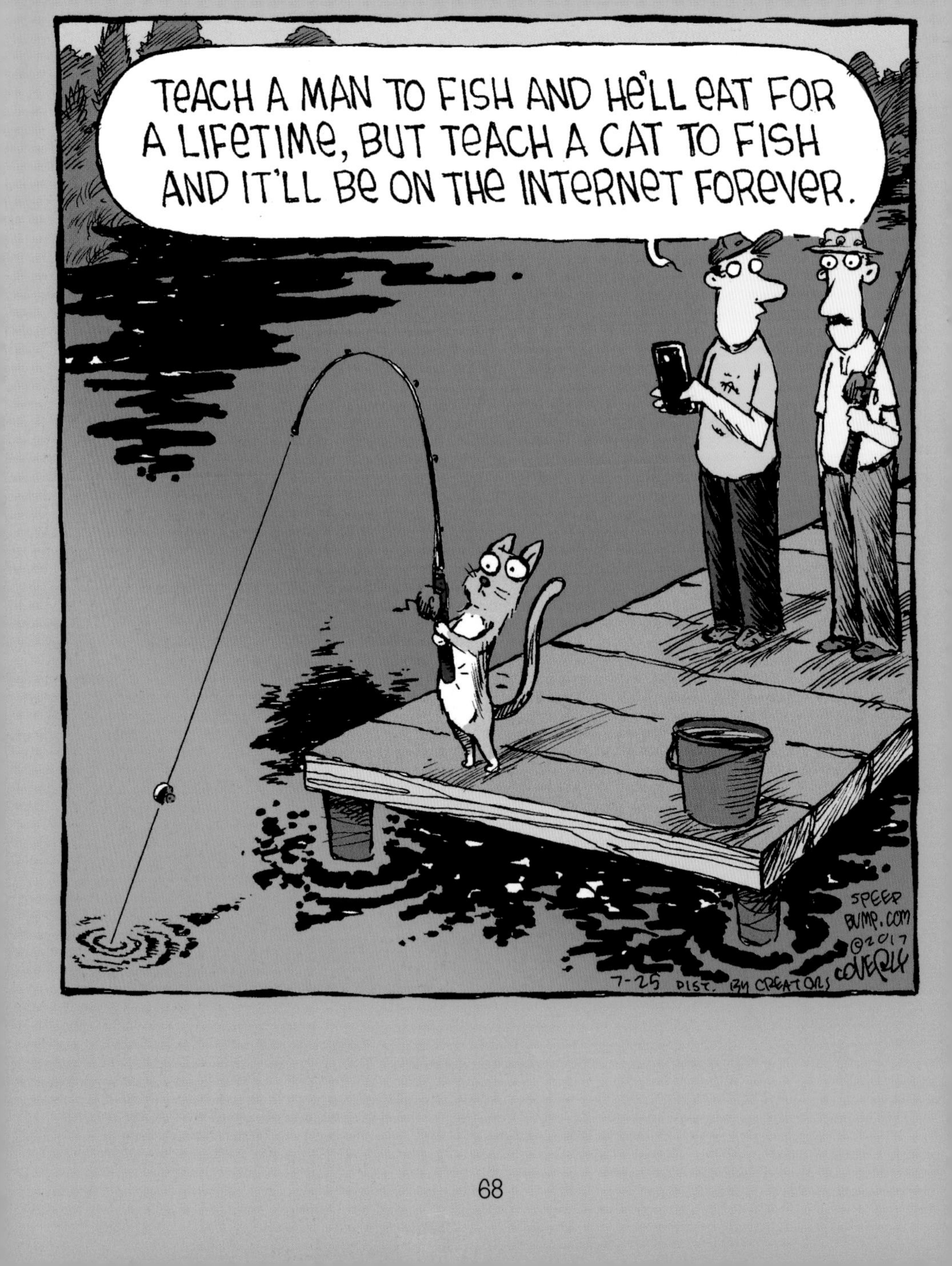
TEACH A MAN TO FISH AND HE'LL EAT FOR A LIFETIME, BUT TEACH A CAT TO FISH AND IT'LL BE ON THE INTERNET FOREVER.
SPEEDBUMP.COM ©2017 COVERLY
7-25 DIST. BY CREATORS

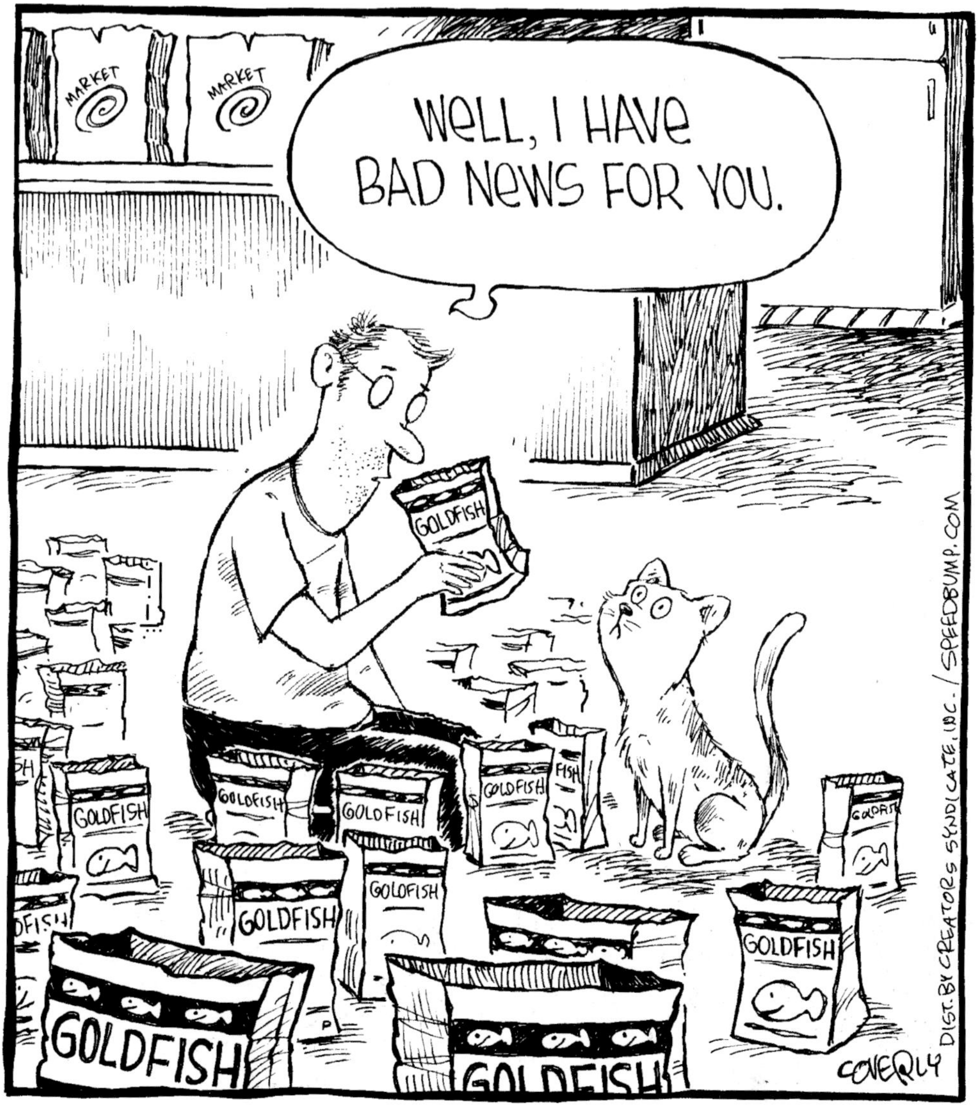
WELL, I HAVE
BAD NEWS FOR YOU.
GOLDFISH
DIST. BY CREATORS SYNDICATE, INC. / SPEEDBUMP.COM
COVERLY

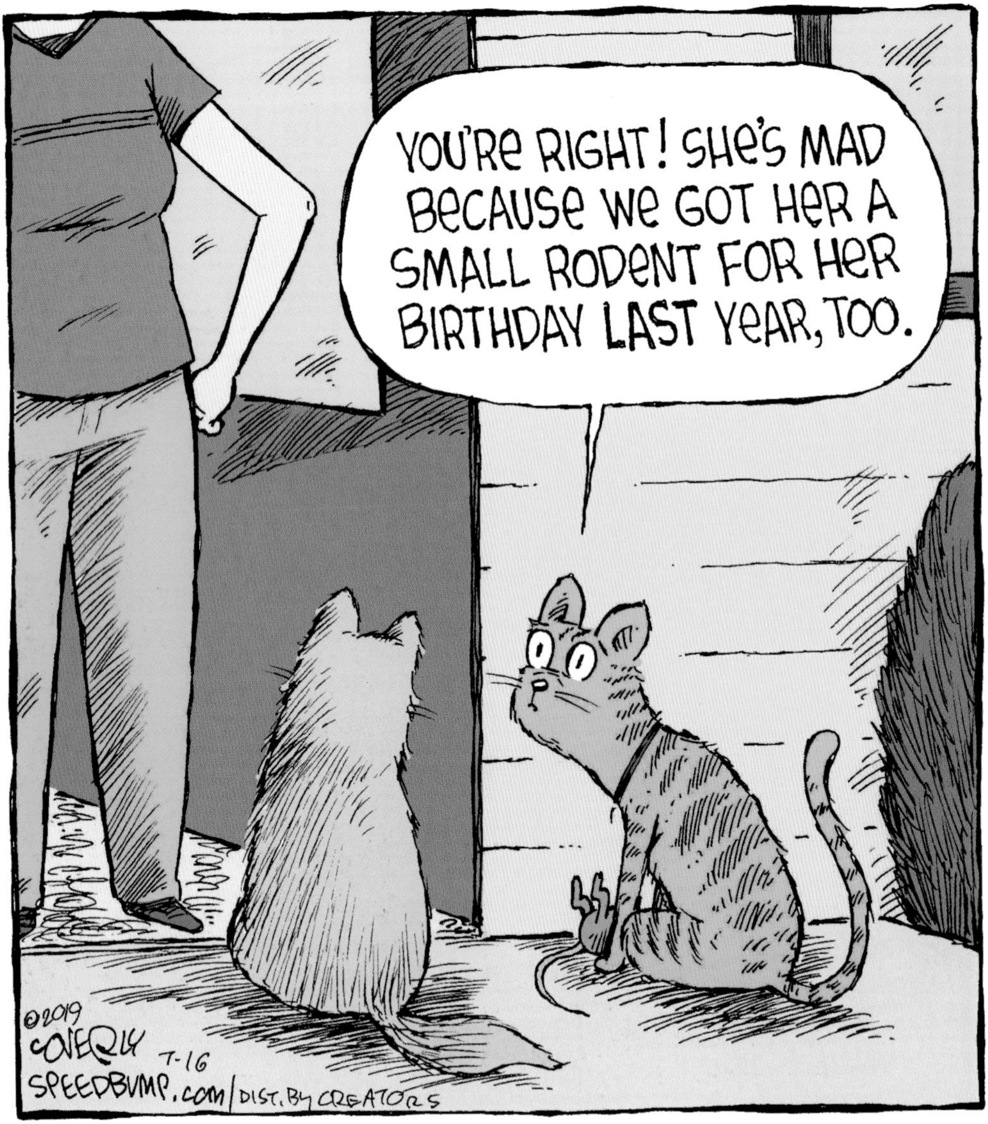
YOU'RE RIGHT! SHE'S MAD BECAUSE WE GOT HER A SMALL RODENT FOR HER BIRTHDAY LAST YEAR, TOO.
©2019 COVERLY 7-16
SPEEDBUMP.com/DIST. BY CREATORS

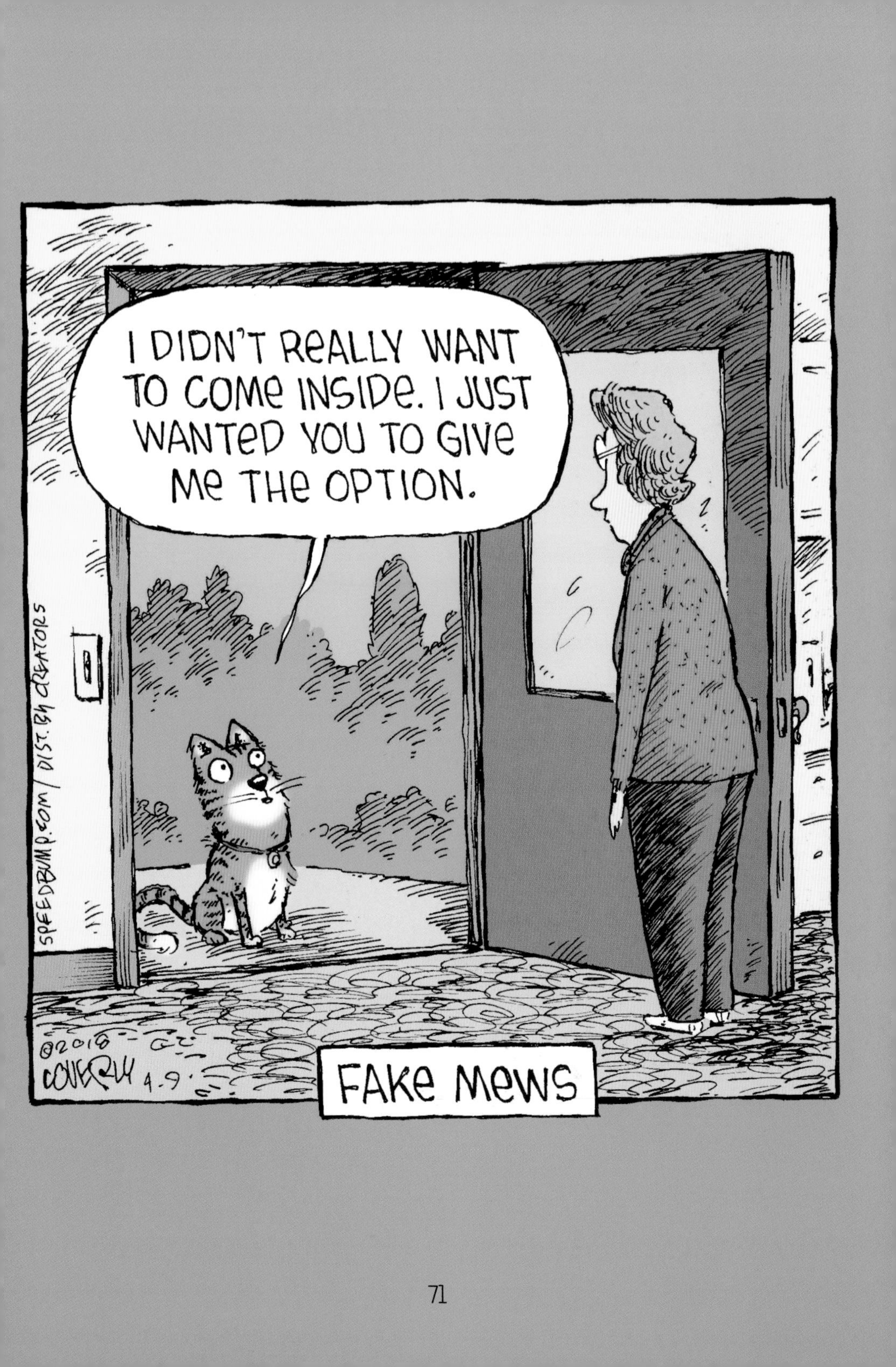
I DIDN'T REALLY WANT TO COME INSIDE. I JUST WANTED YOU TO GIVE ME THE OPTION.
SPEEDBUMP.COM / DIST. BY CREATORS
©2018 COVERLY 4.9
FAKE MEWS

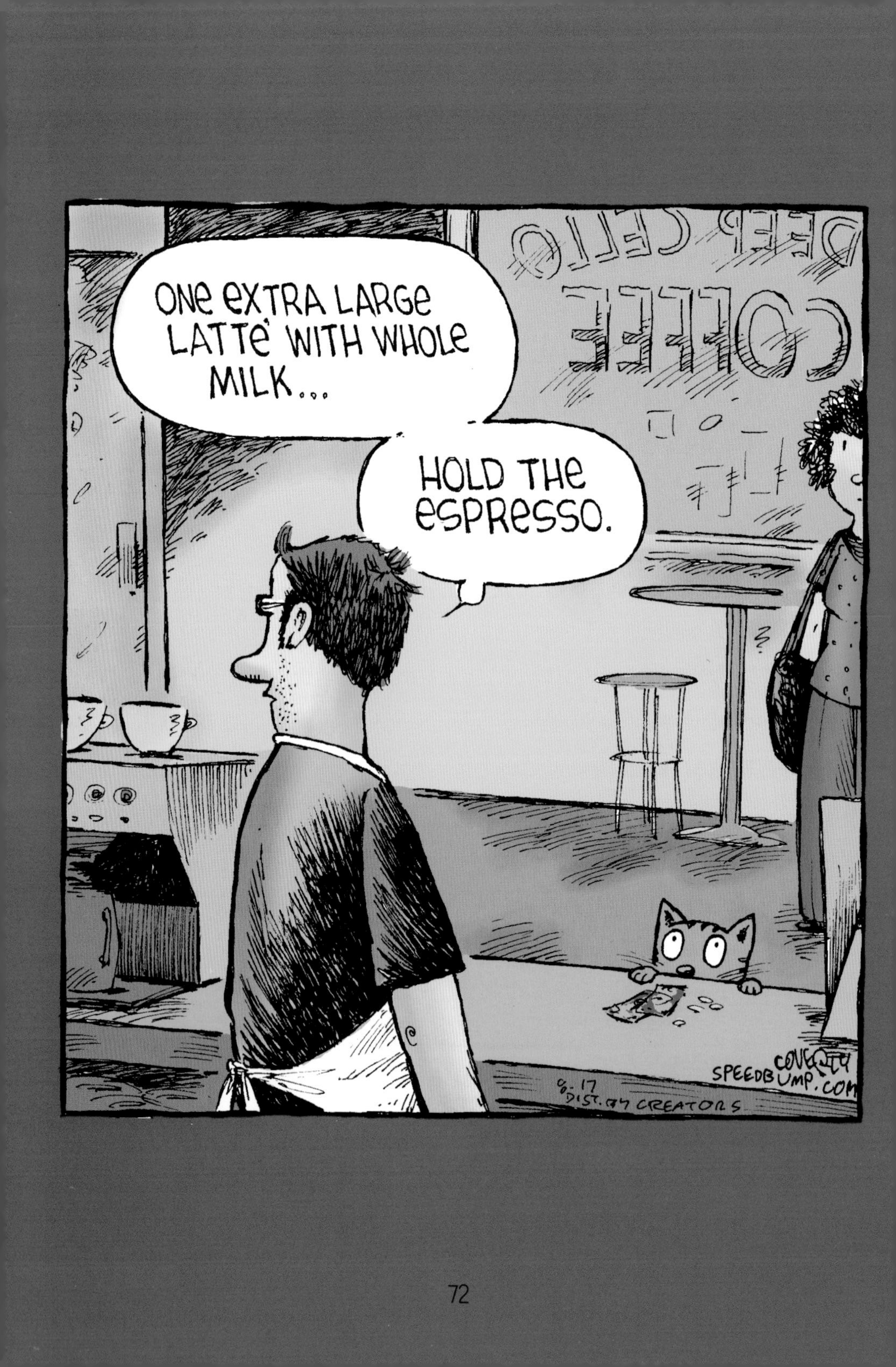
ONE EXTRA LARGE LATTE WITH WHOLE MILK...
HOLD THE ESPRESSO.
COVERLY
SPEEDBUMP.COM
8.17
DIST. BY CREATORS

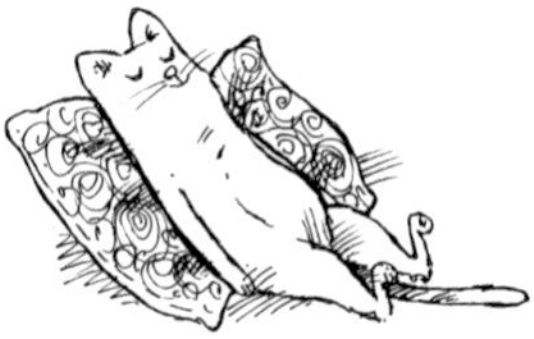

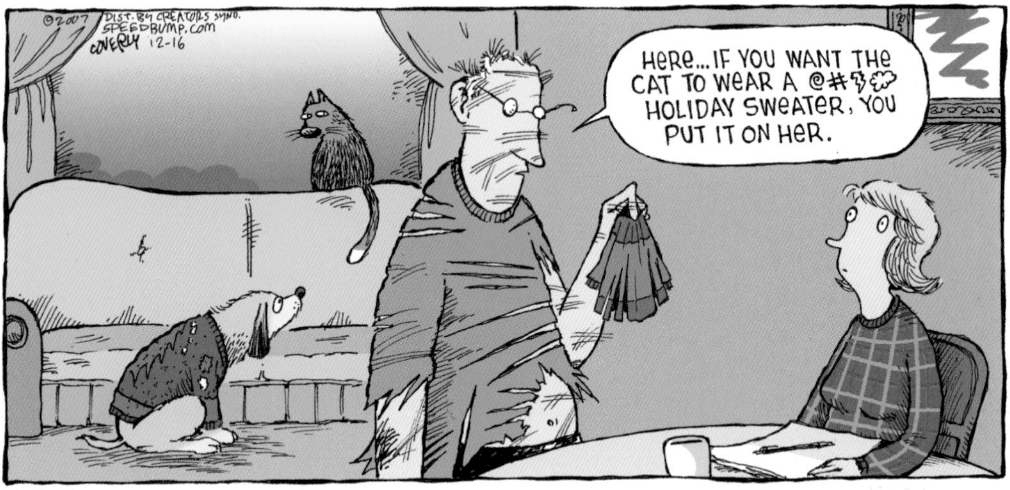
©2007 DIST. BY CREATORS SYND.
SPEEDBUMP.COM
COVERLY 12-16
HERE...IF YOU WANT THE CAT TO WEAR A @#%$ HOLIDAY SWEATER, YOU PUT IT ON HER.

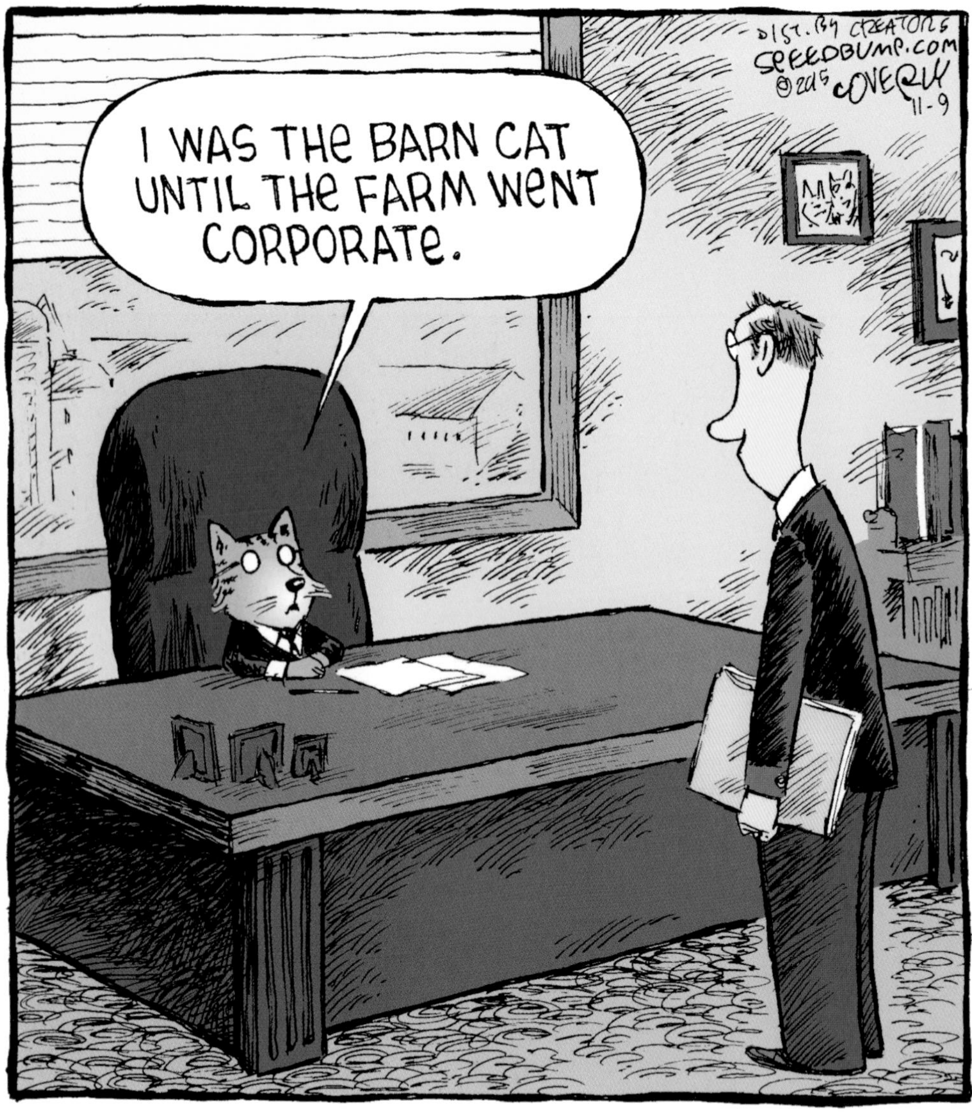
DIST. BY CREATORS
SPEEDBUMP.COM
©2015 COVERLY
11-9
I WAS THE BARN CAT UNTIL THE FARM WENT CORPORATE.

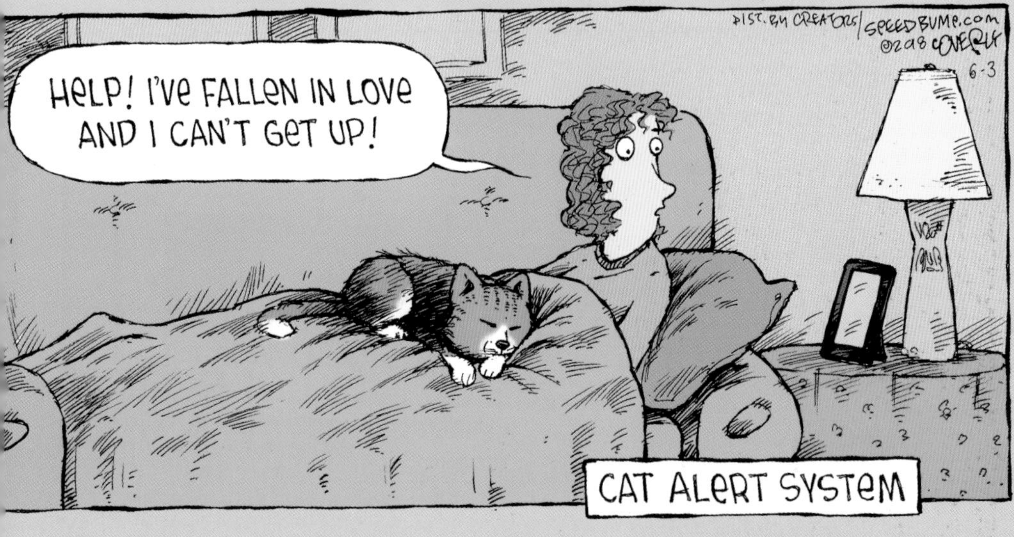
HELP! I'VE FALLEN IN LOVE AND I CAN'T GET UP!
DIST. BY CREATORS/ SPEEDBUMP.COM ©2018 COVERLY
6-3
CAT ALERT SYSTEM

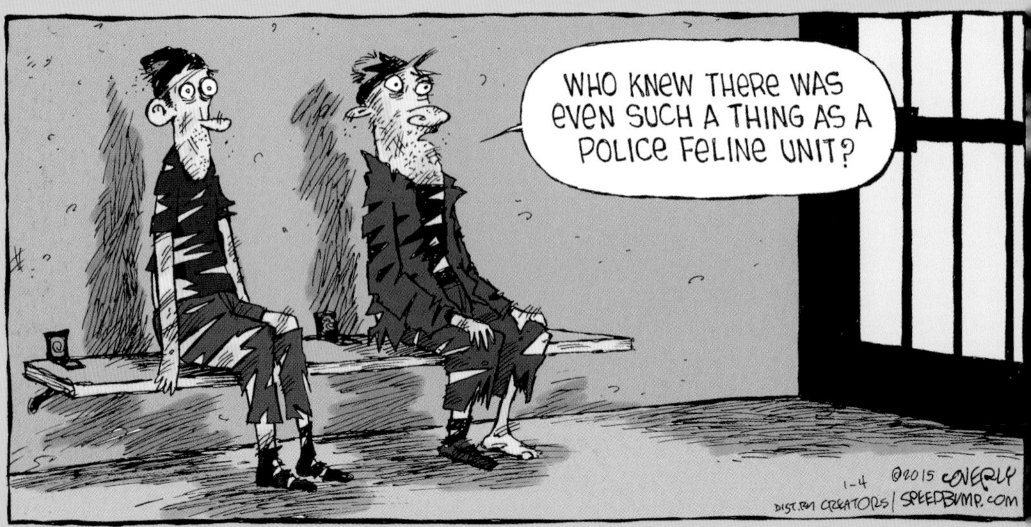
WHO KNEW THERE WAS EVEN SUCH A THING AS A POLICE FELINE UNIT?
1-4
©2015 COVERLY
DIST. BY CREATORS | SPEEDBUMP.COM

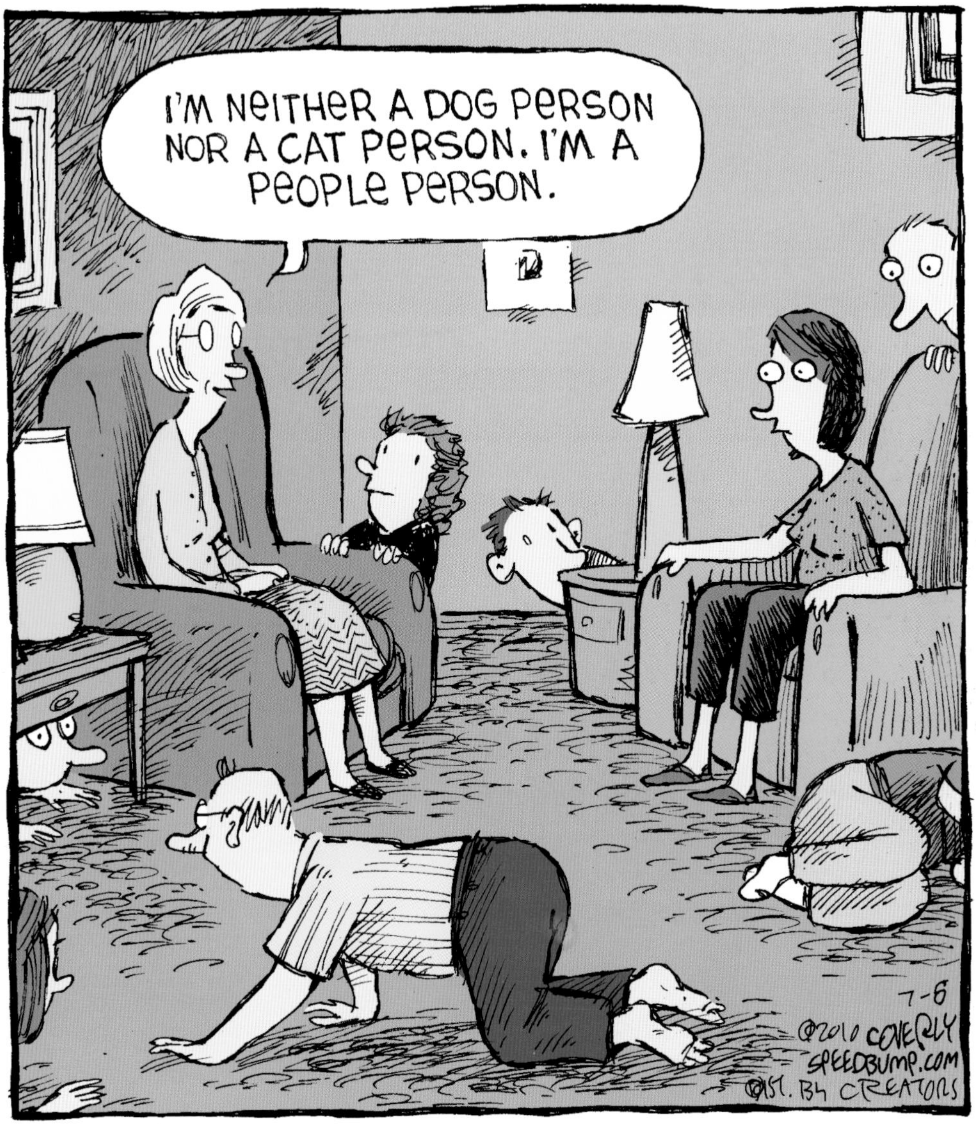
I'M NEITHER A DOG PERSON NOR A CAT PERSON. I'M A PEOPLE PERSON.
7-6
©2010 COVERLY
SPEEDBUMP.COM
DIST. BY CREATORS

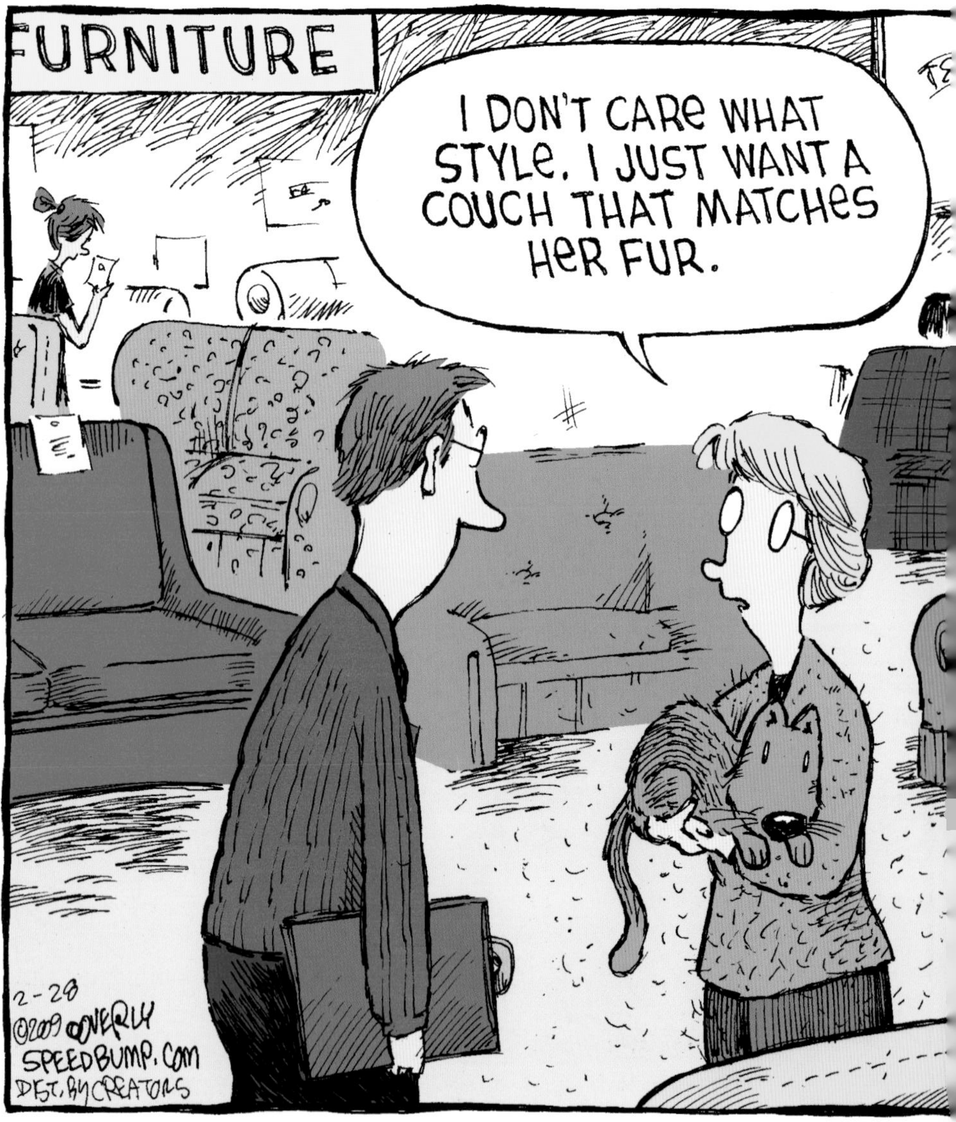
FURNITURE
I DON'T CARE WHAT STYLE. I JUST WANT A COUCH THAT MATCHES HER FUR.
2-28
©2009 COVERLY
SPEEDBUMP.COM
DIST. BY CREATORS

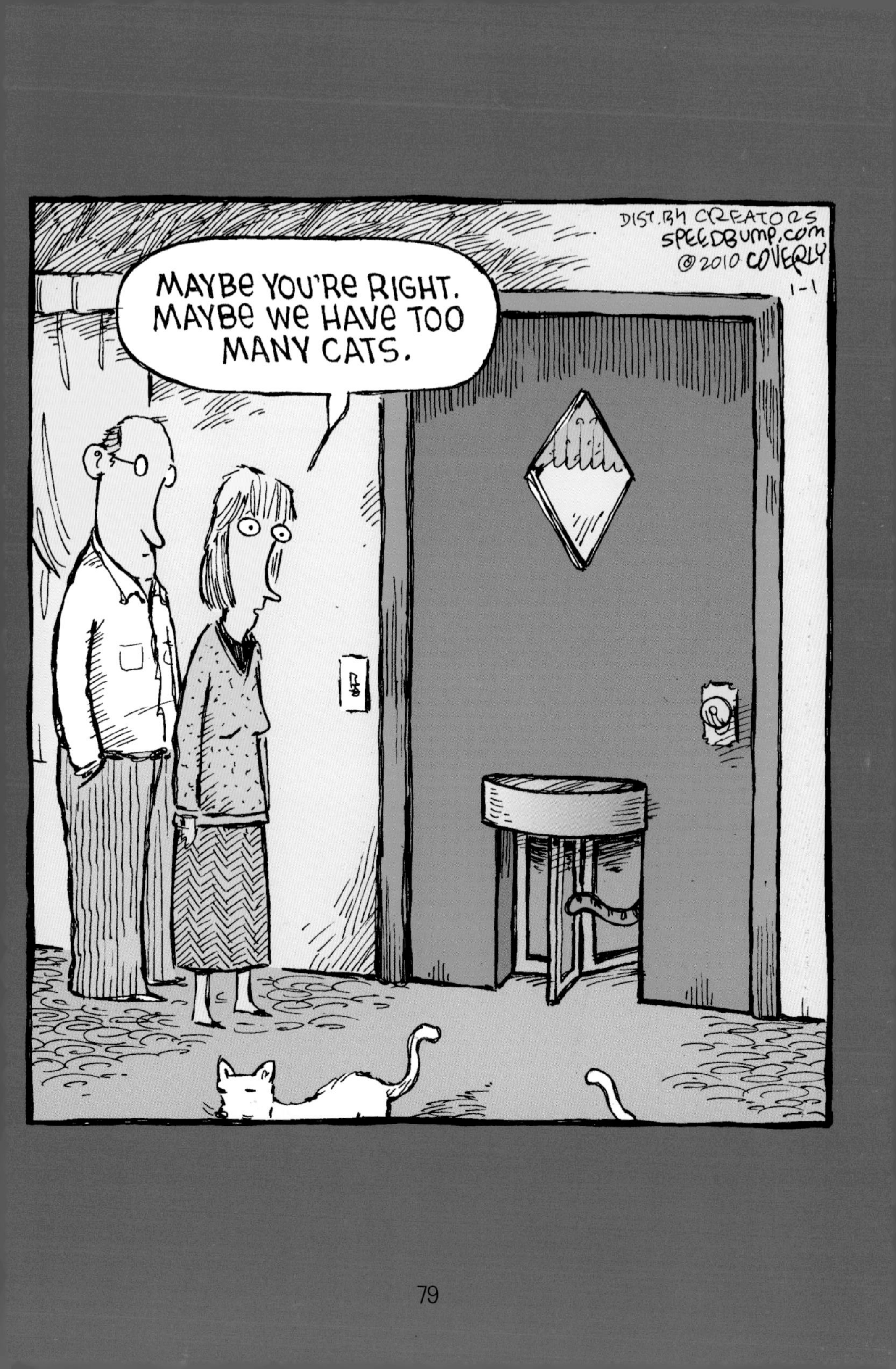
MAYBE YOU'RE RIGHT. MAYBE WE HAVE TOO MANY CATS.
DIST. BY CREATORS
SPEEDBUMP.COM
©2010 COVERLY
1-1

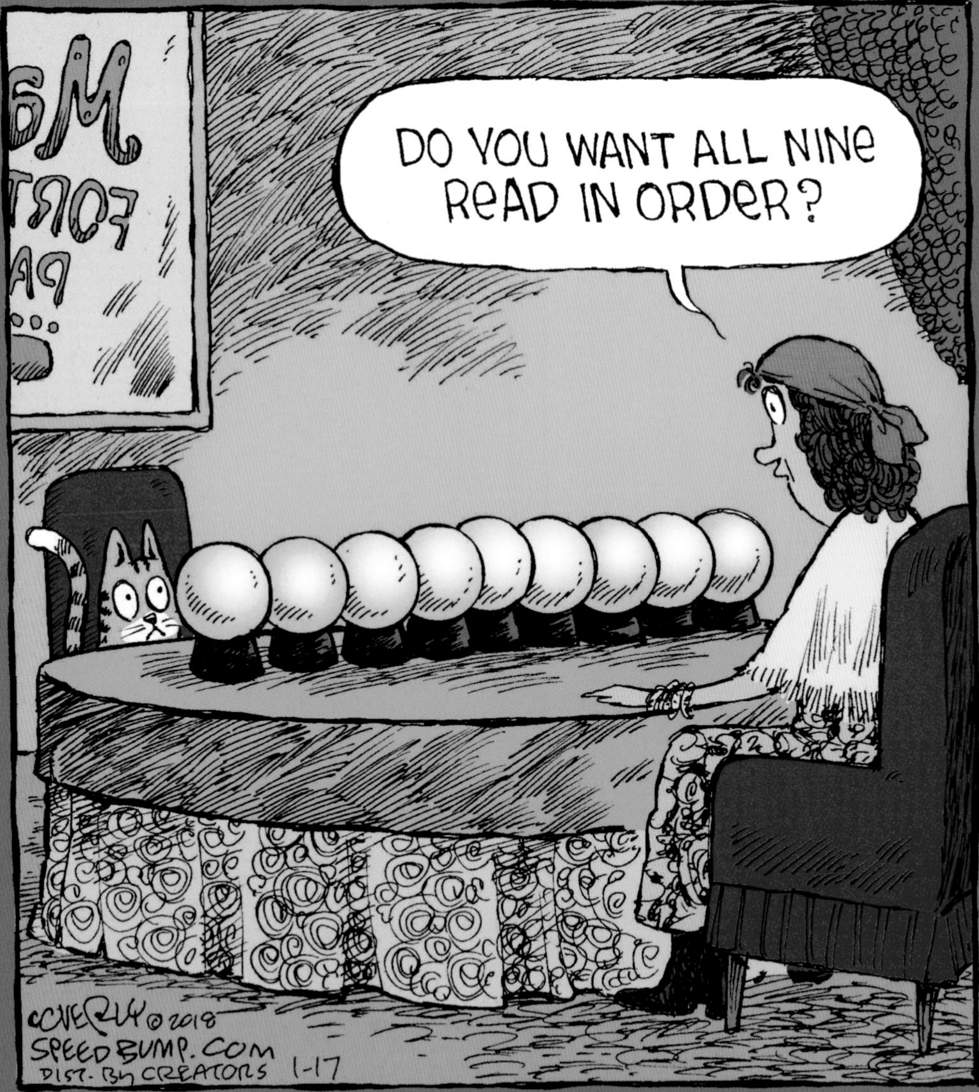
DO YOU WANT ALL NINE READ IN ORDER?
COVERLY ©2018
SPEEDBUMP.COM
DIST. BY CREATORS 1-17

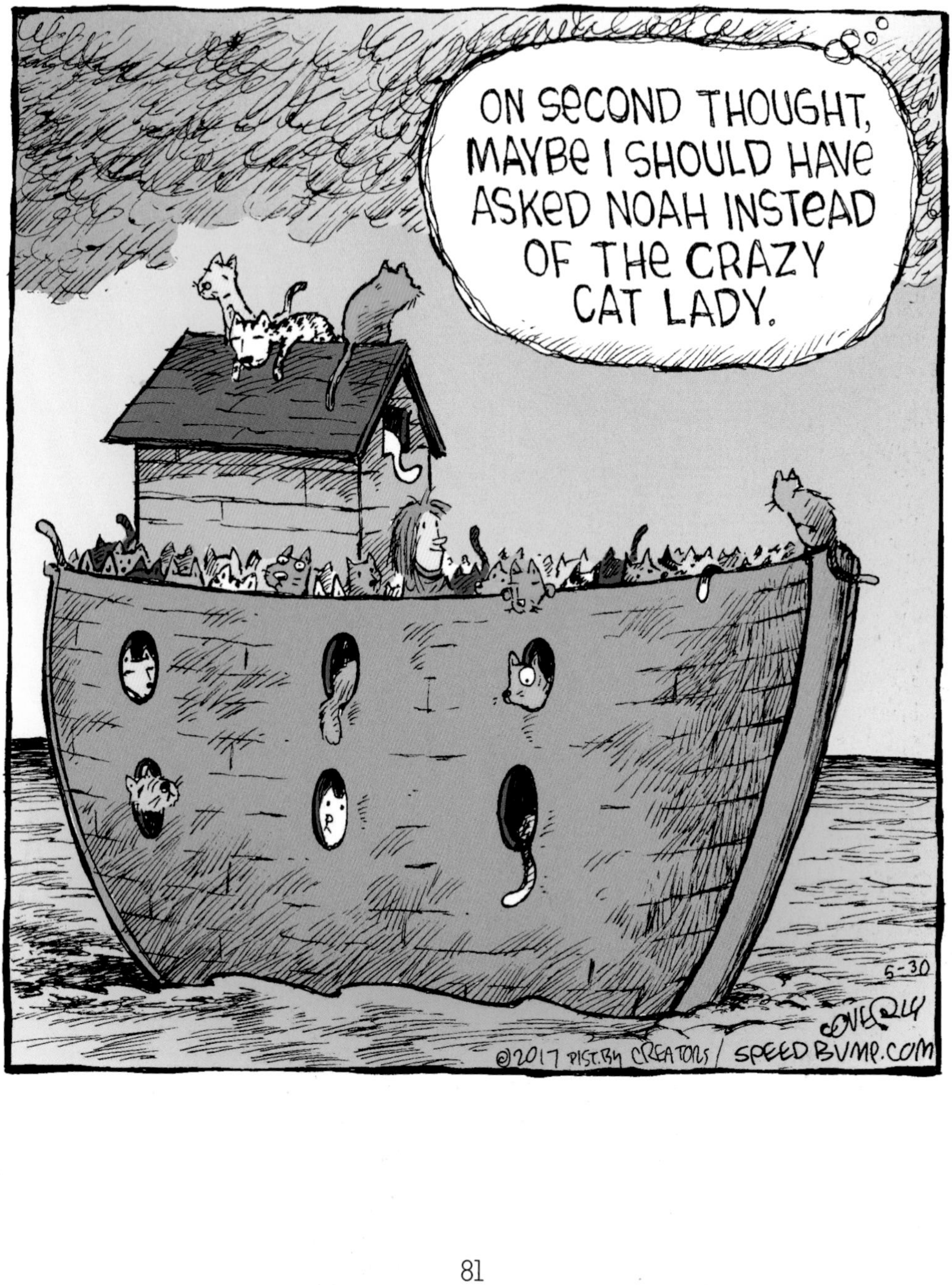
ON SECOND THOUGHT, MAYBE I SHOULD HAVE ASKED NOAH INSTEAD OF THE CRAZY CAT LADY.
5-30
COVERLY
©2017 DIST. BY CREATORS / SPEEDBUMP.COM

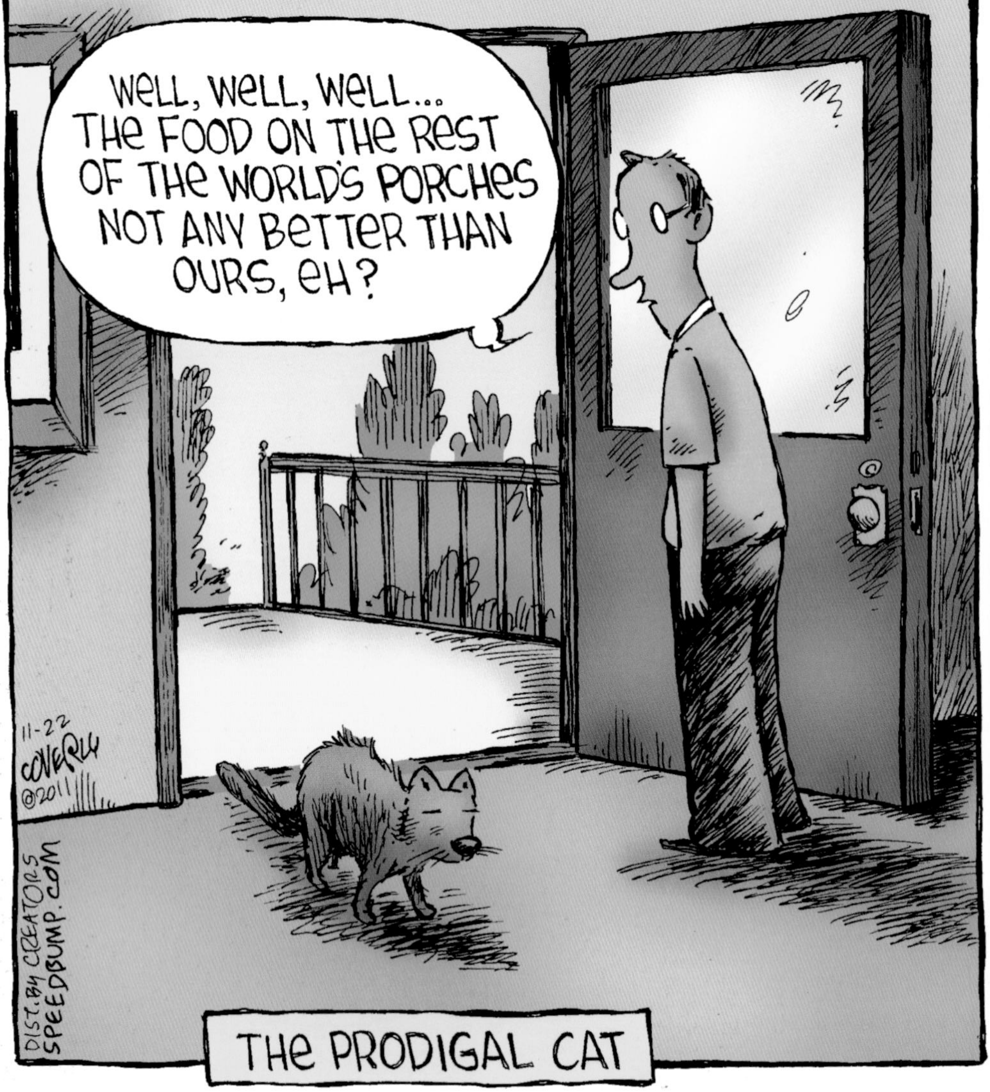
WELL, WELL, WELL... THE FOOD ON THE REST OF THE WORLD'S PORCHES NOT ANY BETTER THAN OURS, EH?
11-22 COVERLY ©2011
DIST. BY CREATORS SPEEDBUMP.COM
THE PRODIGAL CAT

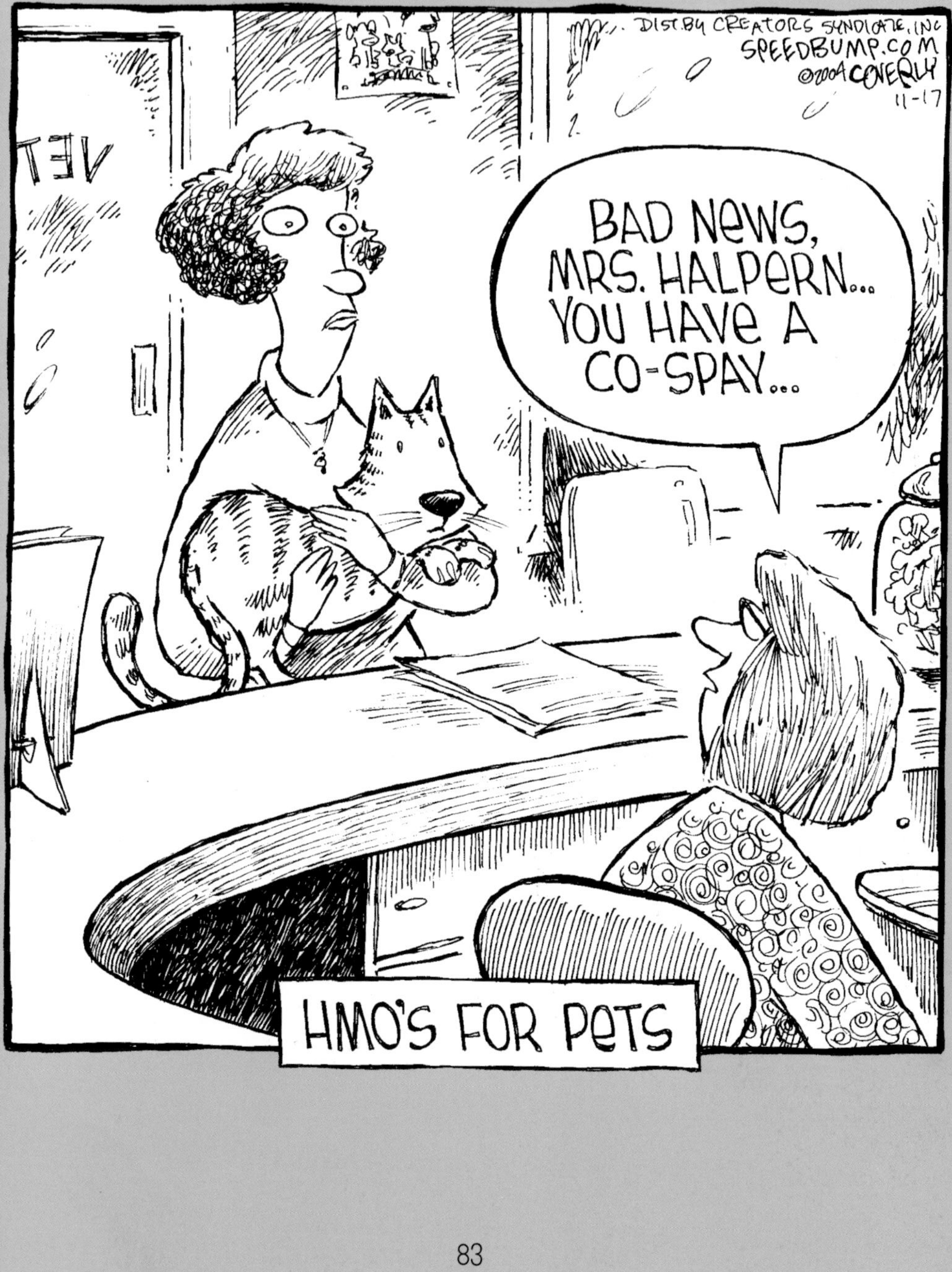
DIST. BY CREATORS SYNDICATE, INC
SPEEDBUMP.COM
©2004 COVERLY
11-17
VET
BAD NEWS, MRS. HALPERN... YOU HAVE A CO-SPAY...
HMO'S FOR PETS

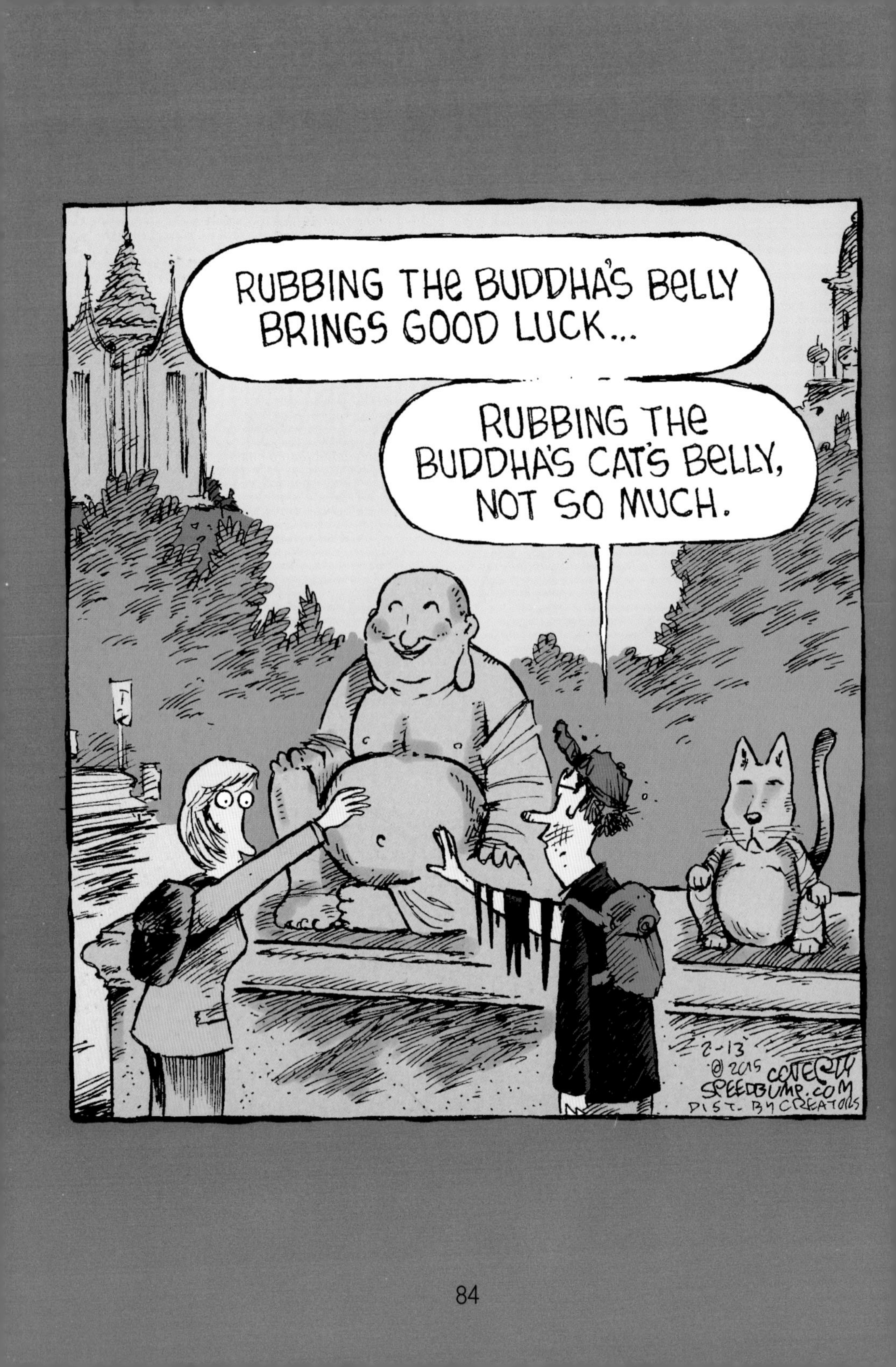
RUBBING THE BUDDHA'S BELLY BRINGS GOOD LUCK...
RUBBING THE BUDDHA'S CAT'S BELLY, NOT SO MUCH.
2-13
© 2015 CONEELY
SPEEDBUMP.COM
DIST. BY CREATORS

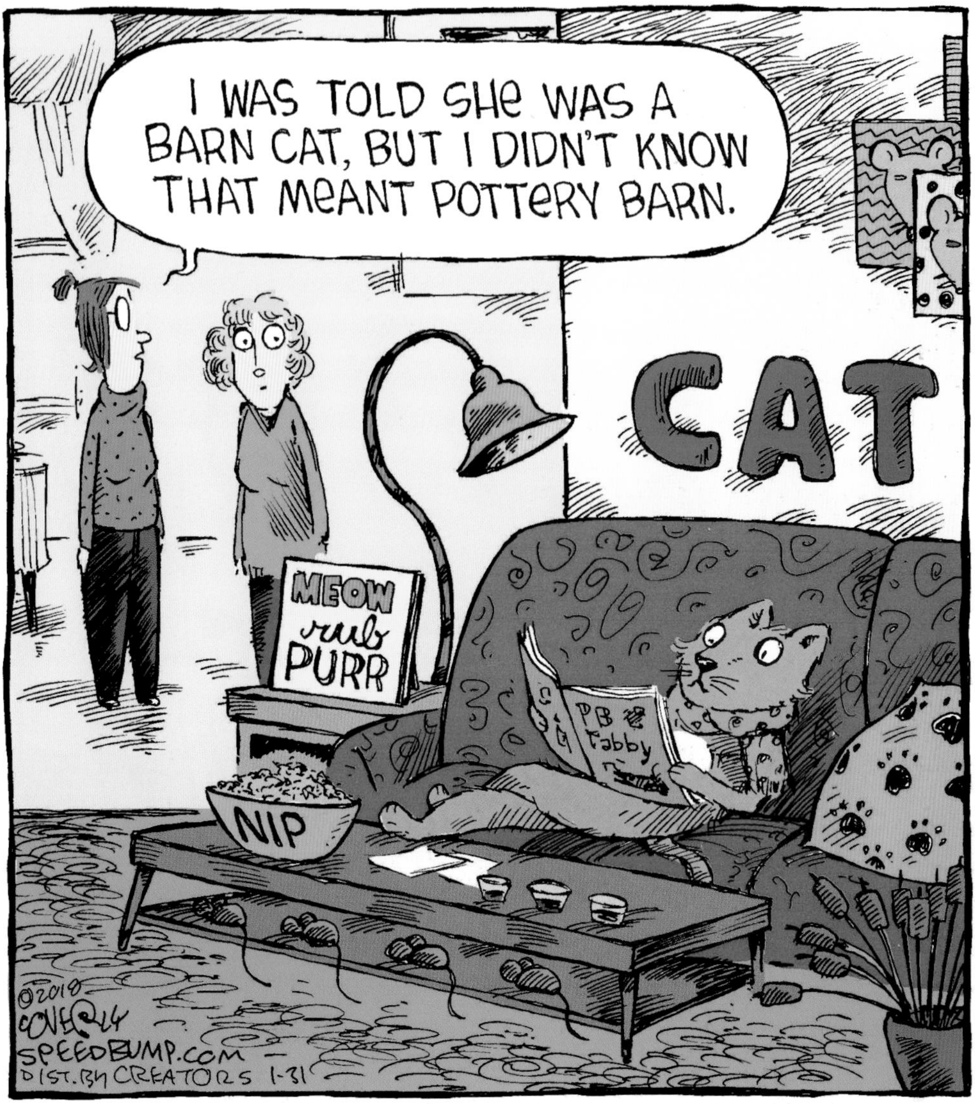
I WAS TOLD SHE WAS A BARN CAT, BUT I DIDN'T KNOW THAT MEANT POTTERY BARN.
CAT
MEOW rub PURR
PB Tabby
NIP
©2018 Coverly
SPEEDBUMP.COM
DIST. BY CREATORS 1-31

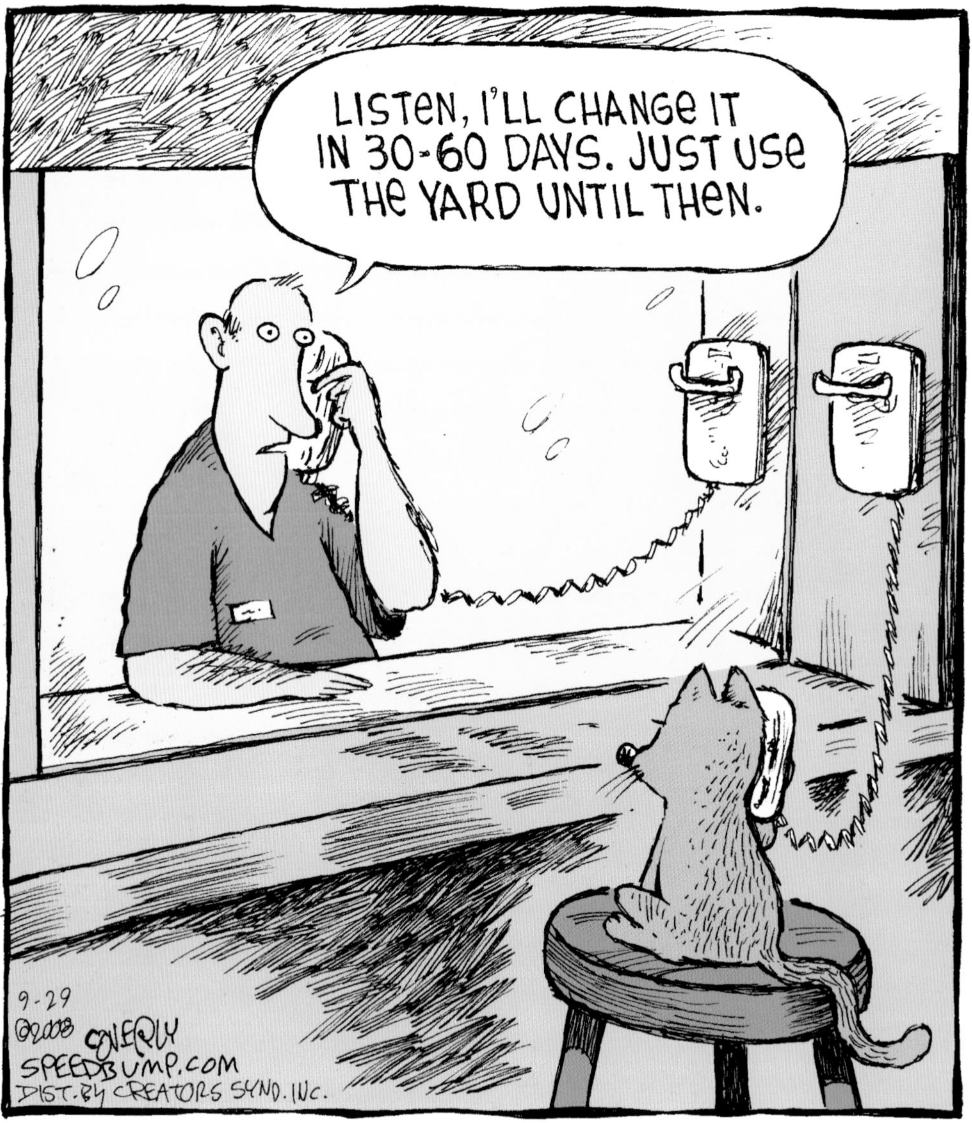
LISTEN, I'LL CHANGE IT IN 30-60 DAYS. JUST USE THE YARD UNTIL THEN.
9-29
©2008 COVERLY
SPEEDBUMP.COM
DIST. BY CREATORS SYND. INC.

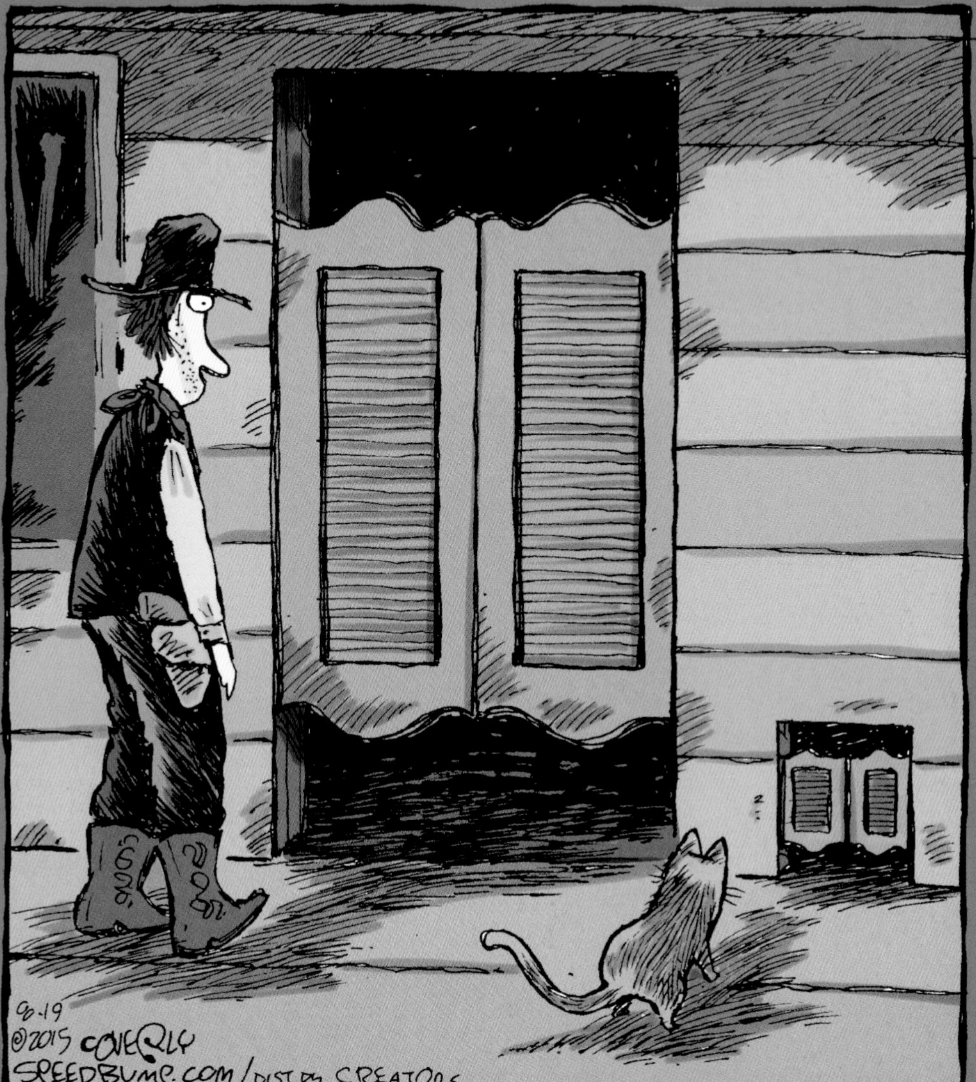

8-19
©2015 COVERLY
SPEEDBUMP.COM/DIST. BY CREATORS

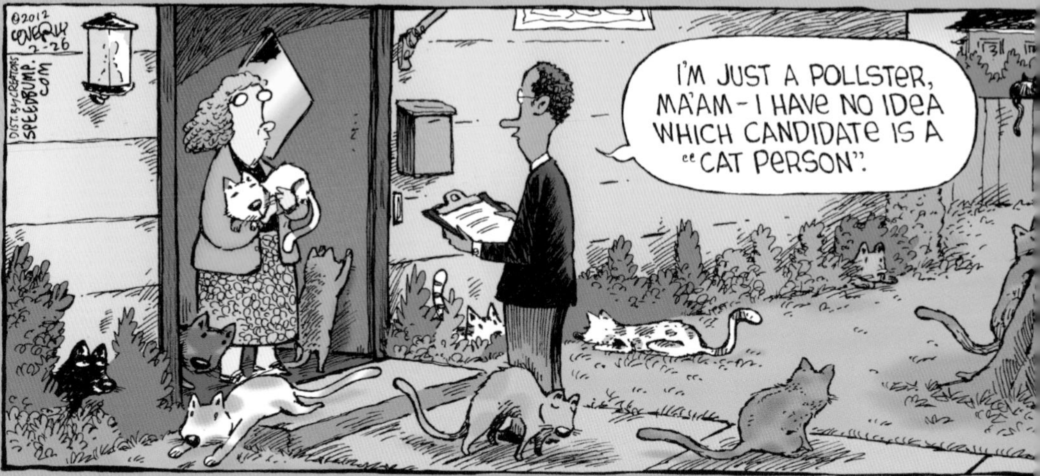
©2012 GENERALLY 2-26
DIST. BY CREATORS SPEEDBUMP.COM
I'M JUST A POLLSTER, MA'AM - I HAVE NO IDEA WHICH CANDIDATE IS A "CAT PERSON".

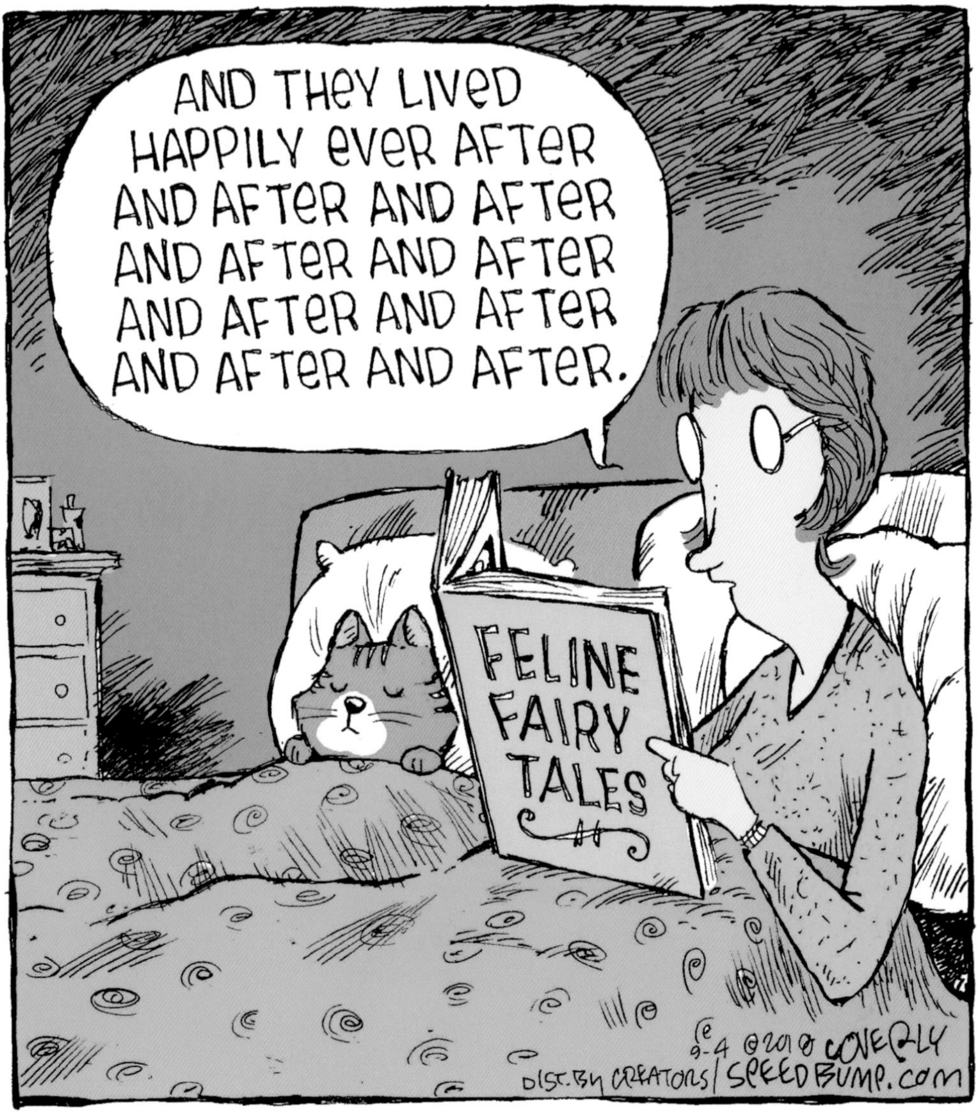
AND THEY LIVED HAPPILY EVER AFTER AND AFTER AND AFTER AND AFTER AND AFTER AND AFTER AND AFTER AND AFTER AND AFTER.
FELINE FAIRY TALES
9-4 ©2018 COVERLY
DIST. BY CREATORS/ SPEEDBUMP.COM

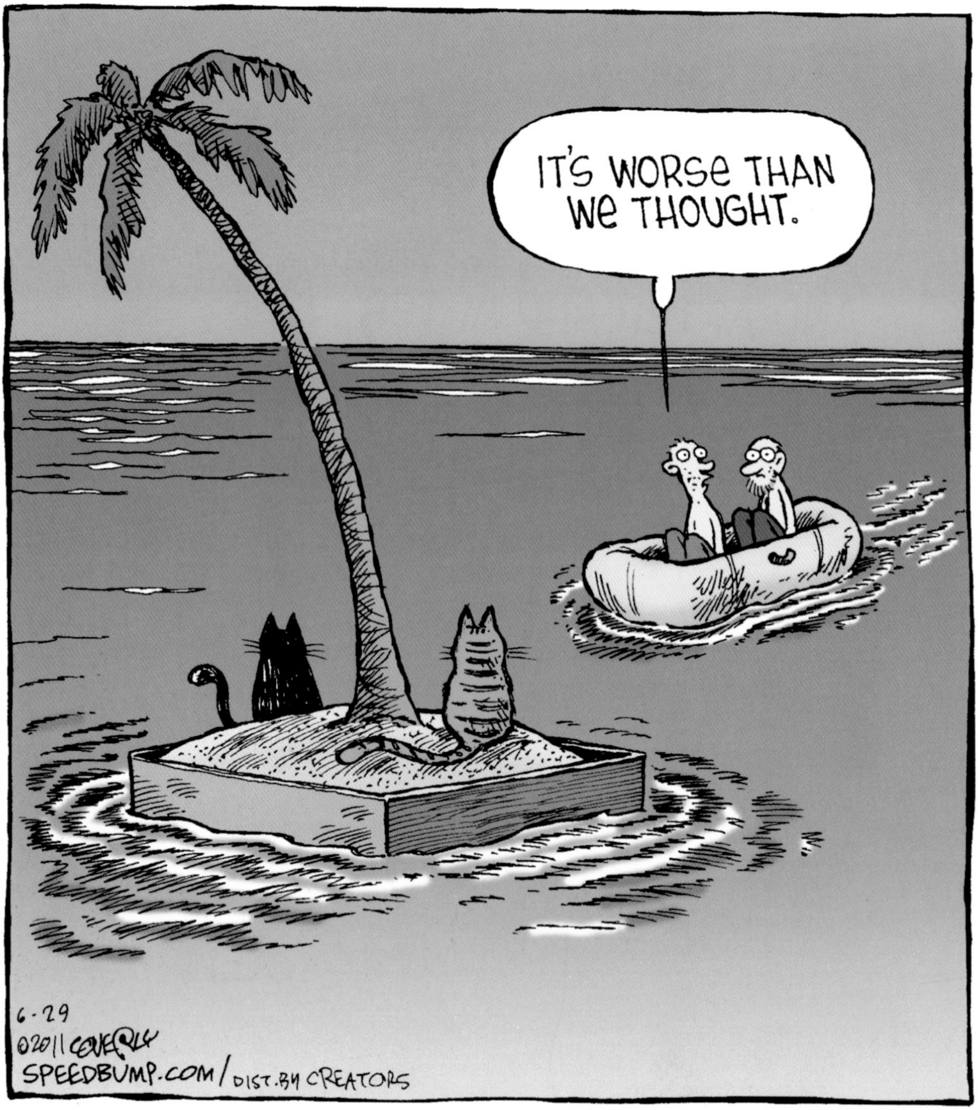
IT'S WORSE THAN WE THOUGHT.
6-29
©2011 COVERLY
SPEEDBUMP.COM/ DIST. BY CREATORS

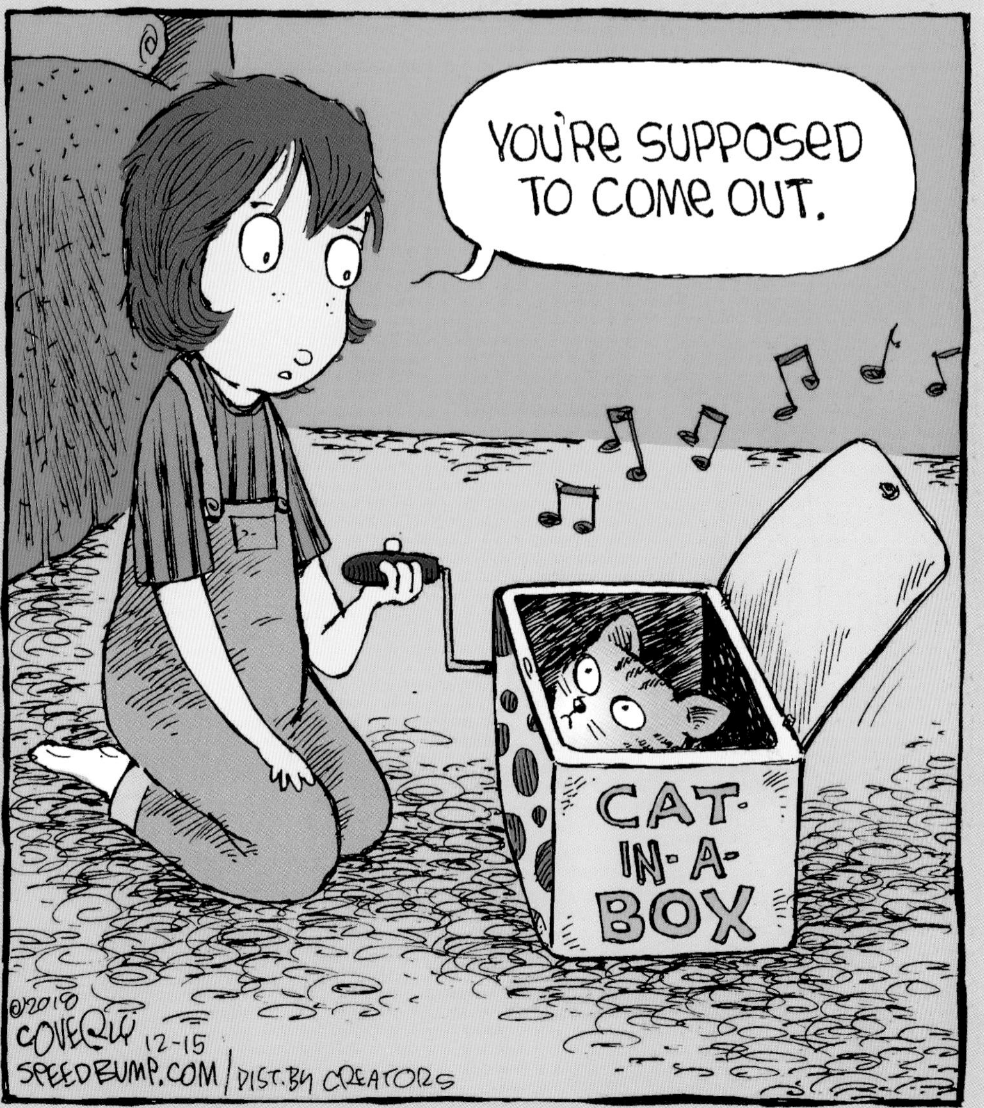
YOU'RE SUPPOSED TO COME OUT.
CAT-IN-A-BOX
©2018 COVERLY 12-15
SPEEDBUMP.COM / DIST. BY CREATORS

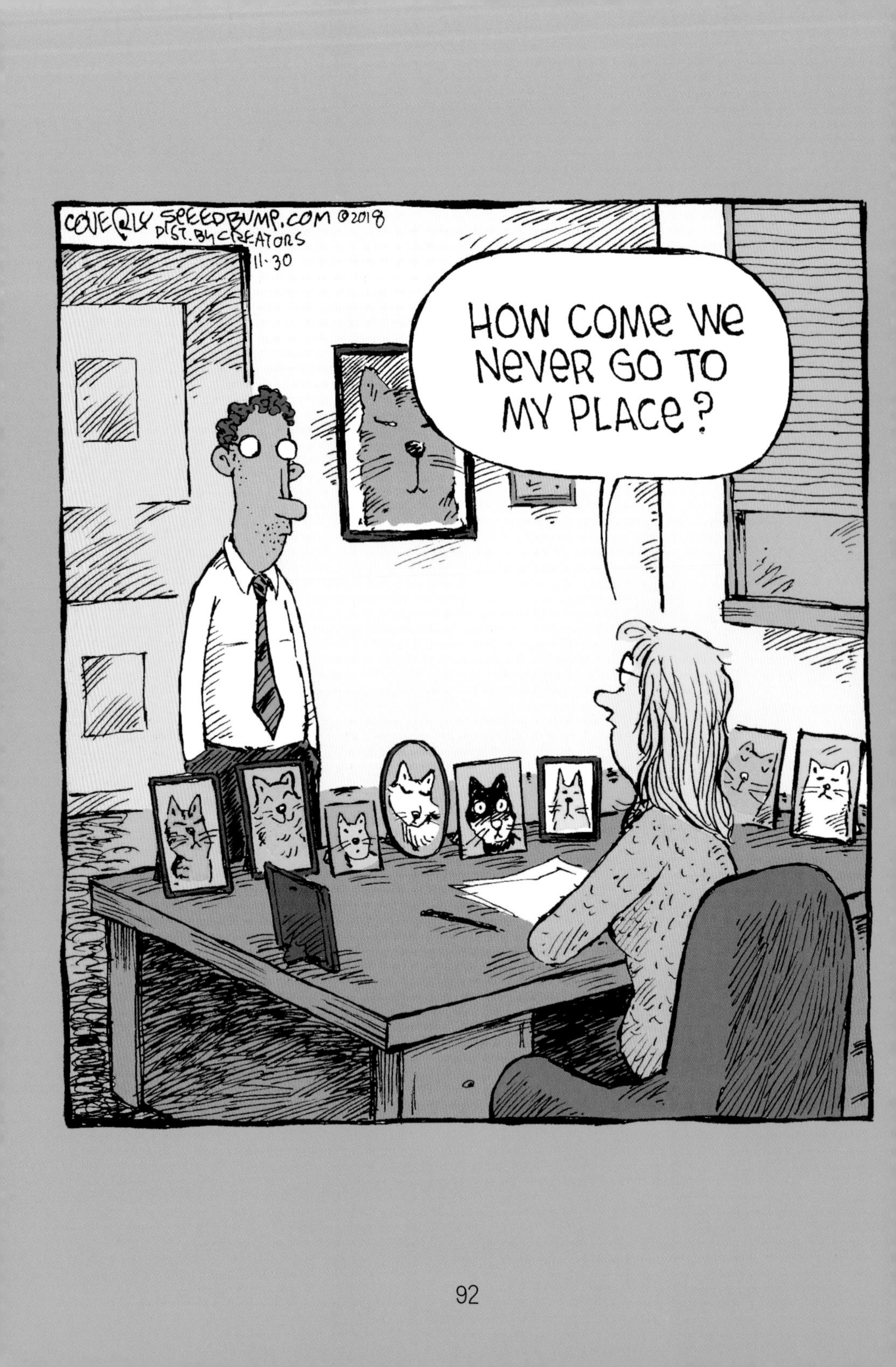
COVERLY SPEEDBUMP.COM ©2018
DIST. BY CREATORS
11-30
HOW COME WE NEVER GO TO MY PLACE?

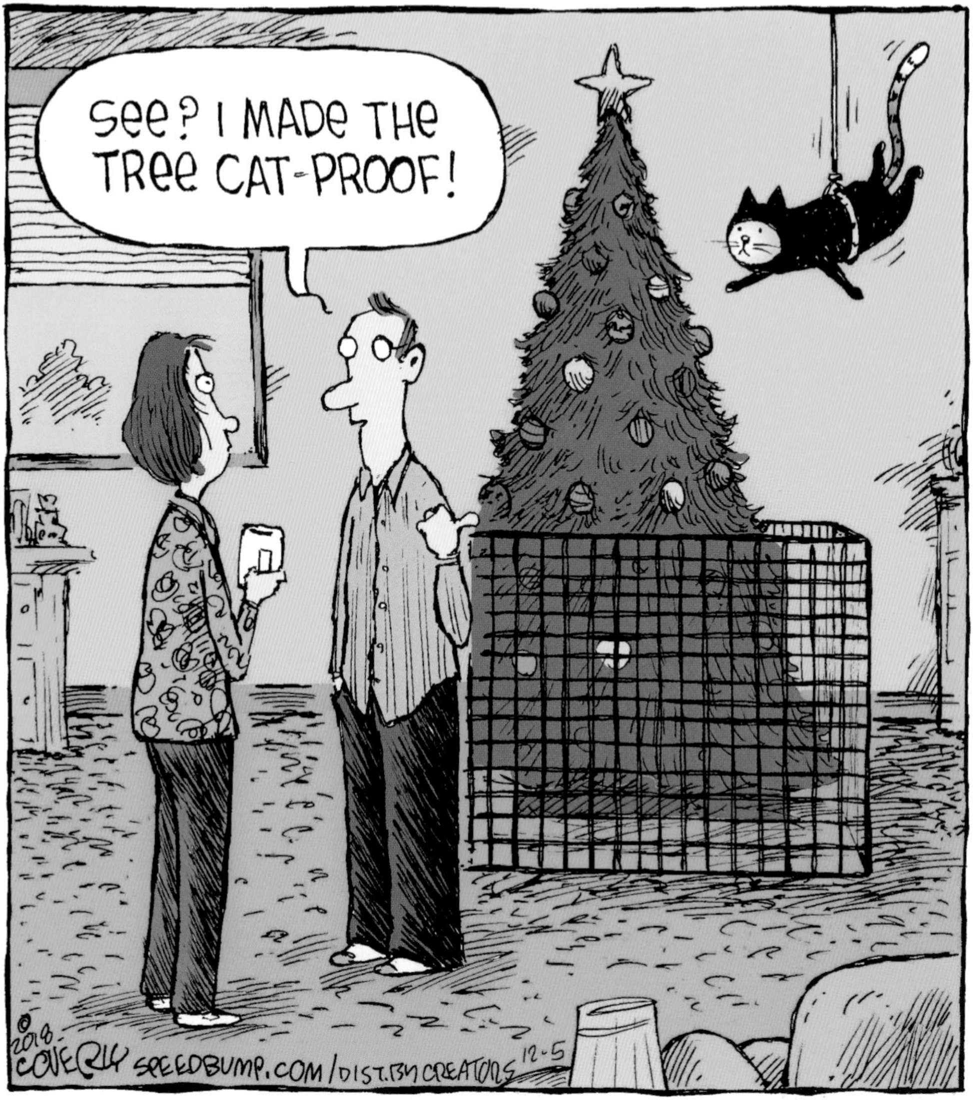
SEE? I MADE THE TREE CAT-PROOF!
© 2018 COVERLY SPEEDBUMP.COM/DIST.BY CREATORS 12-5

Laurie Keller

The moment just before Louie decides to wake Olive by pouncing on her and clamping his teeth around her neck.

About Laurie Keller

Laurie Keller is the acclaimed author-illustrator of many books for kids, including *Potato Pants!*; *Do Unto Otters*; *Arnie, the Doughnut*; *The Scrambled States of America*; and *Open Wide: Tooth School Inside*.

Laurie grew up in Muskegon, Michigan, and always loved to draw, paint, and write stories. She earned a BFA at Kendall College of Art and Design, then worked at Hallmark as a greeting card illustrator for seven and a half years, until the night she got an idea for a children's book. Soon after, she moved to New York City and published her first book. She loved living in New York, but now resides in her home state, in a little cottage in the woods on the shore of Lake Michigan.

lauriekeller.com

CHAPTER 4
CRAZY CATS

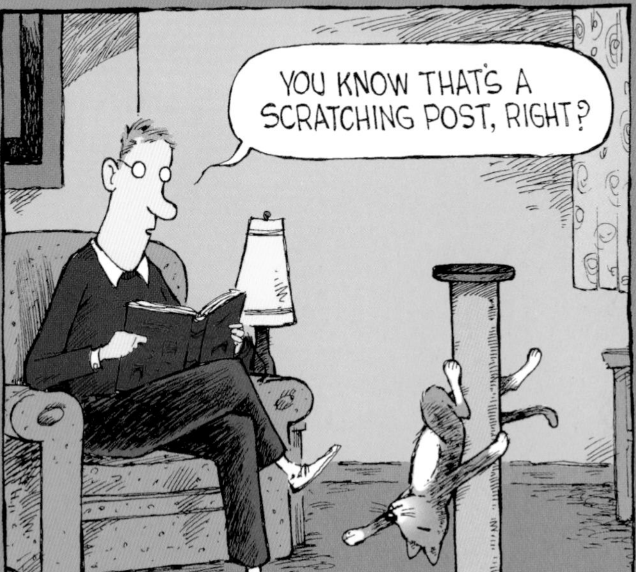
YOU KNOW THAT'S A SCRATCHING POST, RIGHT?
©2017 COVERLY
SPEEDBUMP.COM / 1-25 DIST. BY CREATORS

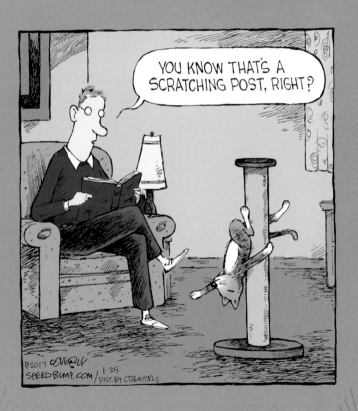

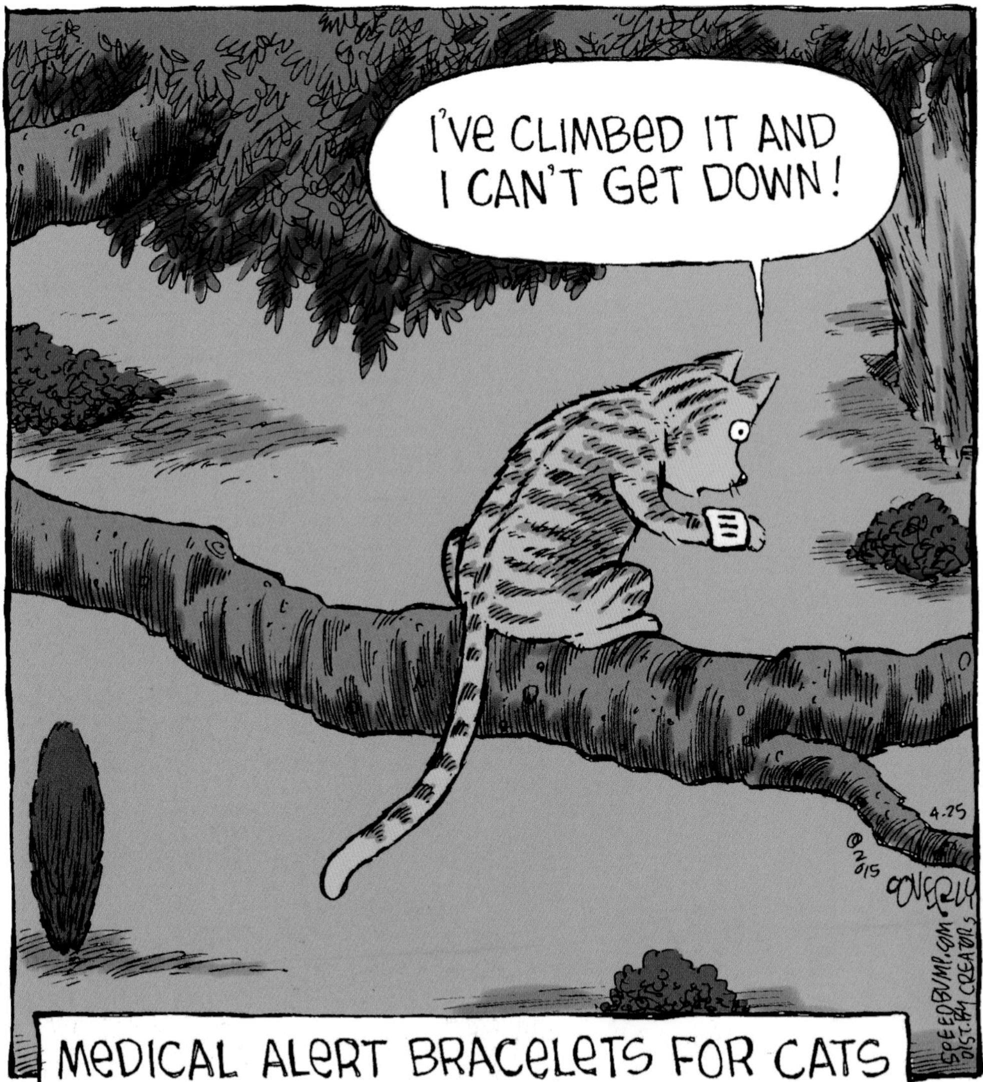
I'VE CLIMBED IT AND I CAN'T GET DOWN!
4.25
©2015 COVERLY
SPEEDBUMP.COM
DIST. BY CREATORS
MEDICAL ALERT BRACELETS FOR CATS

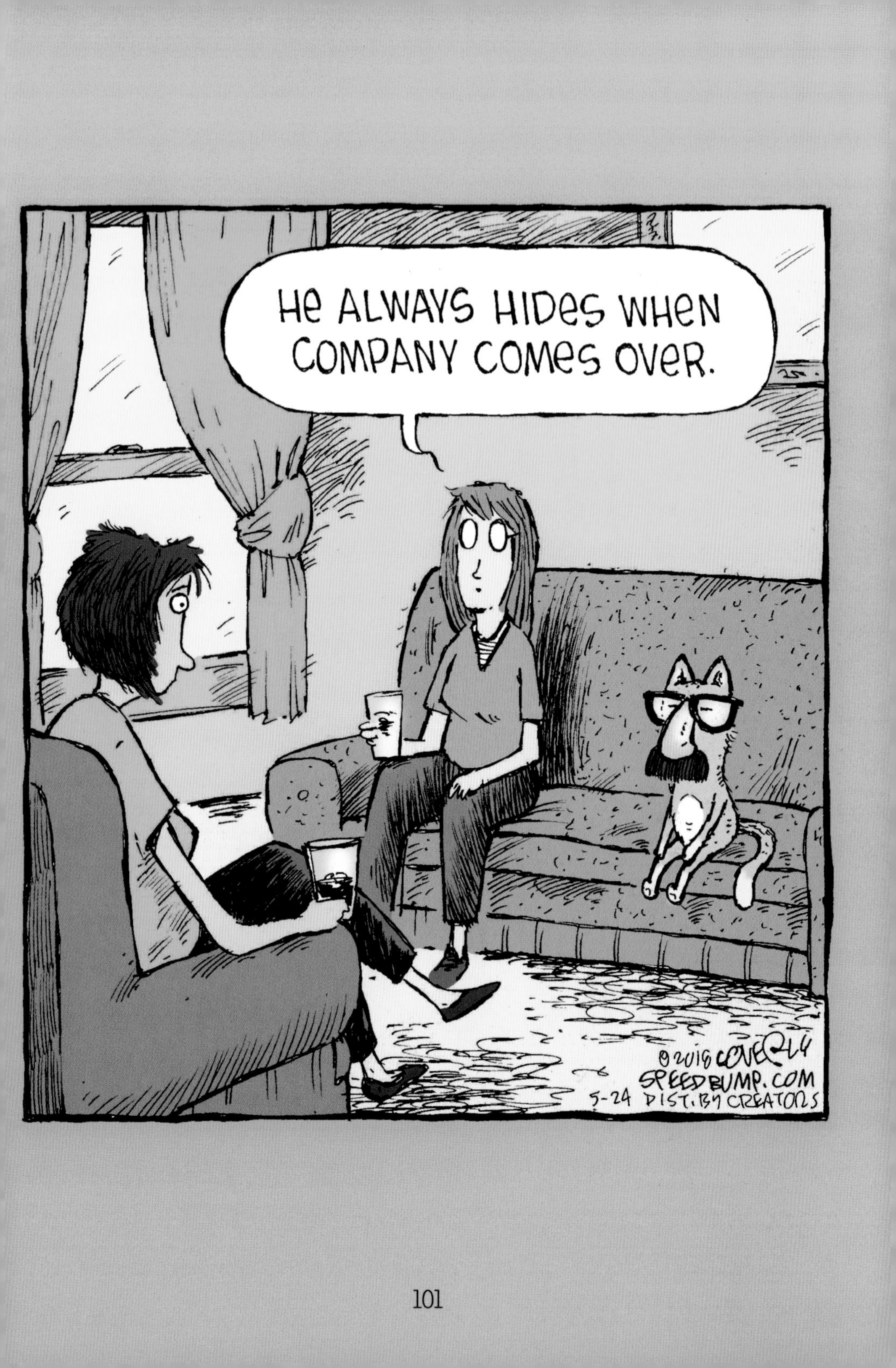
HE ALWAYS HIDES WHEN COMPANY COMES OVER.
© 2018 COVERLY
SPEEDBUMP.COM
5-24 DIST. BY CREATORS

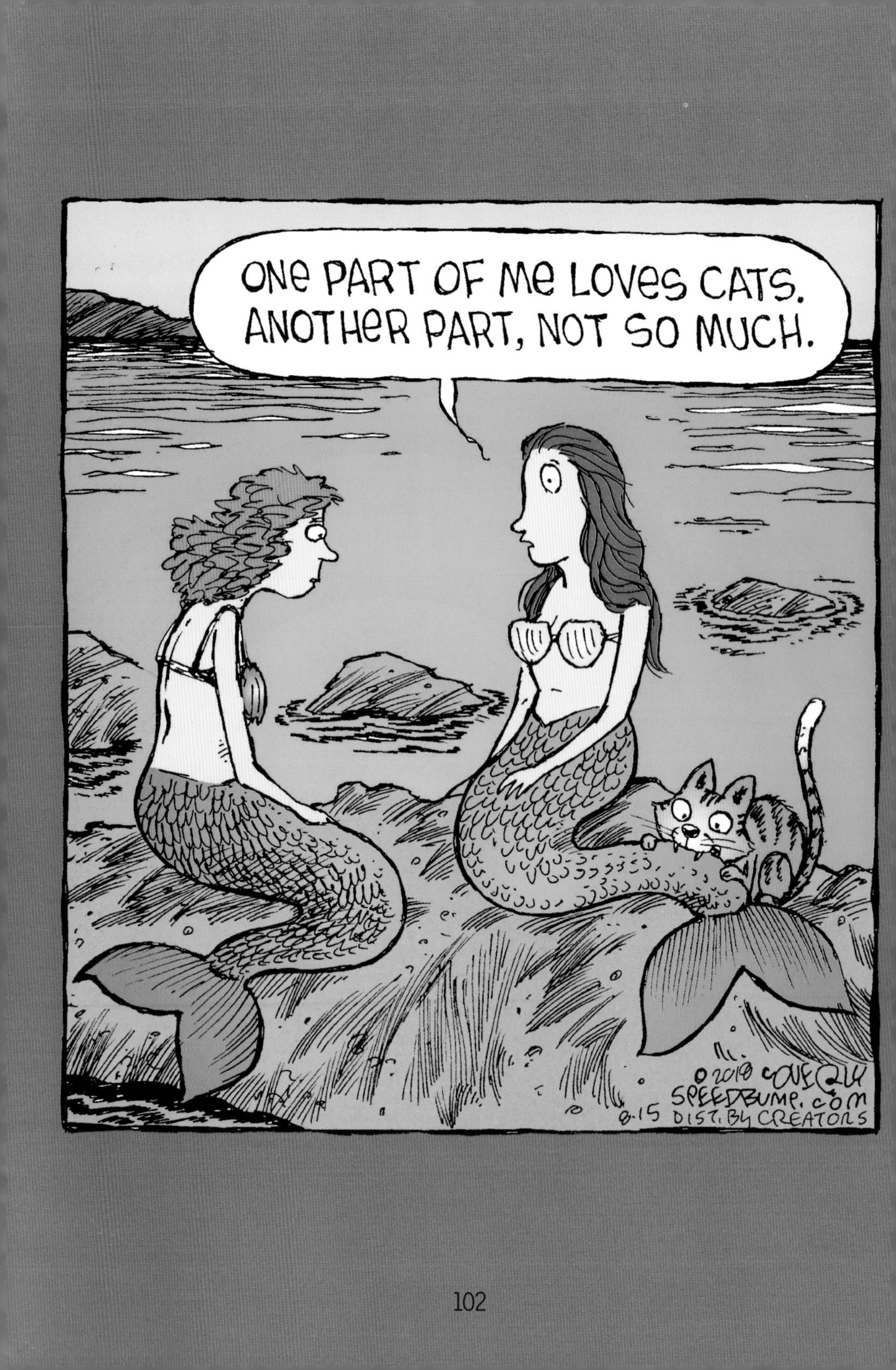
ONE PART OF ME LOVES CATS. ANOTHER PART, NOT SO MUCH.
© 2018 COVERLY
SPEEDBUMP.COM
8-15 DIST. BY CREATORS

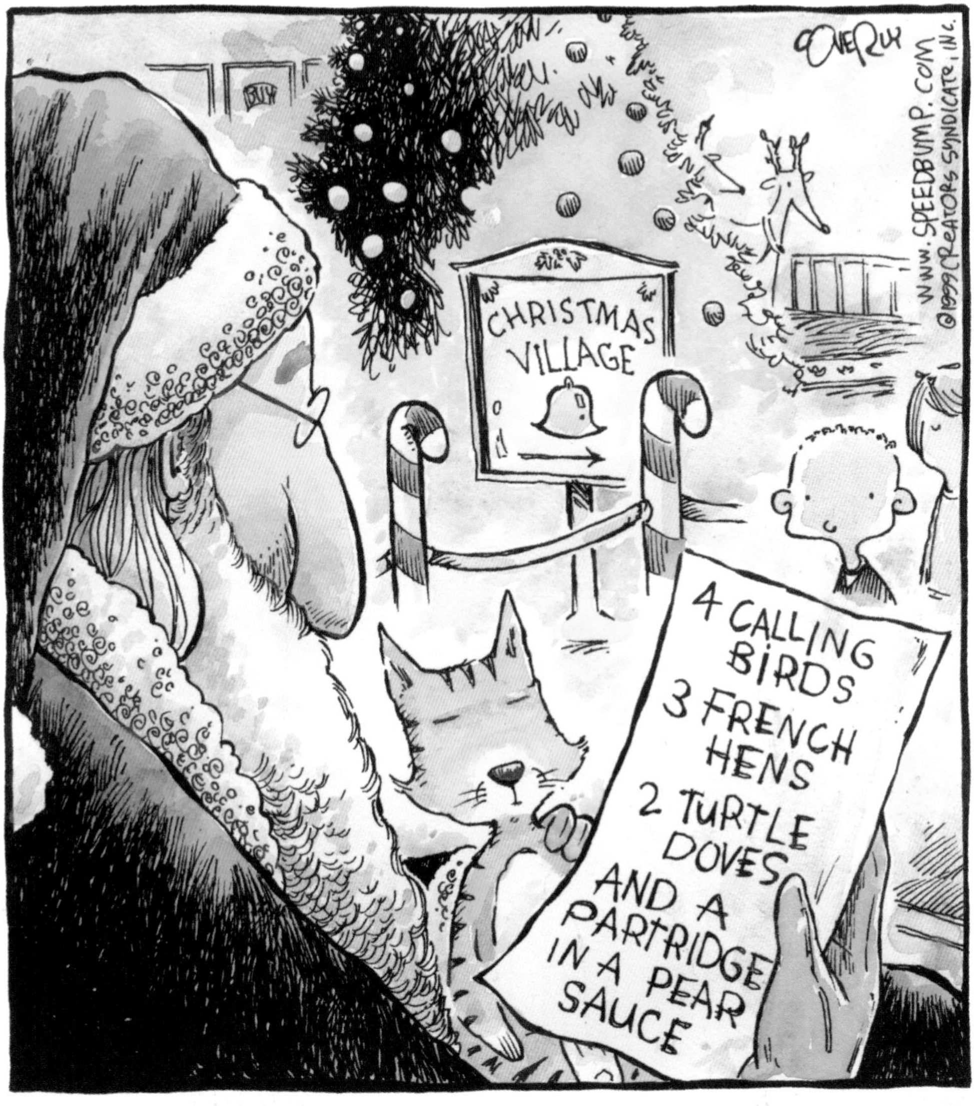
www.SPEEDBUMP.COM
©1999 CREATORS SYNDICATE, INC.
CHRISTMAS VILLAGE
4 CALLING BIRDS
3 FRENCH HENS
2 TURTLE DOVES
AND A PARTRIDGE IN A PEAR SAUCE

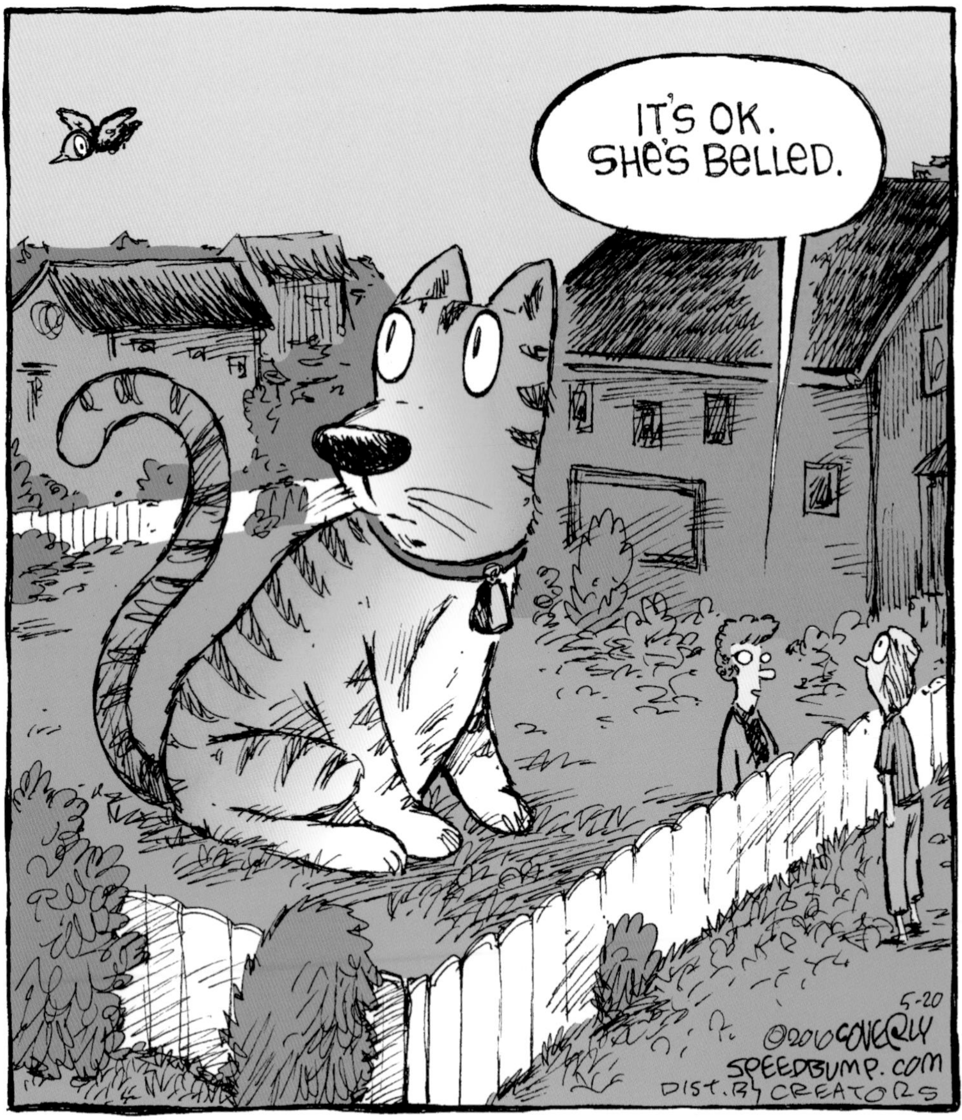
IT'S OK.
SHE'S BELLED.
5-20
©2010 COVERLY
SPEEDBUMP.COM
DIST. BY CREATORS

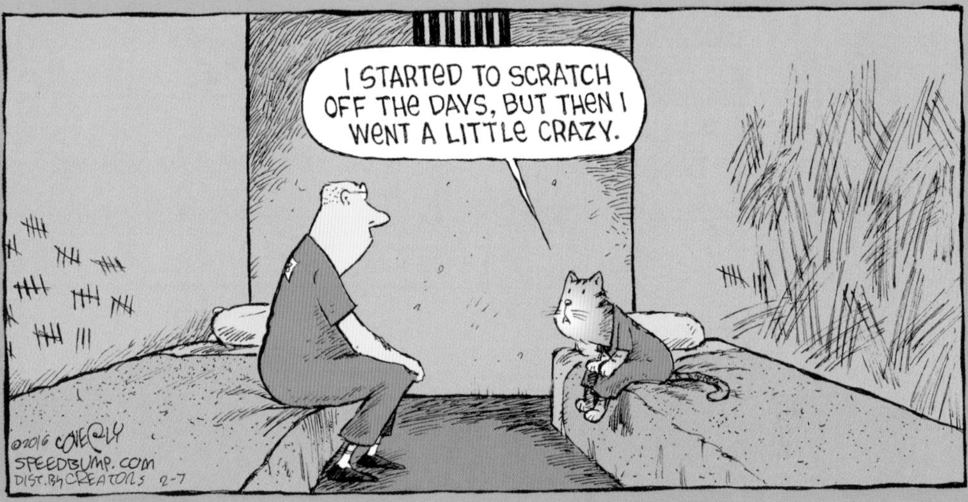
I STARTED TO SCRATCH OFF THE DAYS, BUT THEN I WENT A LITTLE CRAZY.
©2016 COVERLY
SPEEDBUMP.COM
DIST. BY CREATORS 2-7

ENOUGH WITH THE YAPPY DOG RINGTONE, TOM.
10-14 ©2010 COVERLY
DIST. BY CREATORS/ SPEEDBUMP.COM

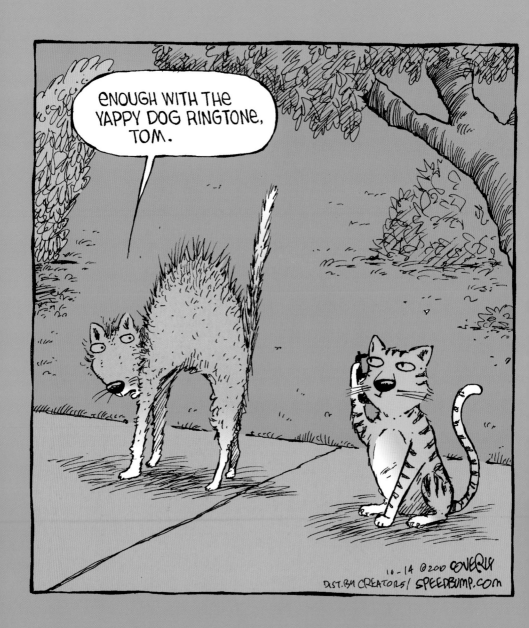

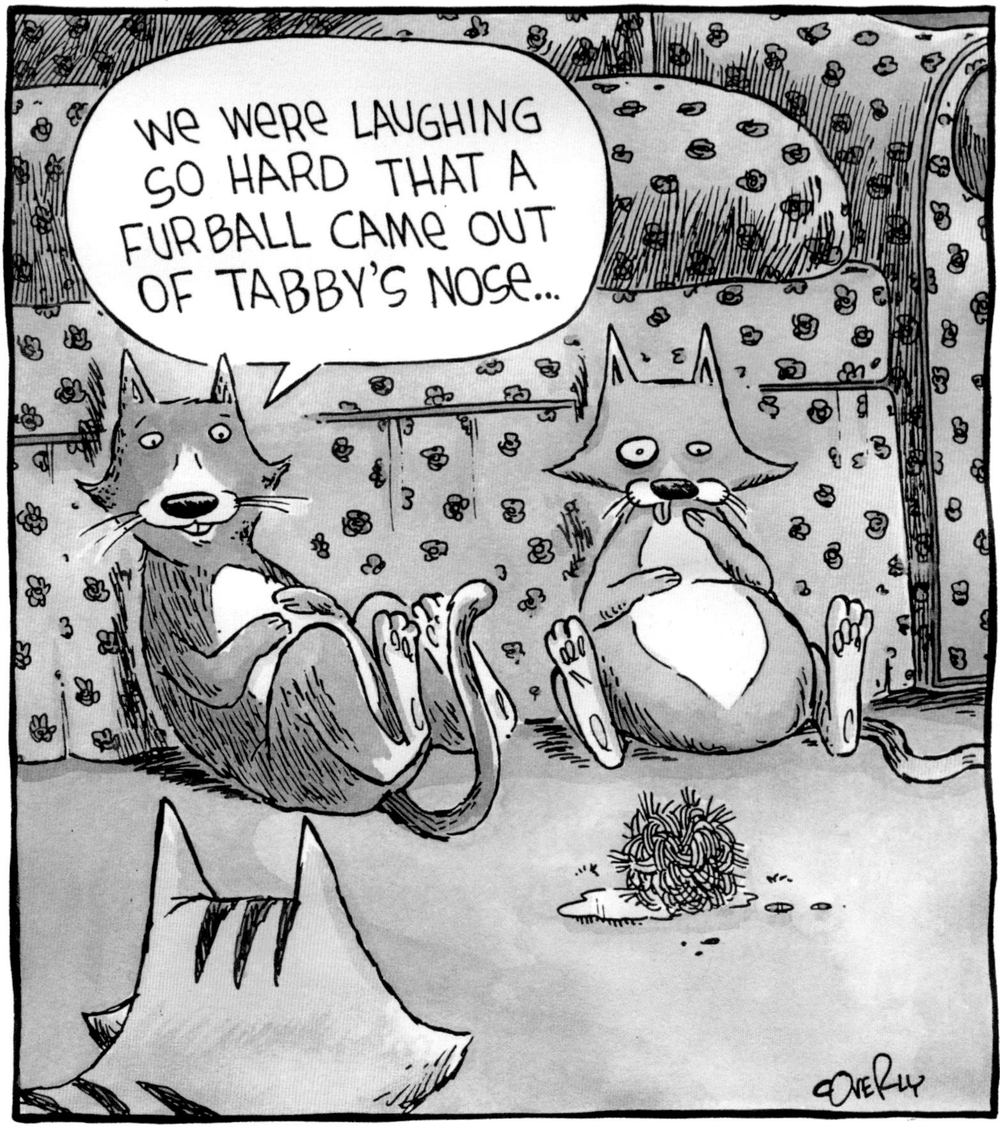
WE WERE LAUGHING SO HARD THAT A FURBALL CAME OUT OF TABBY'S NOSE...
COVERLY

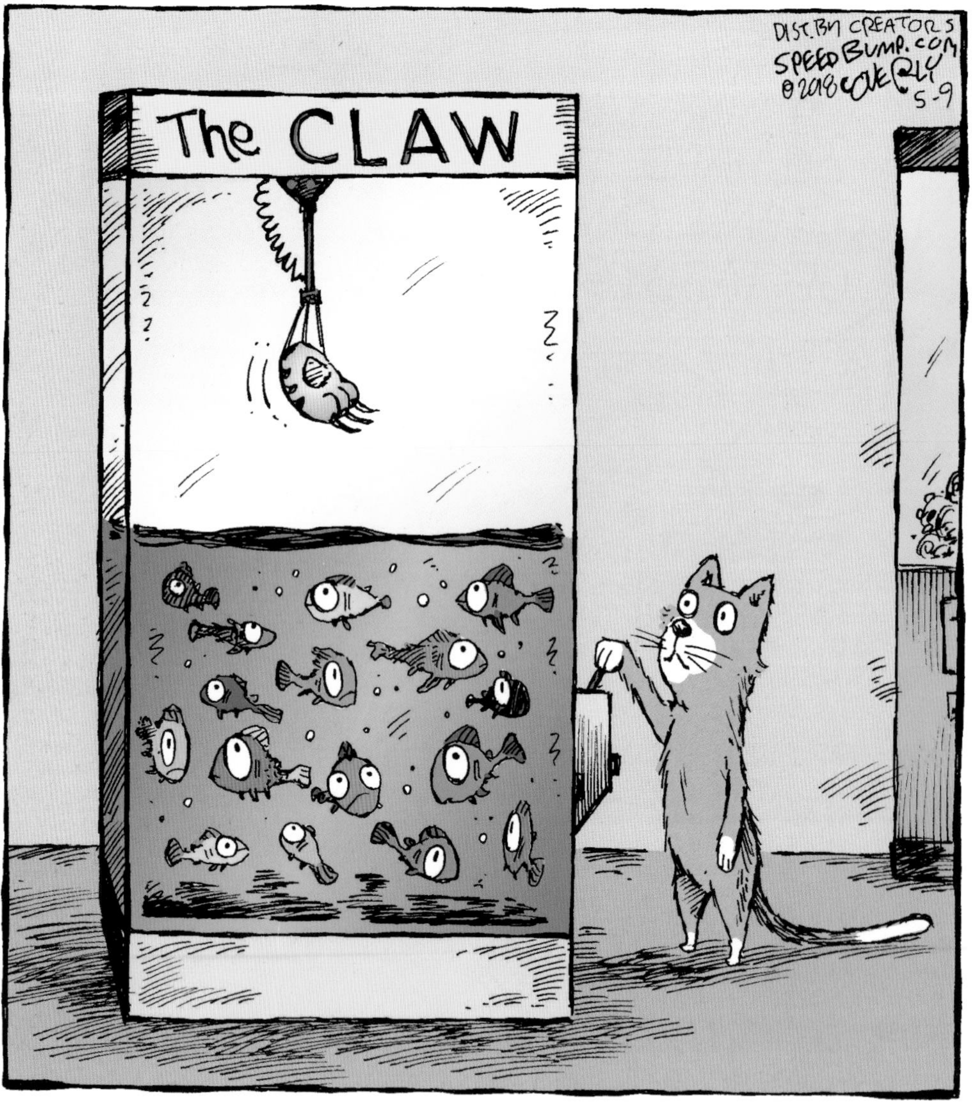
DIST. BY CREATORS
SPEEDBUMP.COM
©2018 DAVE COVERLY
5-9
The CLAW

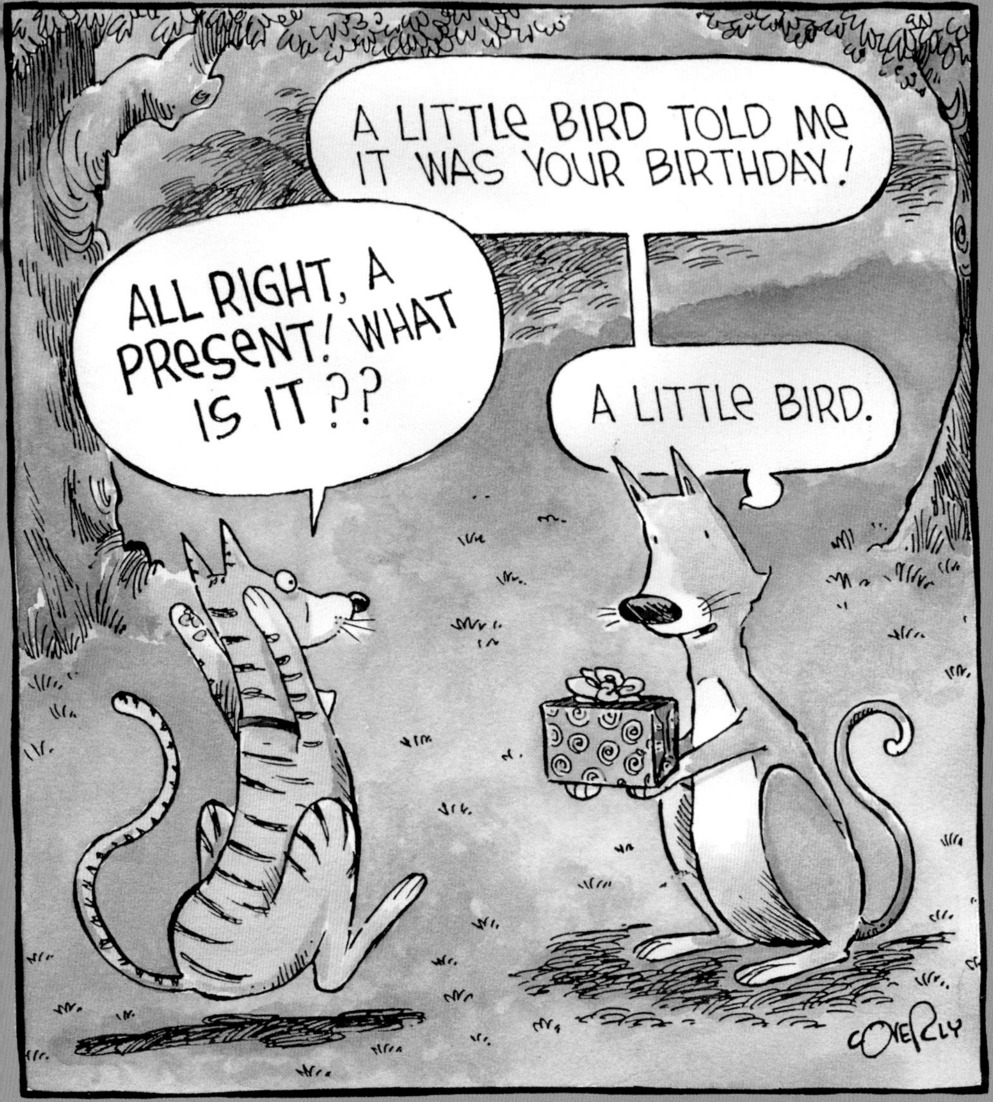
A LITTLE BIRD TOLD ME IT WAS YOUR BIRTHDAY!
ALL RIGHT, A PRESENT! WHAT IS IT??
A LITTLE BIRD.
COVERLY

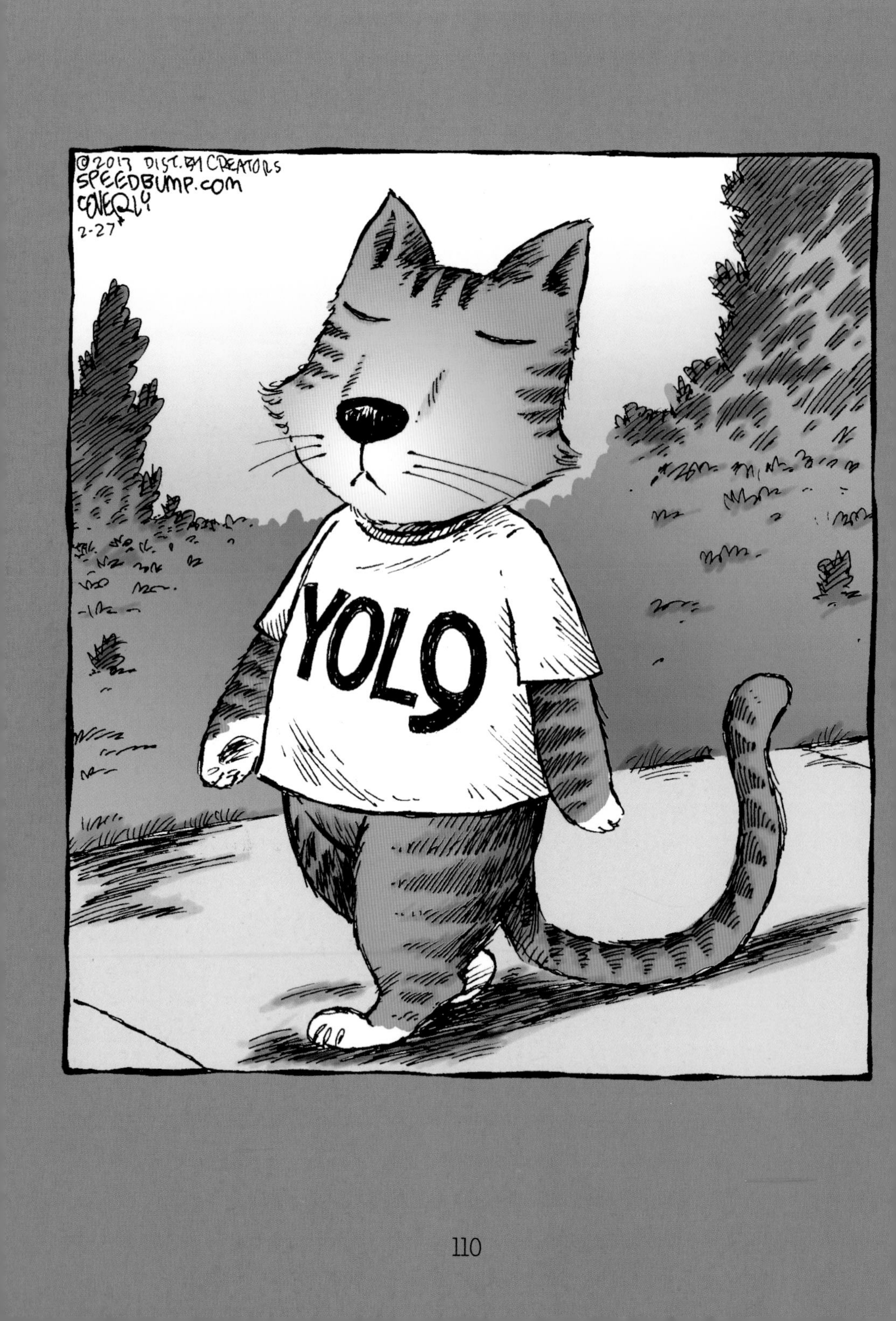
©2017 DIST. BY CREATORS
SPEEDBUMP.COM
COVERLY
2-27
YOLO

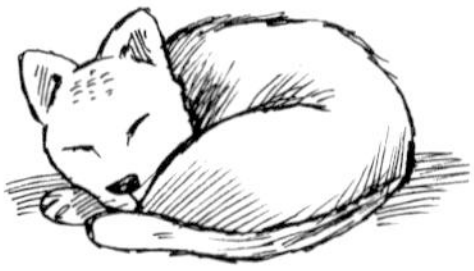

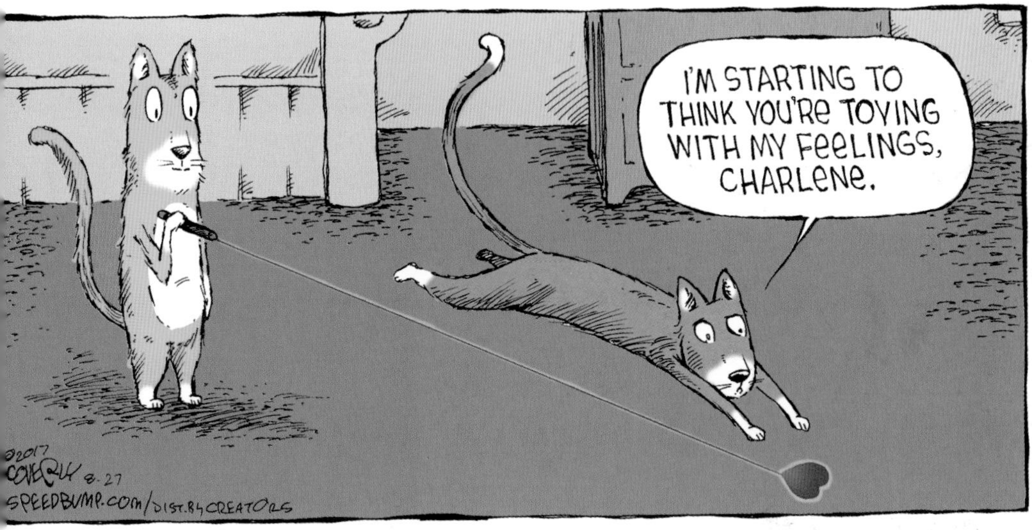
I'M STARTING TO THINK YOU'RE TOYING WITH MY FEELINGS, CHARLENE.
©2017 COVERLY 8-27
SPEEDBUMP.COM/DIST.BY CREATORS

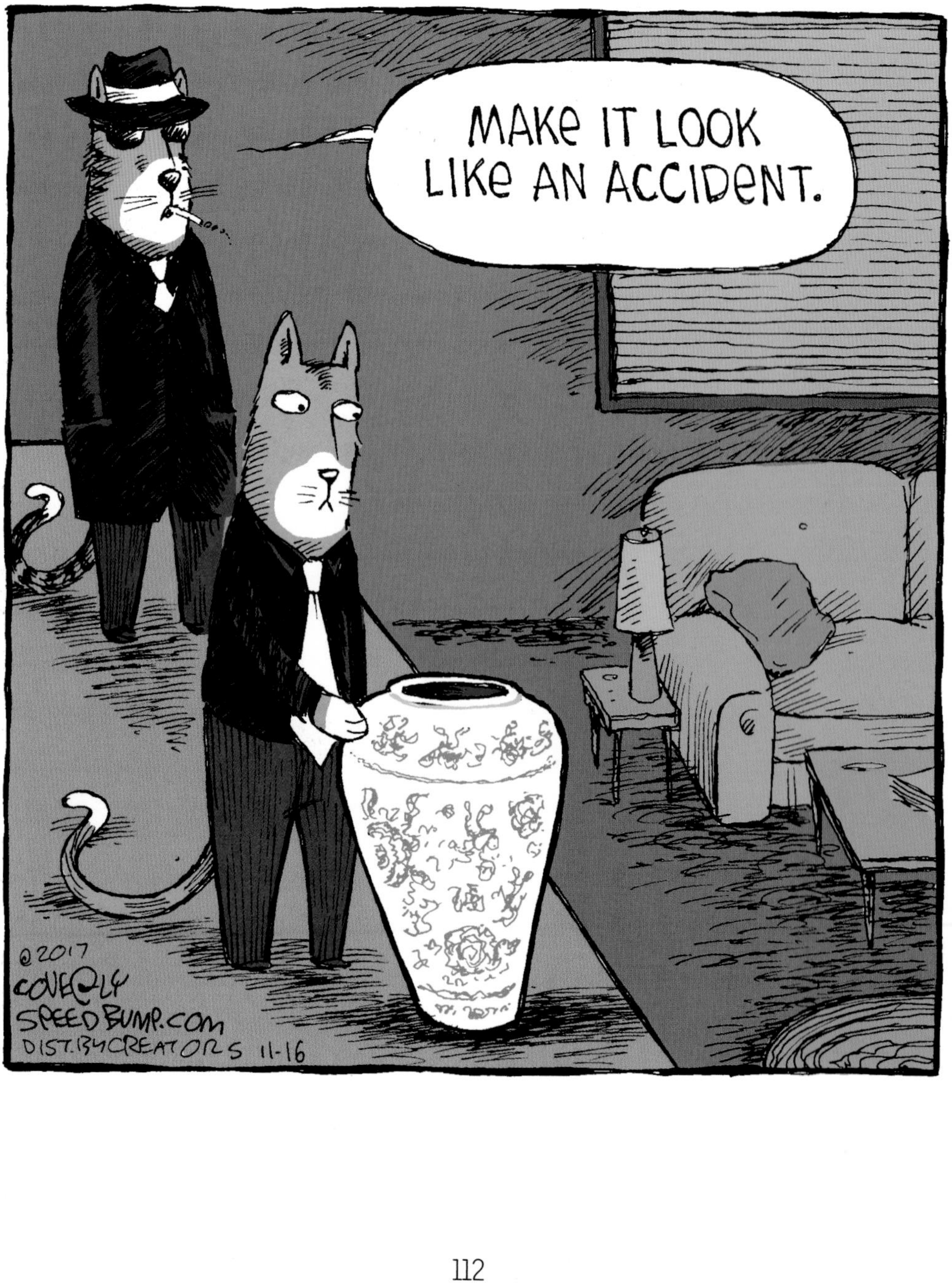
MAKE IT LOOK LIKE AN ACCIDENT.
©2017
COVERLY
SPEEDBUMP.COM
DIST. BY CREATORS 11-16

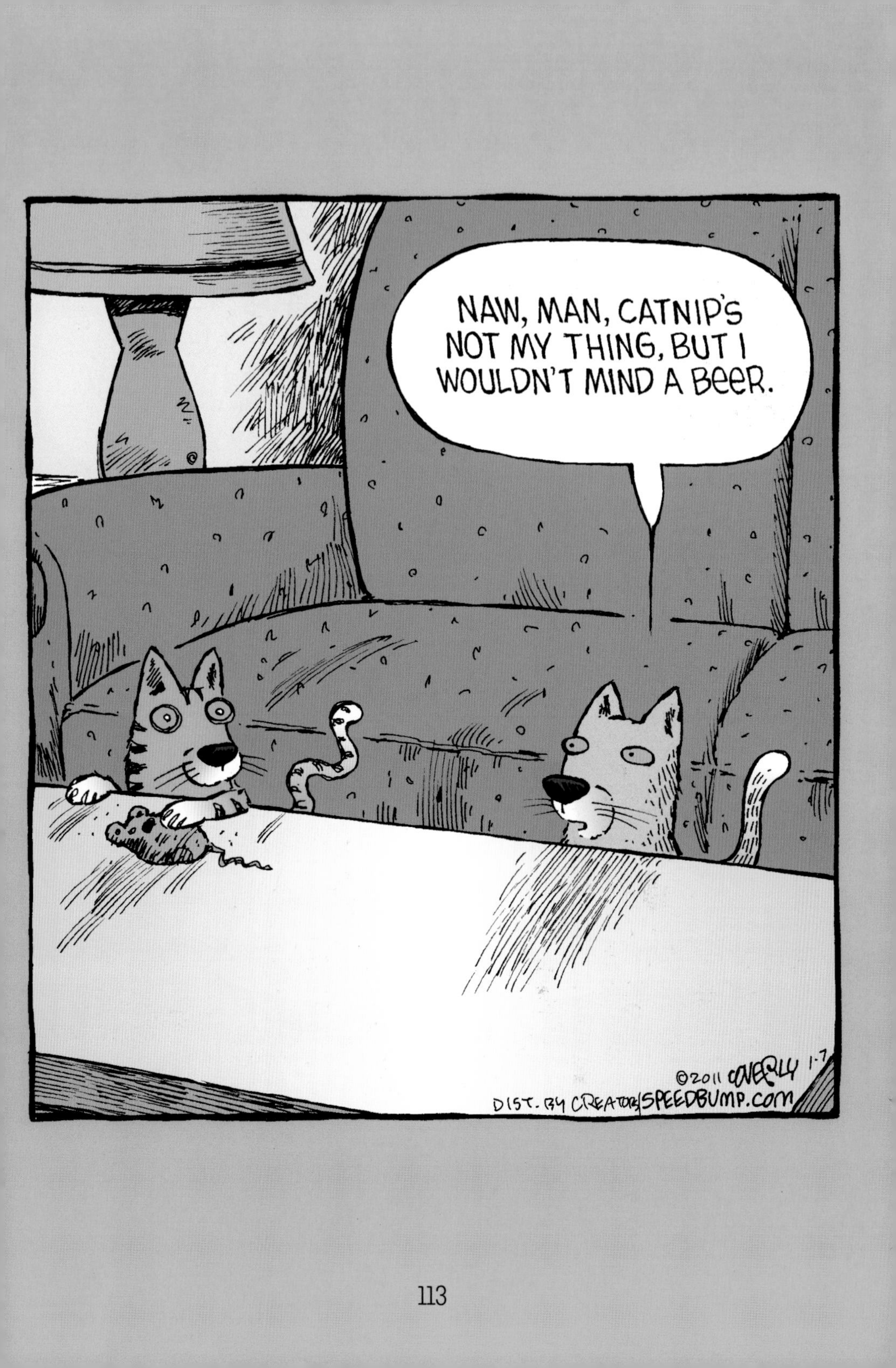
NAW, MAN, CATNIP'S NOT MY THING, BUT I WOULDN'T MIND A BEER.
©2011 COVERLY 1-7
DIST. BY CREATORS SPEEDBUMP.COM

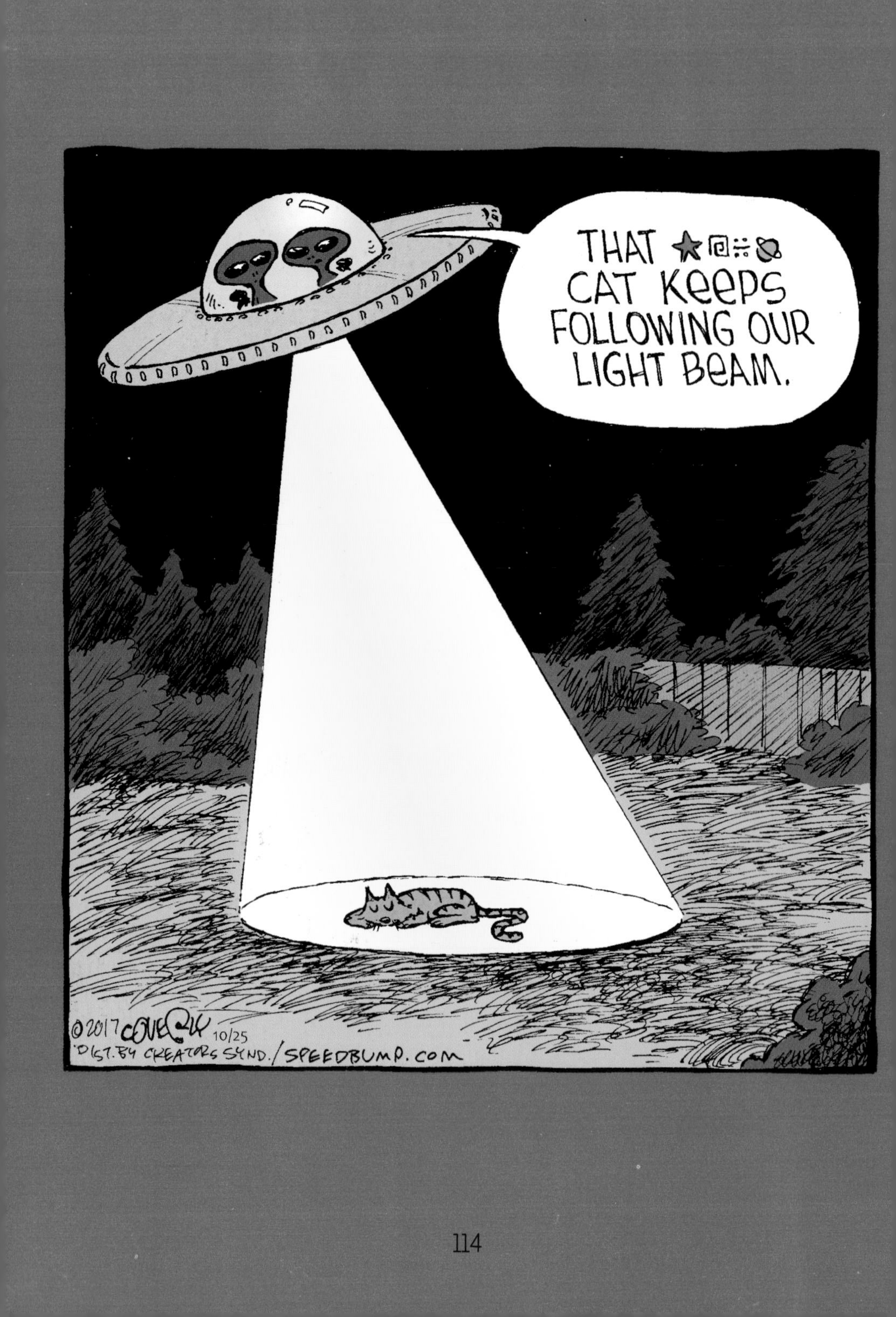
THAT ★@∷♁ CAT KEEPS FOLLOWING OUR LIGHT BEAM.
©2017 COVERLY 10/25
DIST. BY CREATORS SYND./SPEEDBUMP.COM

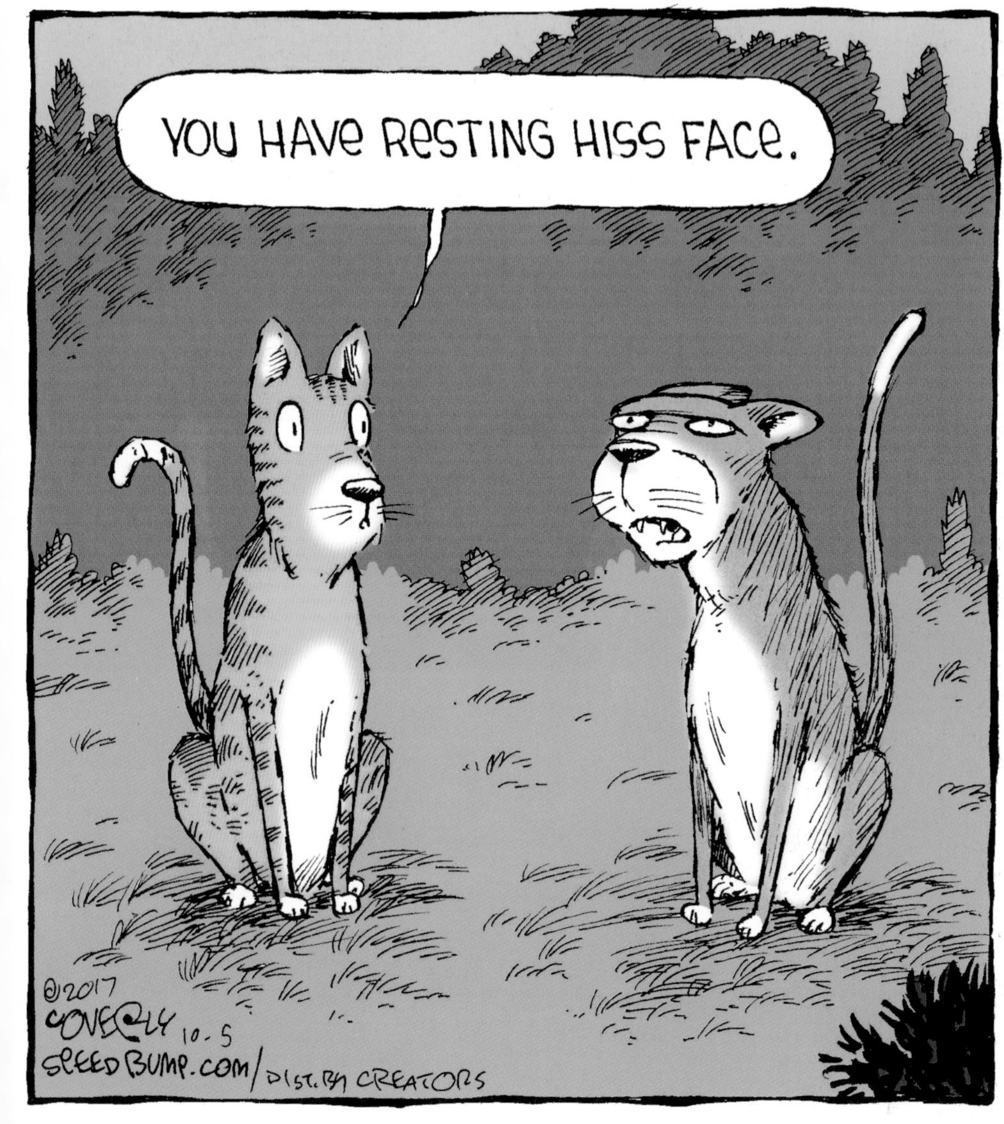
YOU HAVE RESTING HISS FACE.
©2017
COVERLY 10-5
SPEEDBUMP.COM/ DIST. BY CREATORS

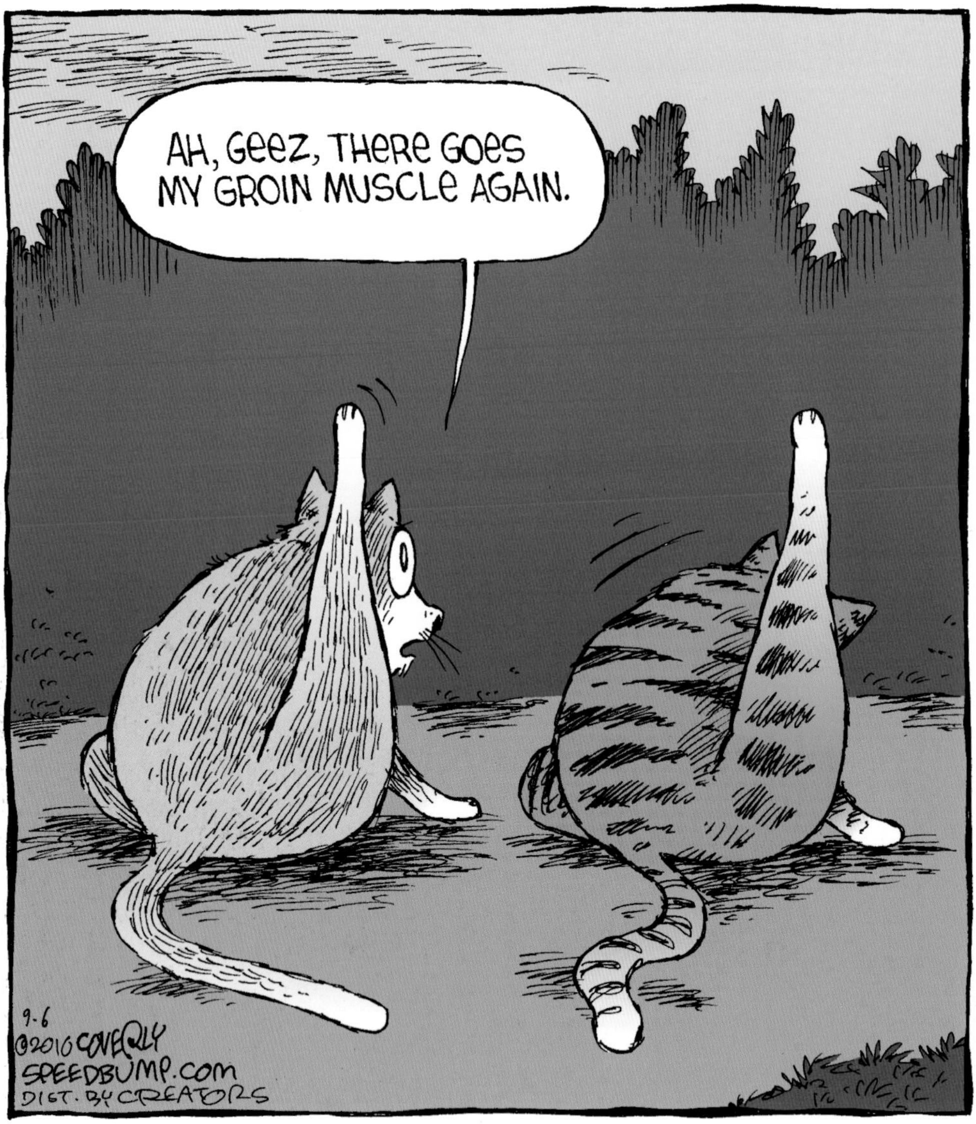
AH, GEEZ, THERE GOES MY GROIN MUSCLE AGAIN.
9-6 ©2010 COVERLY SPEEDBUMP.COM DIST. BY CREATORS

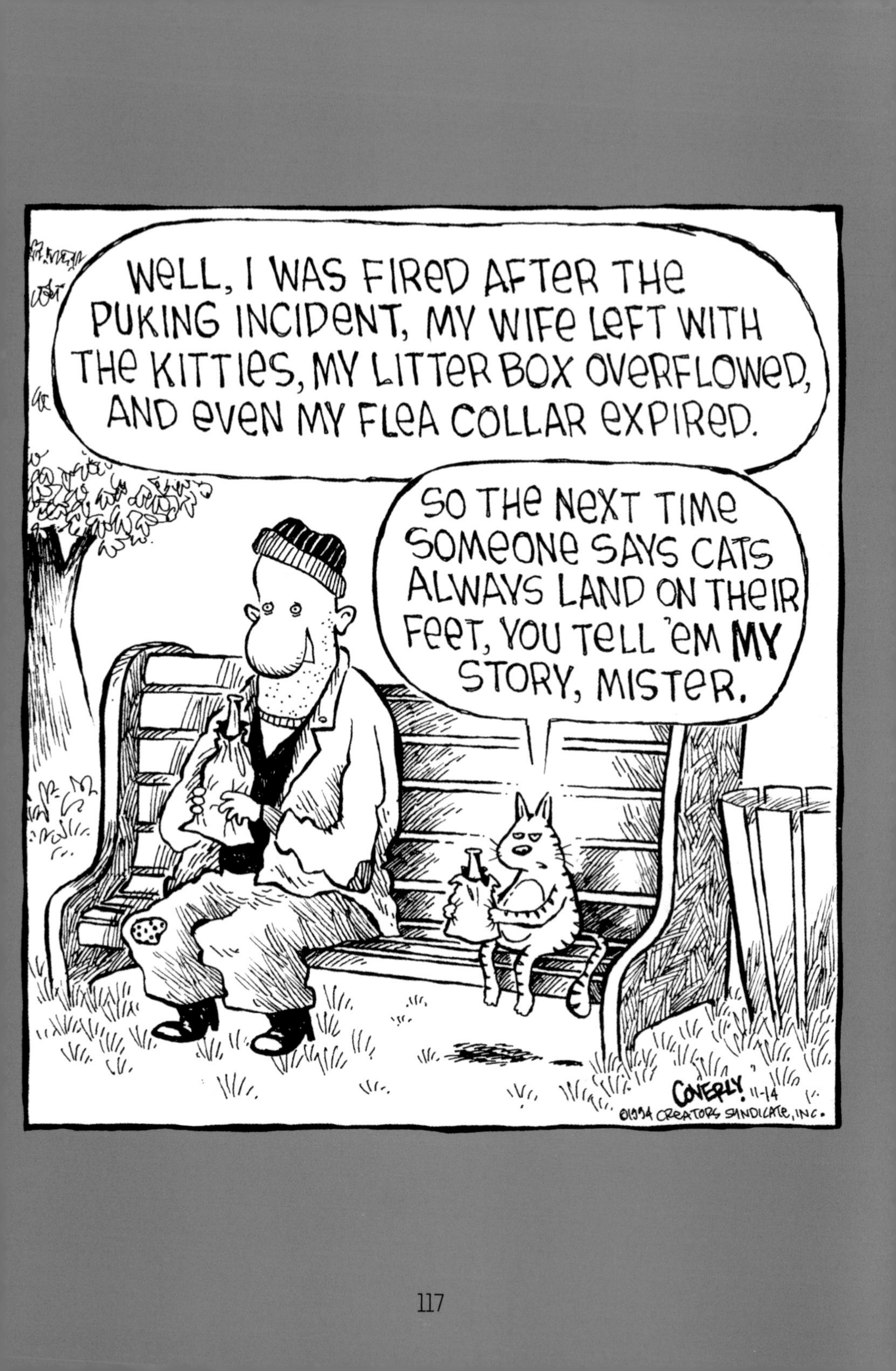
WELL, I WAS FIRED AFTER THE PUKING INCIDENT, MY WIFE LEFT WITH THE KITTIES, MY LITTER BOX OVERFLOWED, AND EVEN MY FLEA COLLAR EXPIRED.
SO THE NEXT TIME SOMEONE SAYS CATS ALWAYS LAND ON THEIR FEET, YOU TELL 'EM MY STORY, MISTER.
COVERLY 11-14
©1994 CREATORS SYNDICATE, INC.

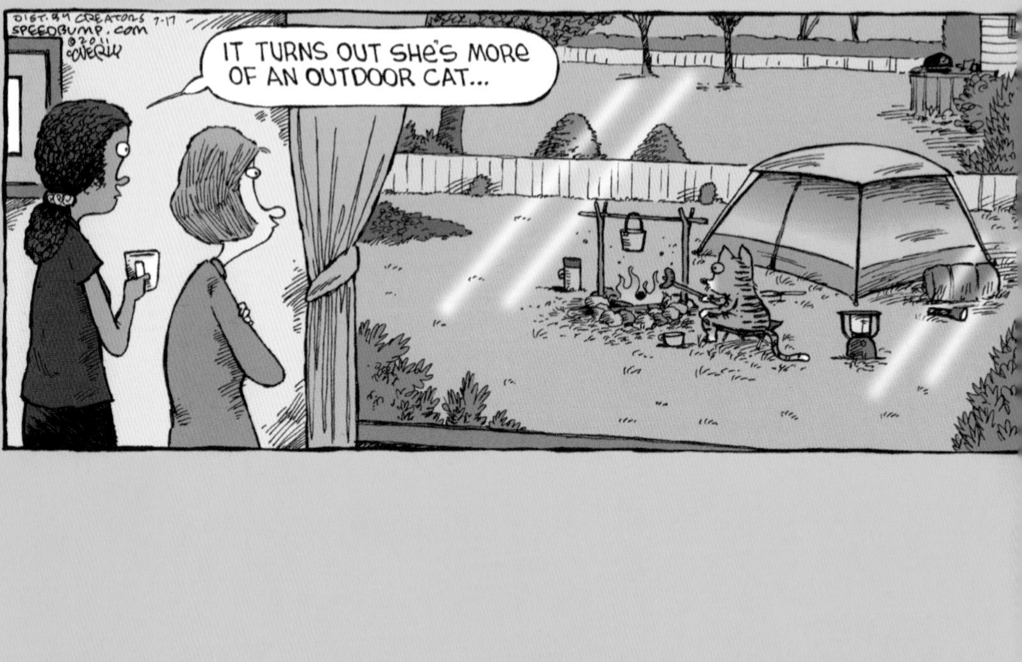
DIST. BY CREATORS 7-17
SPEEDBUMP.COM
©2011
COVERLY
IT TURNS OUT SHE'S MORE OF AN OUTDOOR CAT...

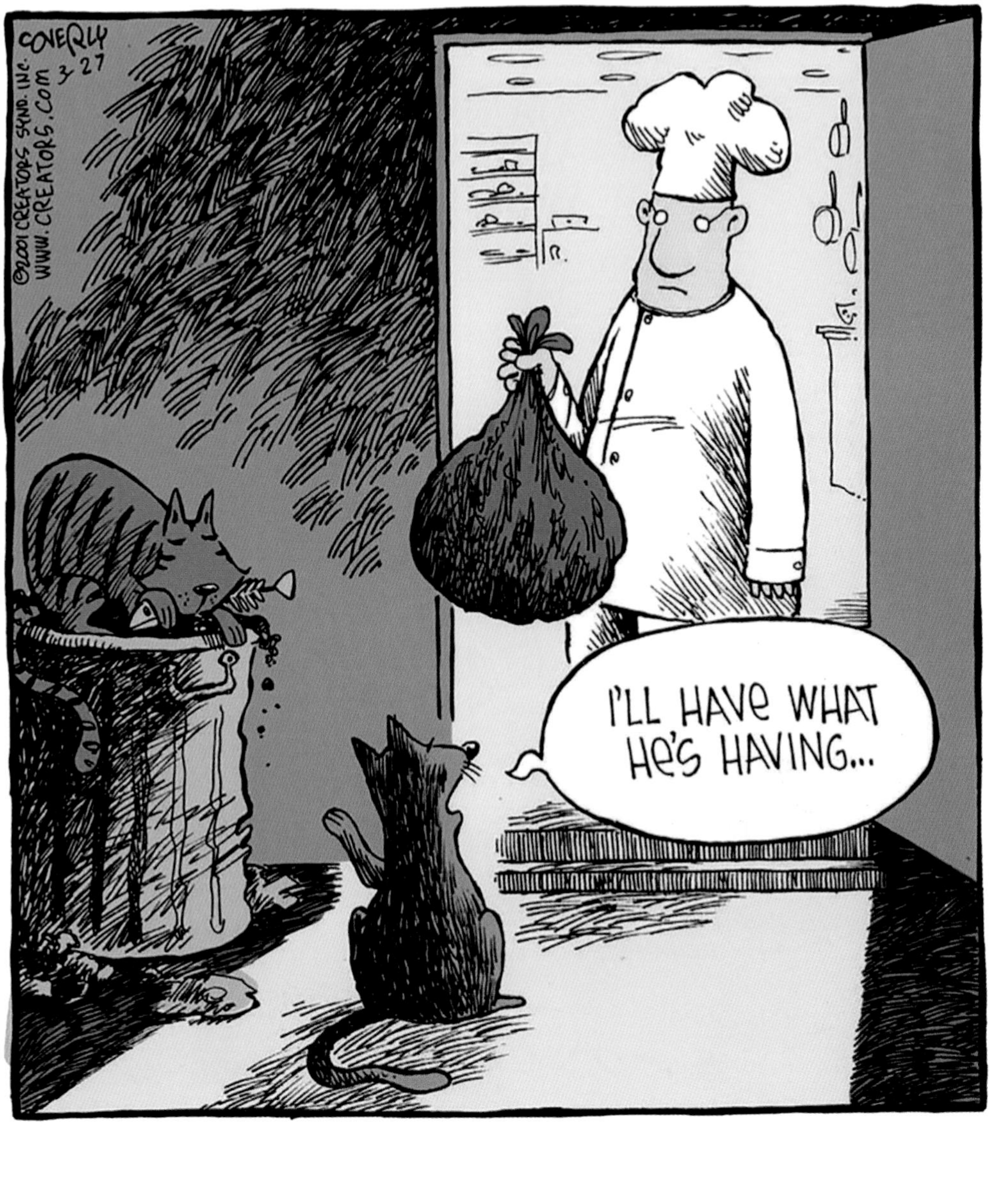
COVERLY 3-27
©2001 CREATORS SYND. INC.
WWW.CREATORS.COM
I'LL HAVE WHAT HE'S HAVING...

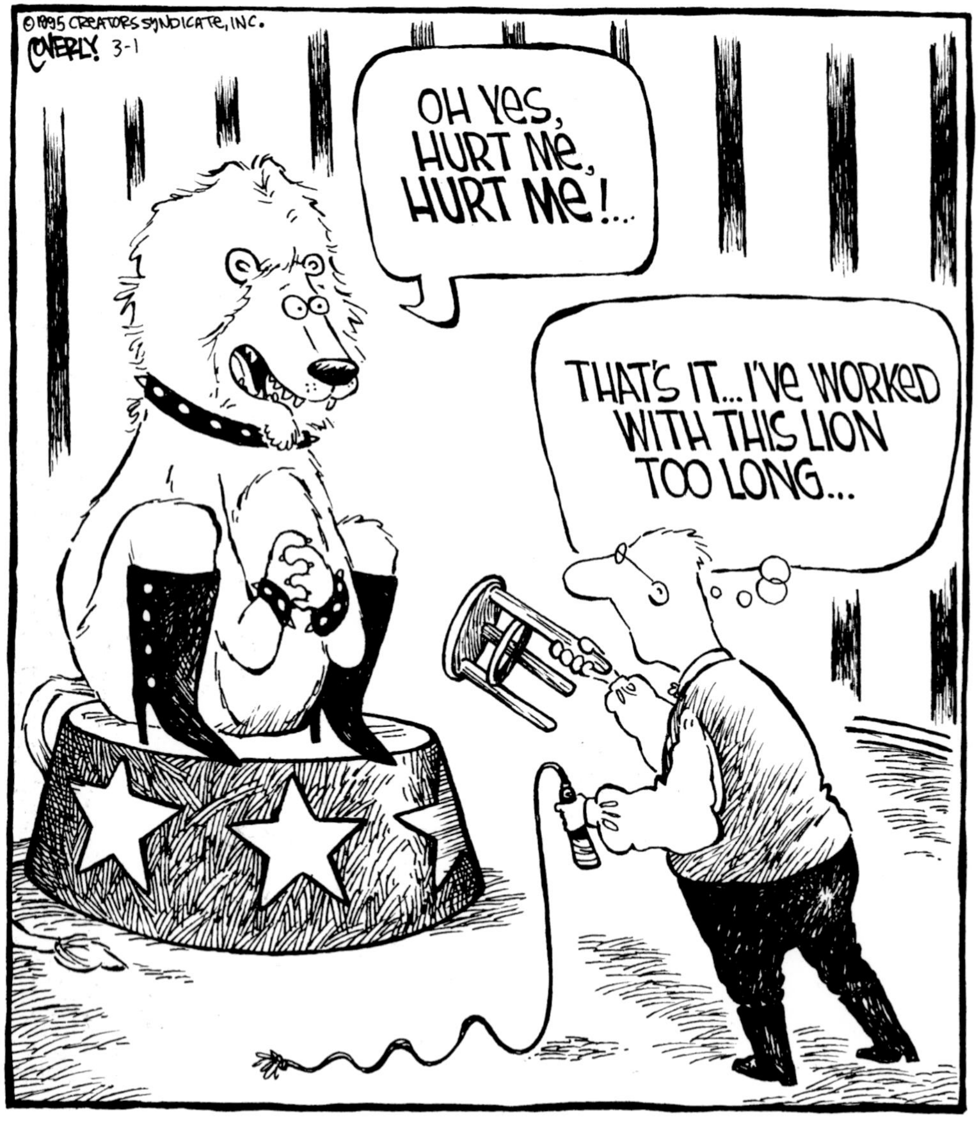
©1995 CREATORS SYNDICATE, INC.
COVERLY! 3-1
OH YES, HURT ME, HURT ME!...
THAT'S IT... I'VE WORKED WITH THIS LION TOO LONG...

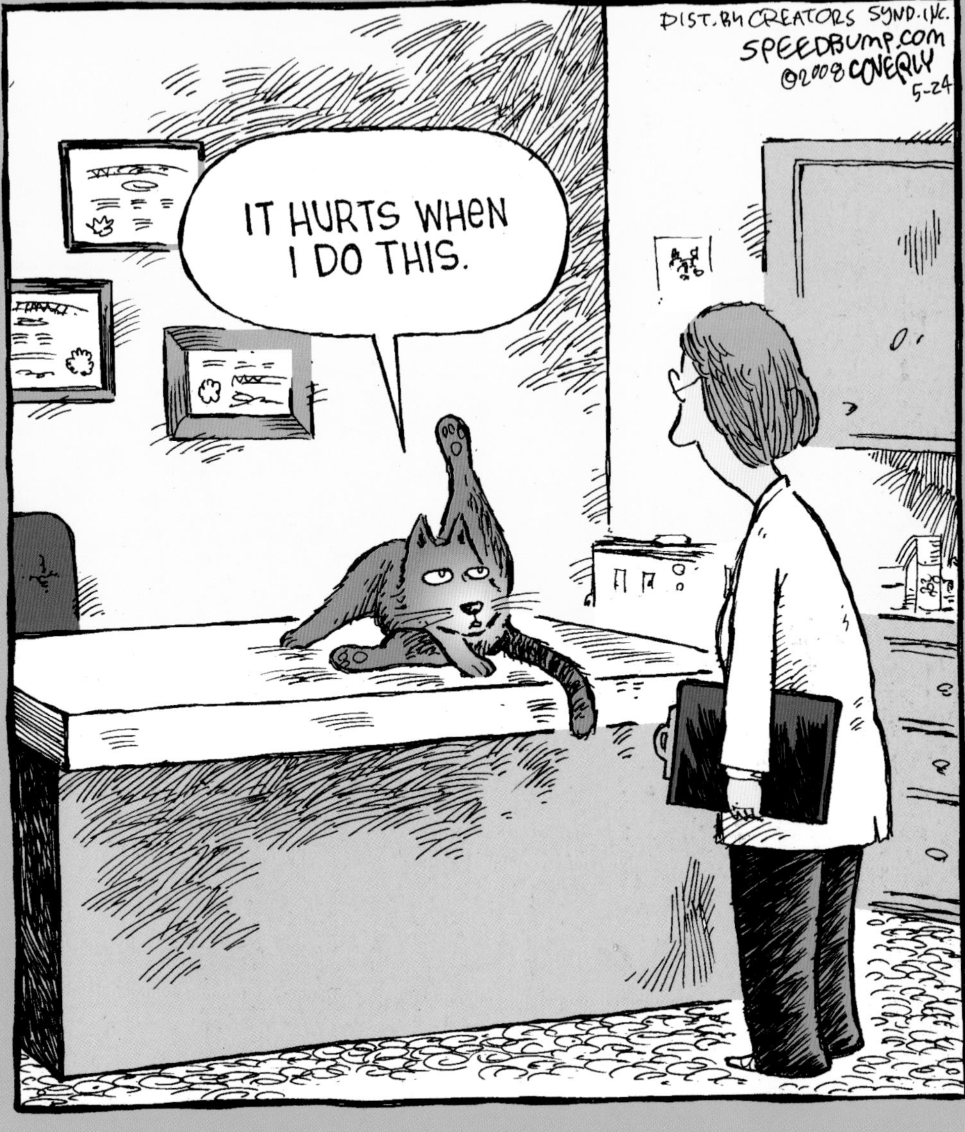
DIST. BY CREATORS SYND. INC.
SPEEDBUMP.COM
©2008 COVERLY
5-24
IT HURTS WHEN I DO THIS.

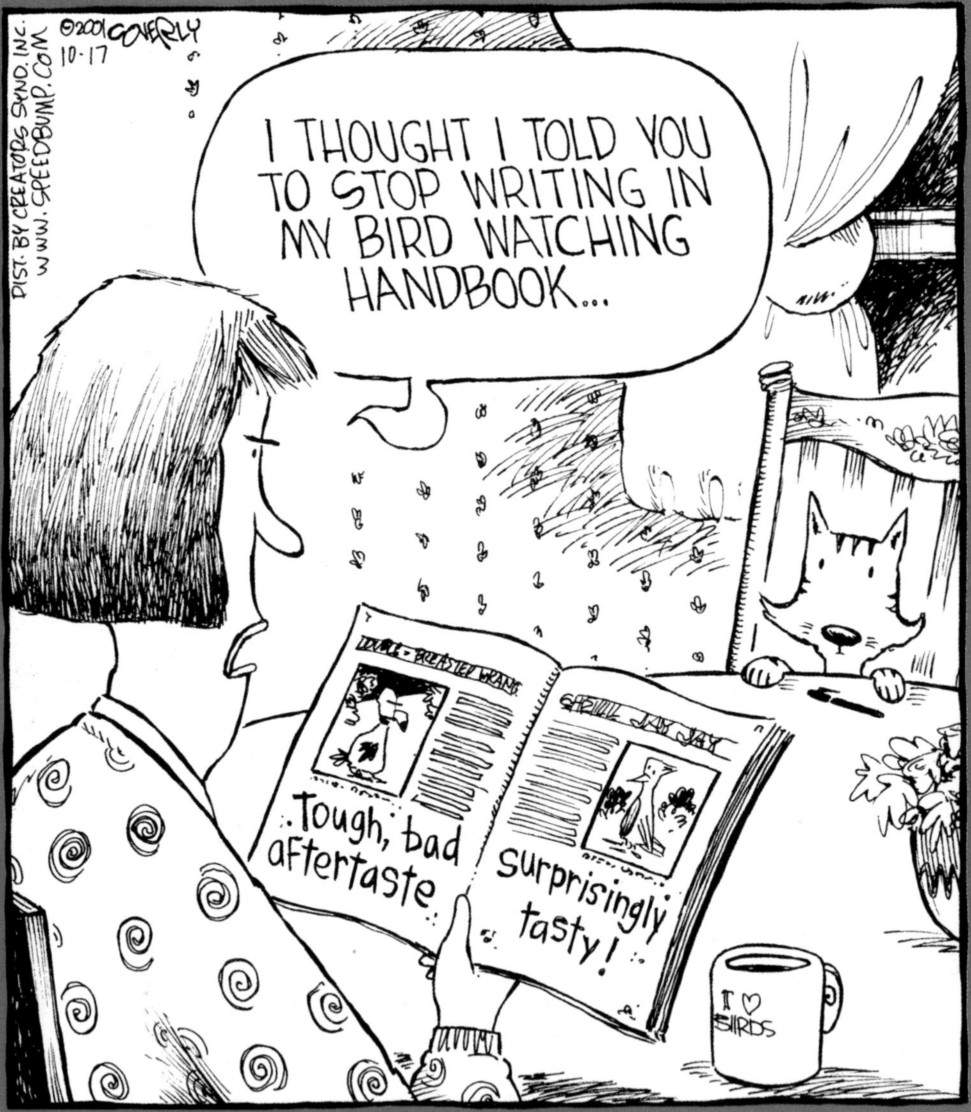
©2001 COVERLY
10-17
DIST. BY CREATORS SYND. INC.
WWW.SPEEDBUMP.COM
I THOUGHT I TOLD YOU TO STOP WRITING IN MY BIRD WATCHING HANDBOOK...
Tough, bad aftertaste
surprisingly tasty!
I ♡ BIRDS

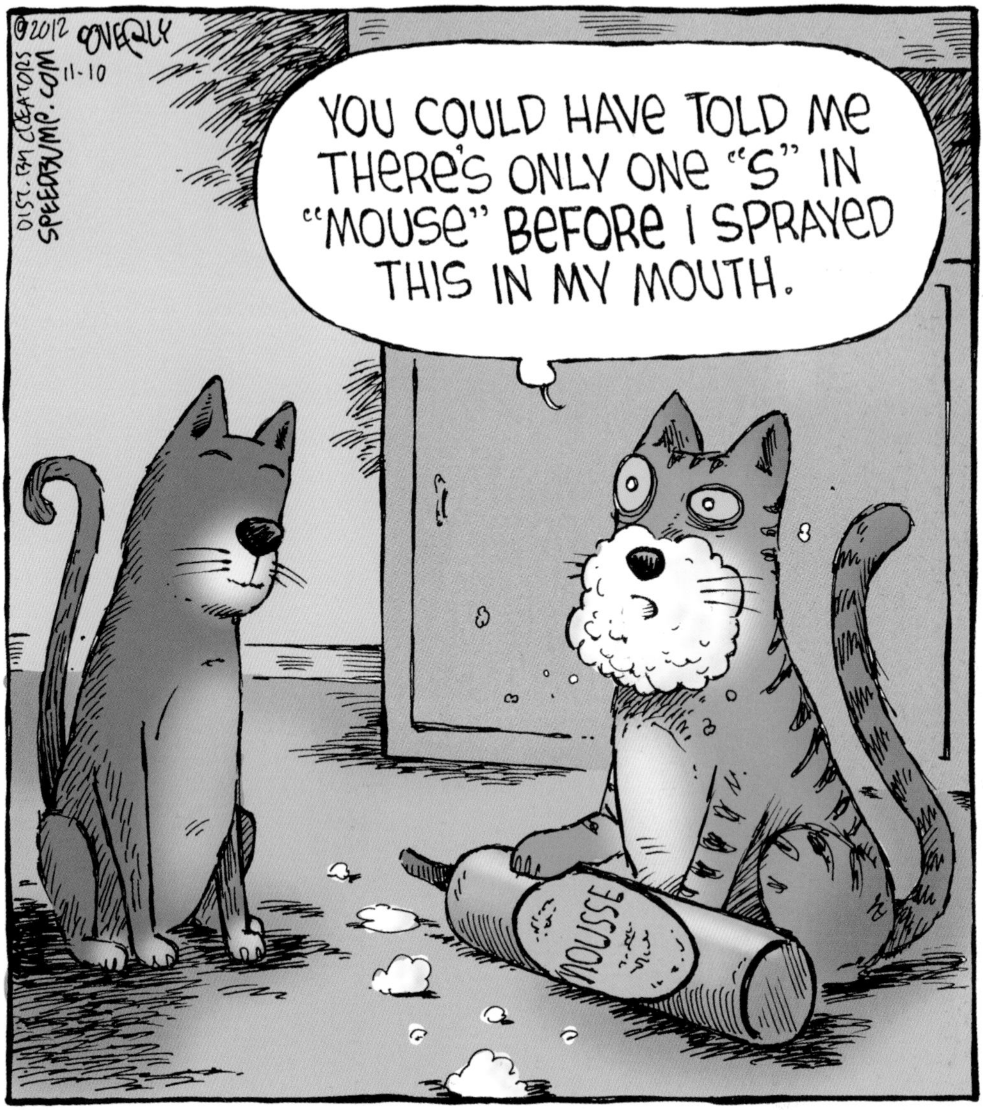
©2012 COVERLY
11-10
DIST. BY CREATORS
SPEEDBUMP.COM
YOU COULD HAVE TOLD ME THERE'S ONLY ONE "S" IN "MOUSE" BEFORE I SPRAYED THIS IN MY MOUTH.
MOUSSE

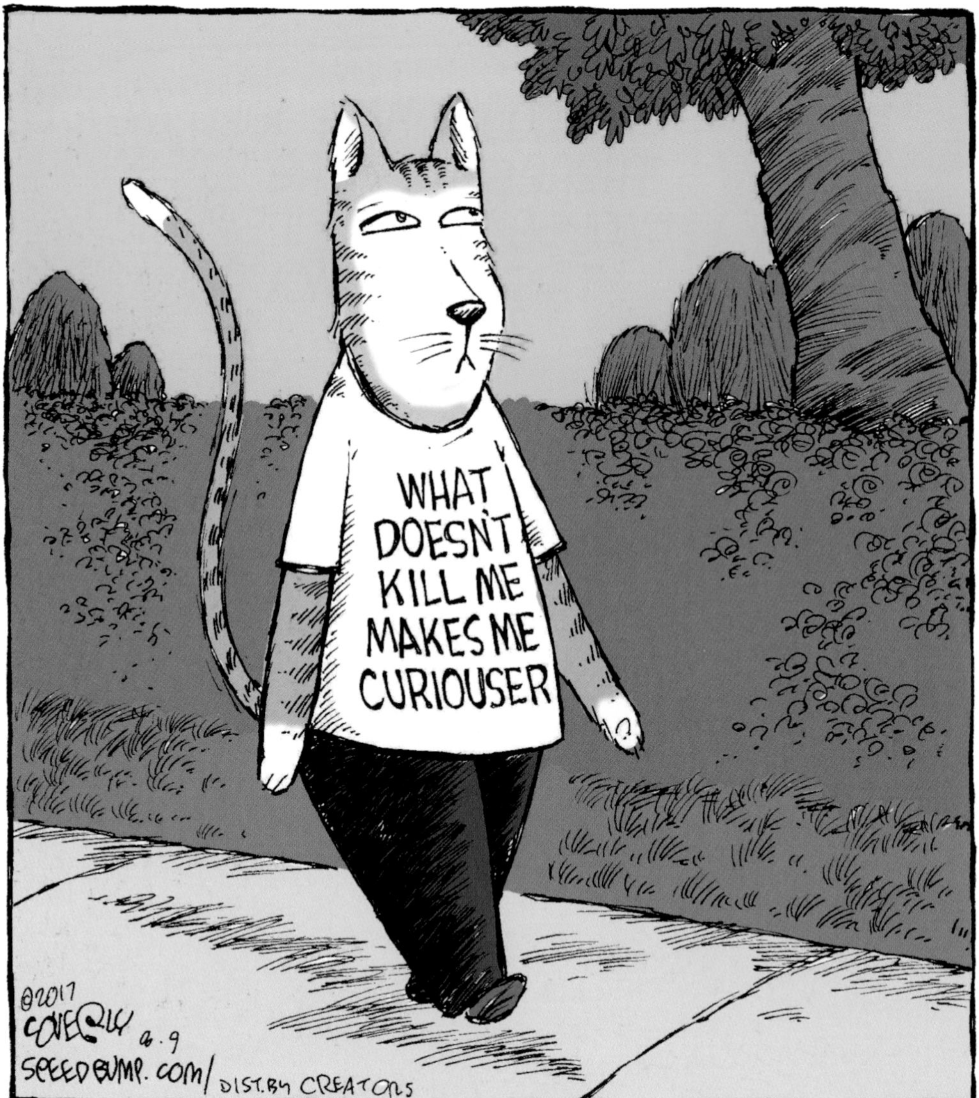
WHAT DOESN'T KILL ME MAKES ME CURIOUSER
©2017 COVERLY 6.9
SPEEDBUMP.COM/ DIST. BY CREATORS

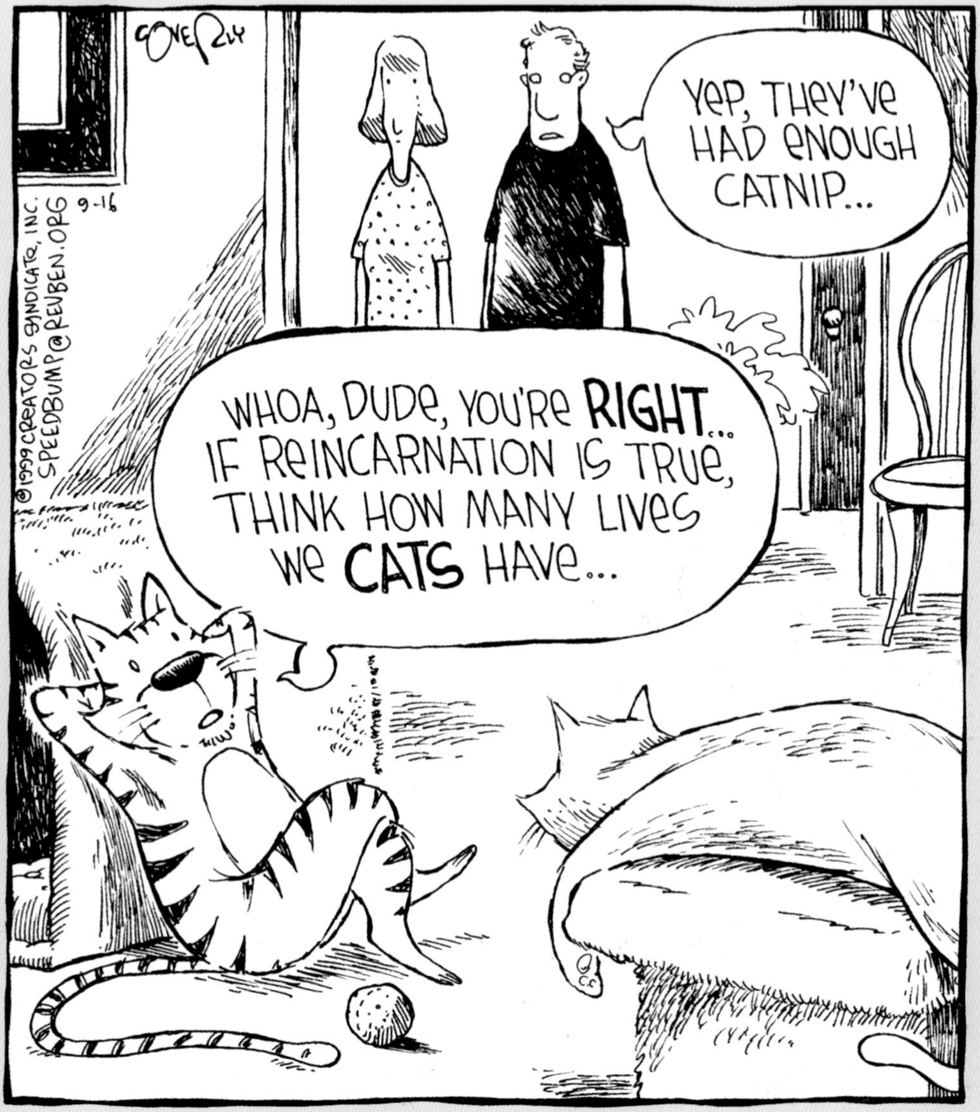

Yep, They've had enough catnip...
Whoa, dude, you're **RIGHT**... If reincarnation is true, think how many lives we **CATS** have...
©1999 Creators Syndicate, Inc. speedbump@reuben.org 9-16

HILARY PRICE

I took this with my iPhone. It's a good thing my iPad
didn't snap a photo at the same moment.

My hoodlum cat's name is Tom. He was found near a barn,
but it seemed he had lived in a home before because he
kept trying to break into people's houses. In fact, after I had
him for a while, I got a call from the neighbor down the street.
Tom had gone in through their cat door, jumped on the kitchen
counter, eaten something on a cookie sheet, knocked it over,
and then went away. They knew it was Tom because he'd left
his collar behind. Great—not only did I have a cat burglar on my
hands, I had a streaker.

About Hilary Price

Hilary Price has been drawing and writing *Rhymes with Orange,* her daily newspaper comic strip, since 1995. It appears in newspapers all over the world and has won Best Newspaper Panel four times from the National Cartoonists Society. Her work has also appeared in *Parade* magazine, the *Funny Times, People,* and *Glamour.* When she began drawing *Rhymes with Orange,* she was the youngest woman to ever have a syndicated strip.

Hilary draws the strip in an old toothbrush factory that has since been converted to studio space for artists. She lives in western Massachusetts with her overly large dog and hoodlum cat.

rhymeswithorange.com

HILARY B. PRICE

CHAPTER 5
BIG CATS

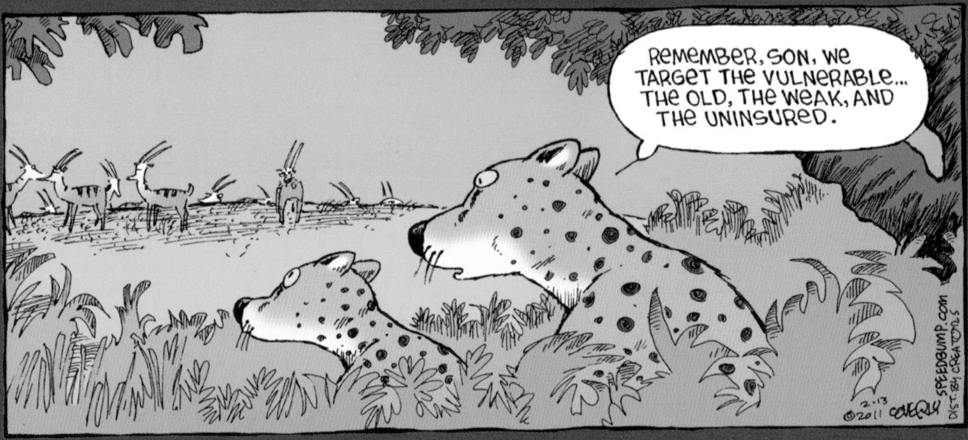
REMEMBER, SON, WE TARGET THE VULNERABLE... THE OLD, THE WEAK, AND THE UNINSURED.

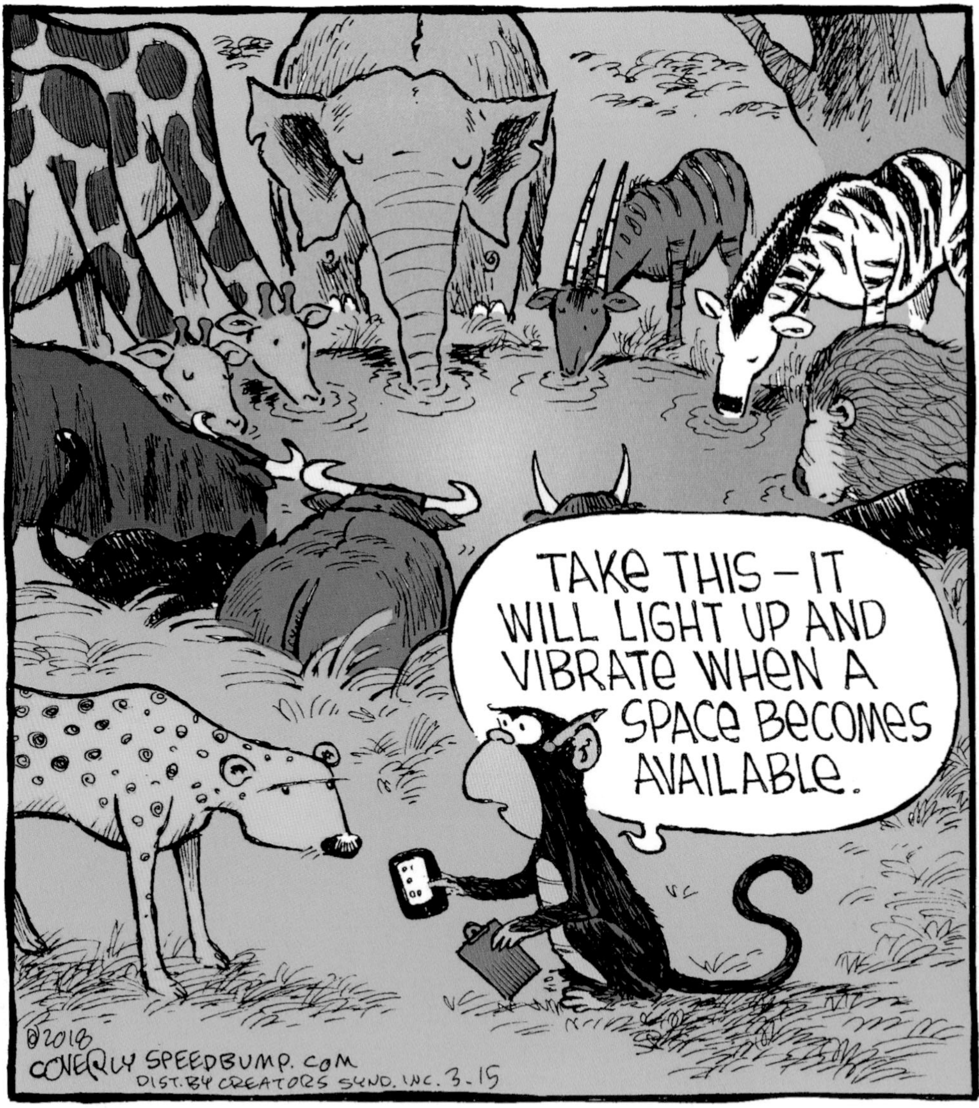
TAKE THIS – IT WILL LIGHT UP AND VIBRATE WHEN A SPACE BECOMES AVAILABLE.
©2018 COVERLY SPEEDBUMP.COM
DIST. BY CREATORS SYND. INC. 3-15

WE'RE PREDATORS, SON, WE PREY ON THE OLD, SICK AND WEAK.
NOW WATCH...
3-2
©2003 COVERLY
WWW.SPEEDBUMP.COM
DIST. BY CREATORS SYNDICATE, INC.
THAT'S RIGHT, MS. GAZELLE, I JUST NEED YOUR CREDIT CARD NUMBER TO LET YOU IN ON AN EXTRAORDINARY OPPORTUNITY.

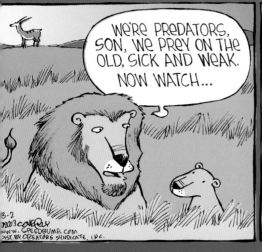

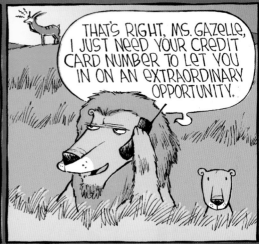

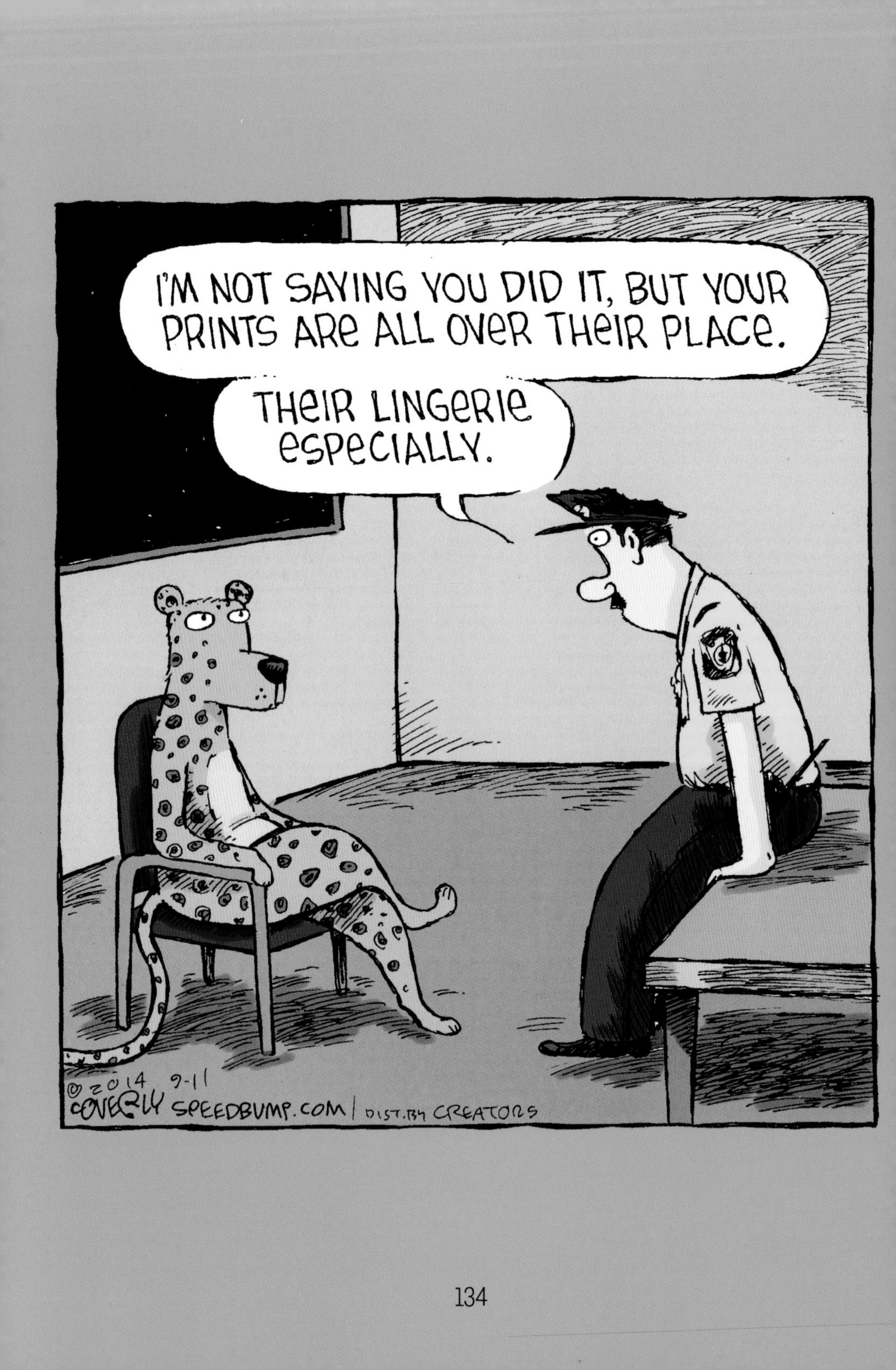
I'M NOT SAYING YOU DID IT, BUT YOUR PRINTS ARE ALL OVER THEIR PLACE.
THEIR LINGERIE ESPECIALLY.
© 2014 9-11
COVERLY SPEEDBUMP.COM / DIST. BY CREATORS

©2006 COVERLY 6-25
SPEEDBUMP.COM DIST. BY CREATORS SYND, INC.

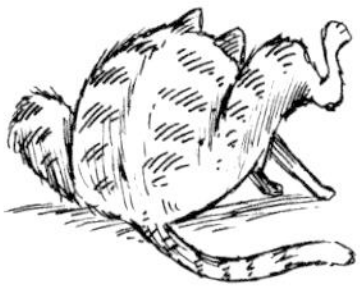

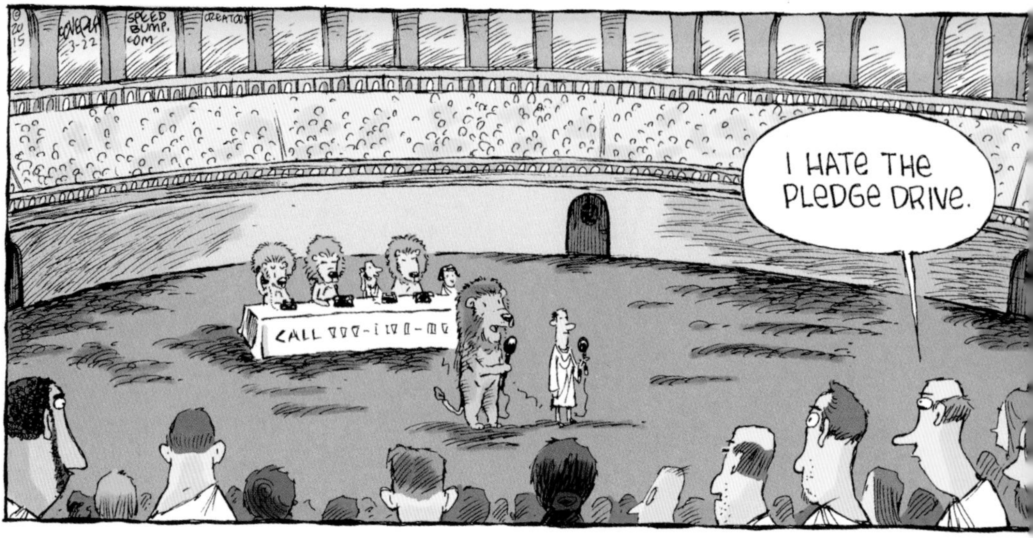
I HATE THE PLEDGE DRIVE.

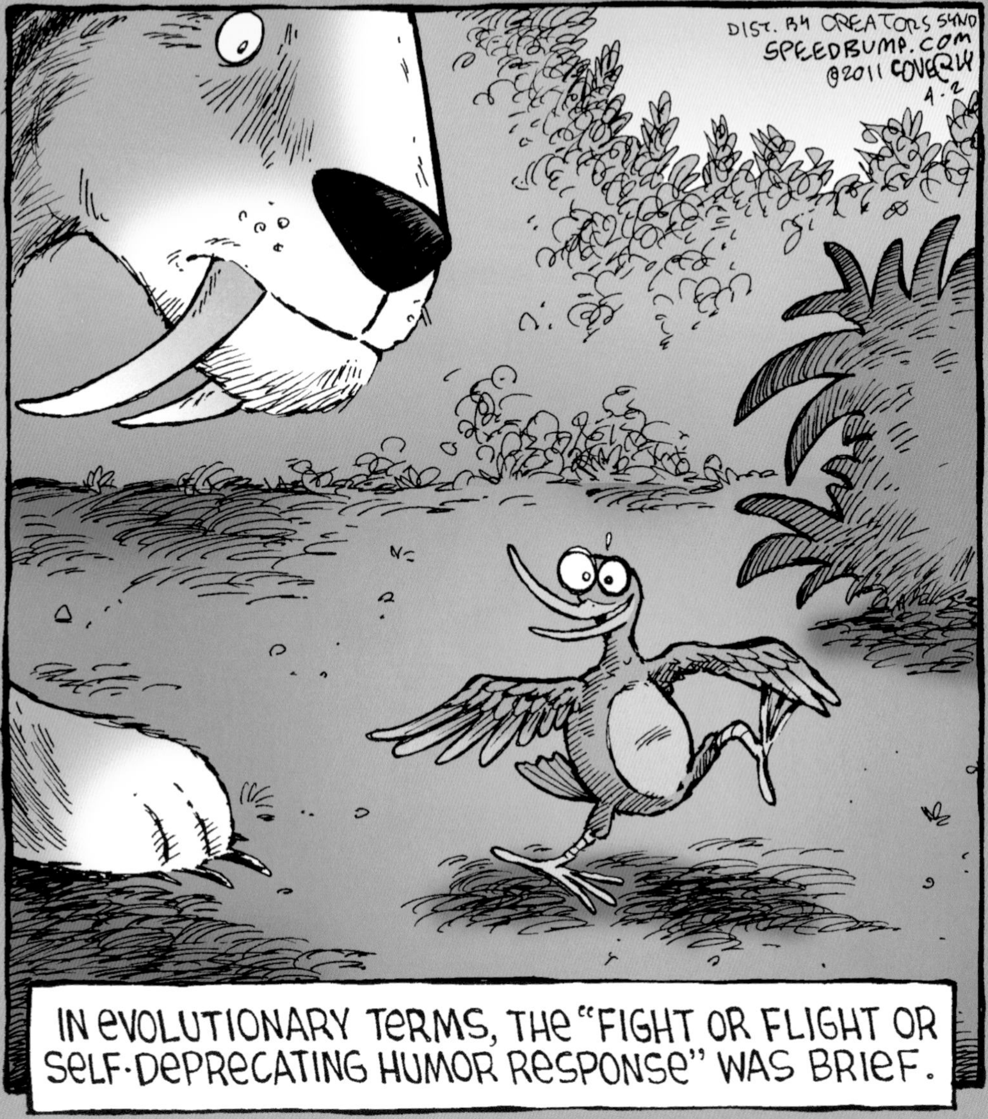
DIST. BY CREATORS SYND
SPEEDBUMP.COM
©2011 COVERLY
IN EVOLUTIONARY TERMS, THE "FIGHT OR FLIGHT OR SELF-DEPRECATING HUMOR RESPONSE" WAS BRIEF.

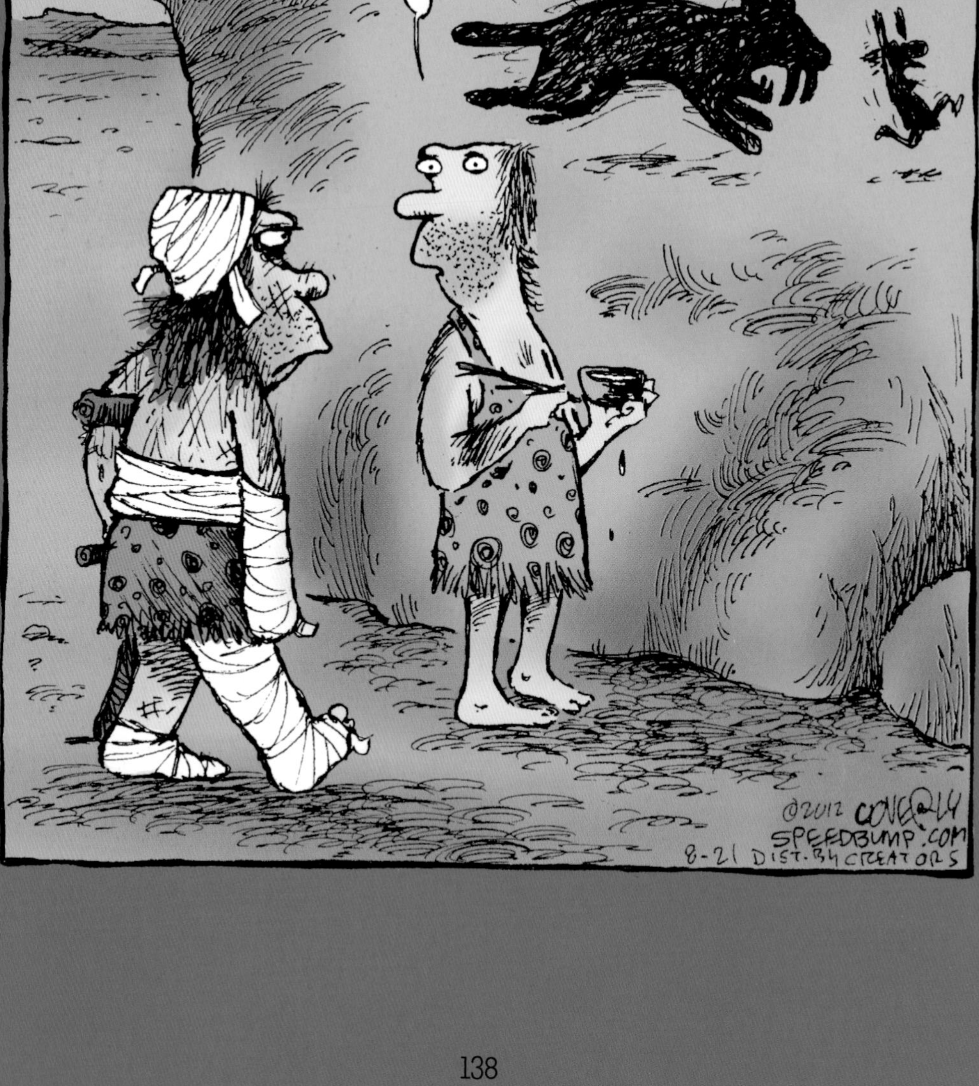
TOO SOON?
©2012 COVERLY
SPEEDBUMP.COM
8-21 DIST. BY CREATORS

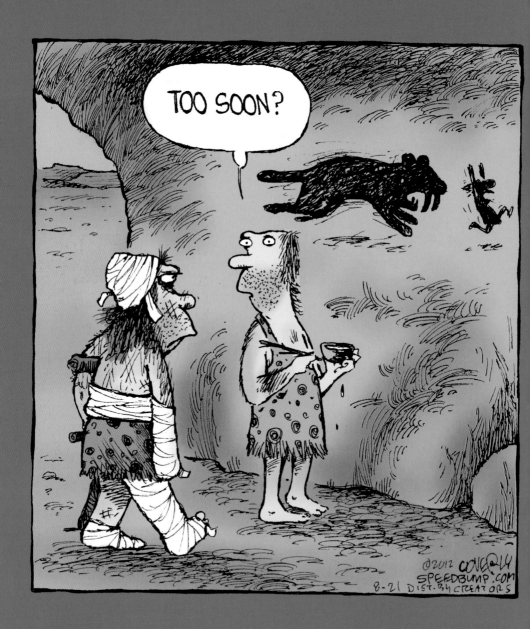

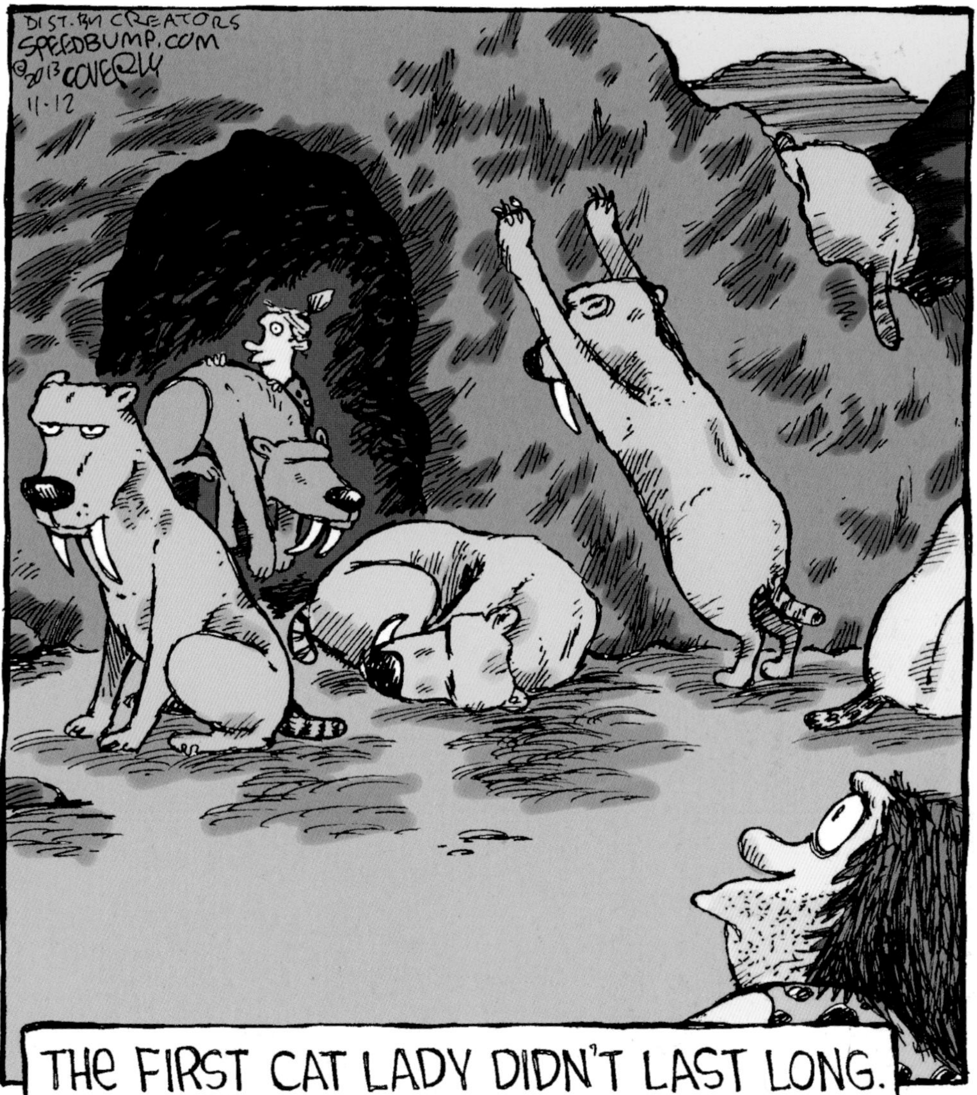
DIST. BY CREATORS
SPEEDBUMP.COM
©2013 COVERLY
11-12

THE FIRST CAT LADY DIDN'T LAST LONG.

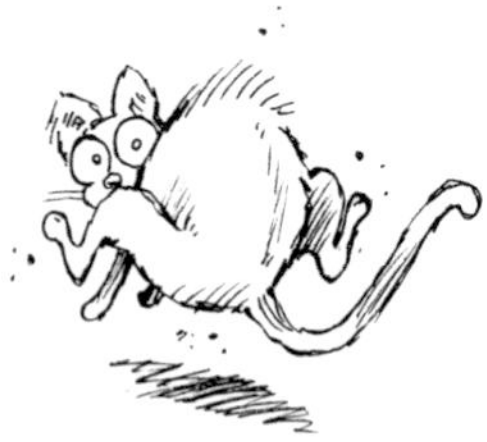

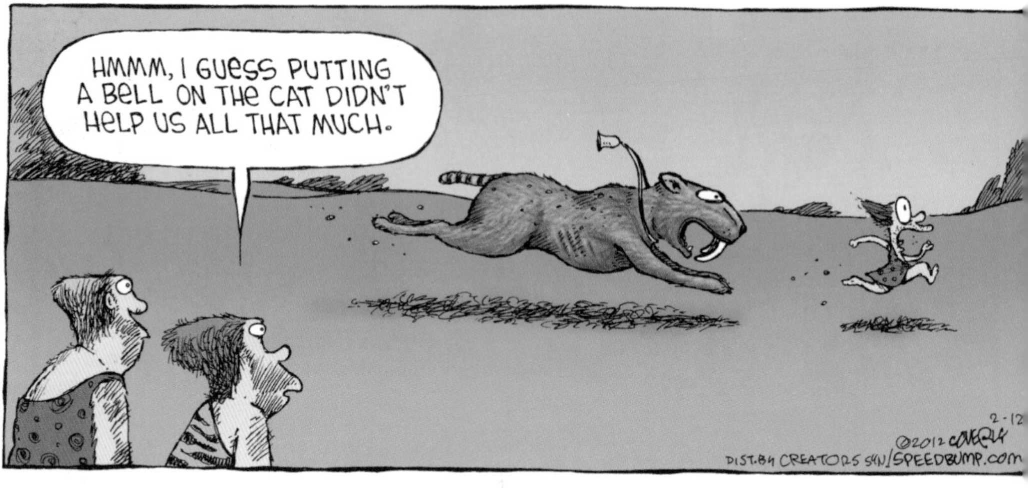
HMMM, I GUESS PUTTING A BELL ON THE CAT DIDN'T HELP US ALL THAT MUCH.
2-12
©2012 COVERLY
DIST. BY CREATORS SYN/SPEEDBUMP.COM

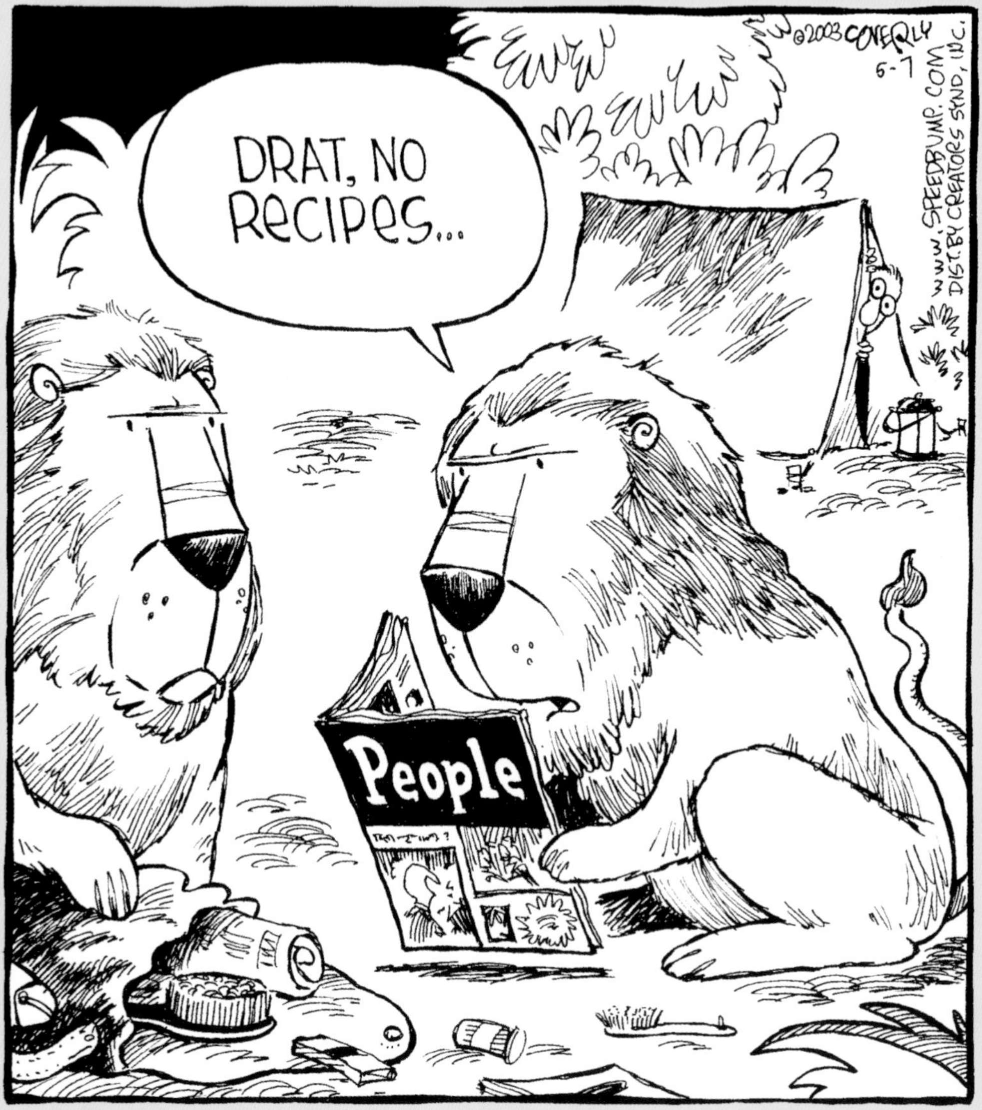
DRAT, NO RECIPES...
People
©2003 COVERLY
6-7
WWW.SPEEDBUMP.COM
DIST. BY CREATORS SYND, INC.

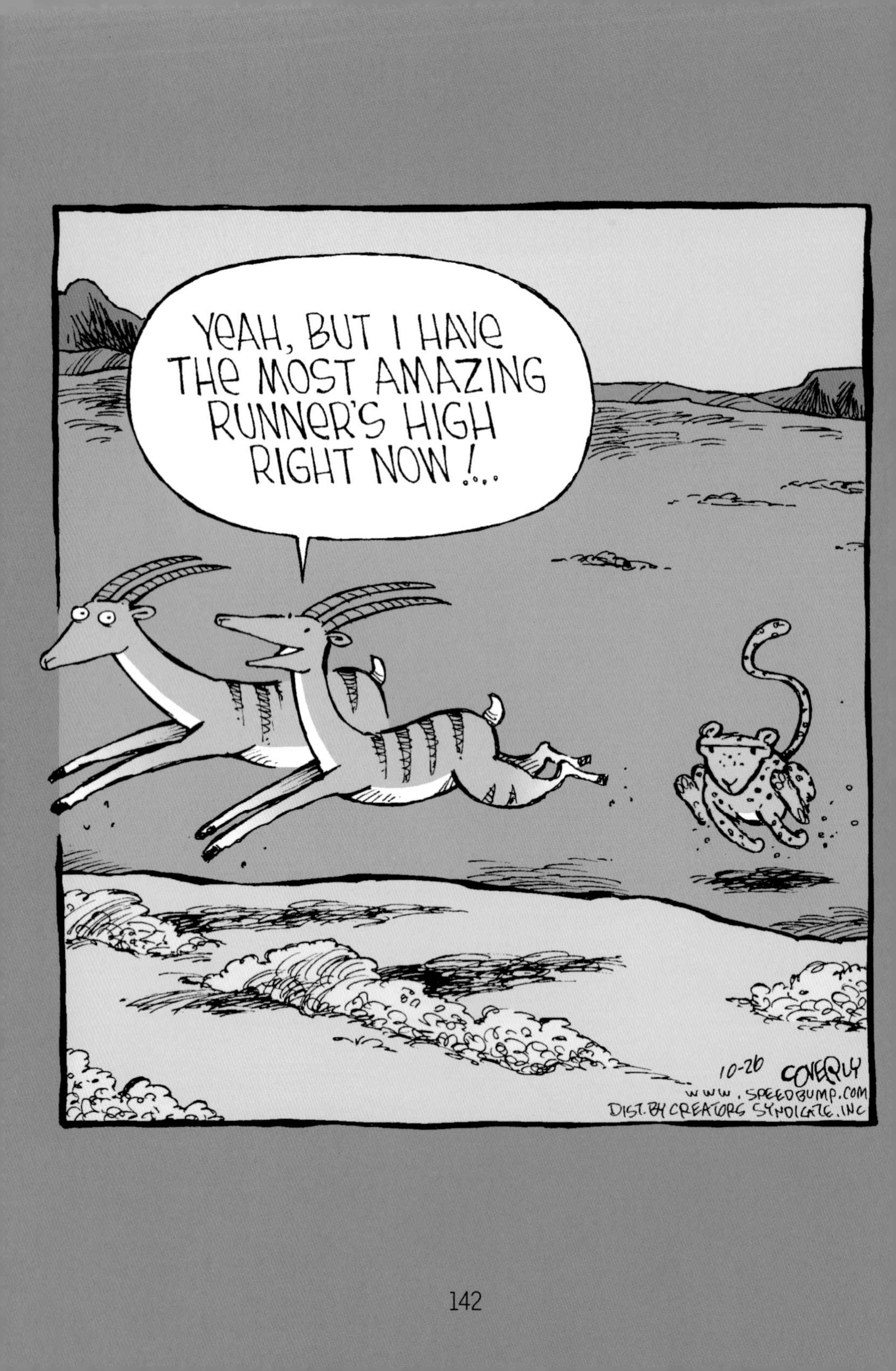
YEAH, BUT I HAVE THE MOST AMAZING RUNNER'S HIGH RIGHT NOW!...
10-26 COVERLY
WWW.SPEEDBUMP.COM
DIST. BY CREATORS SYNDICATE, INC

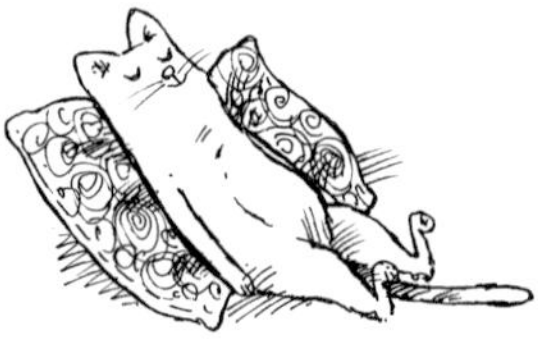

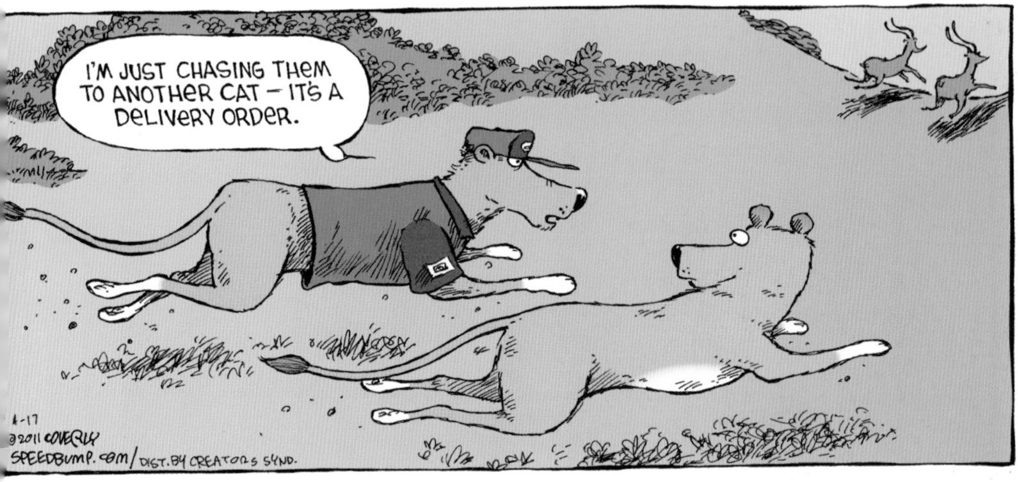
I'M JUST CHASING THEM TO ANOTHER CAT — IT'S A DELIVERY ORDER.
4-17
©2011 COVERLY
SPEEDBUMP.com/ DIST. BY CREATORS SYND.

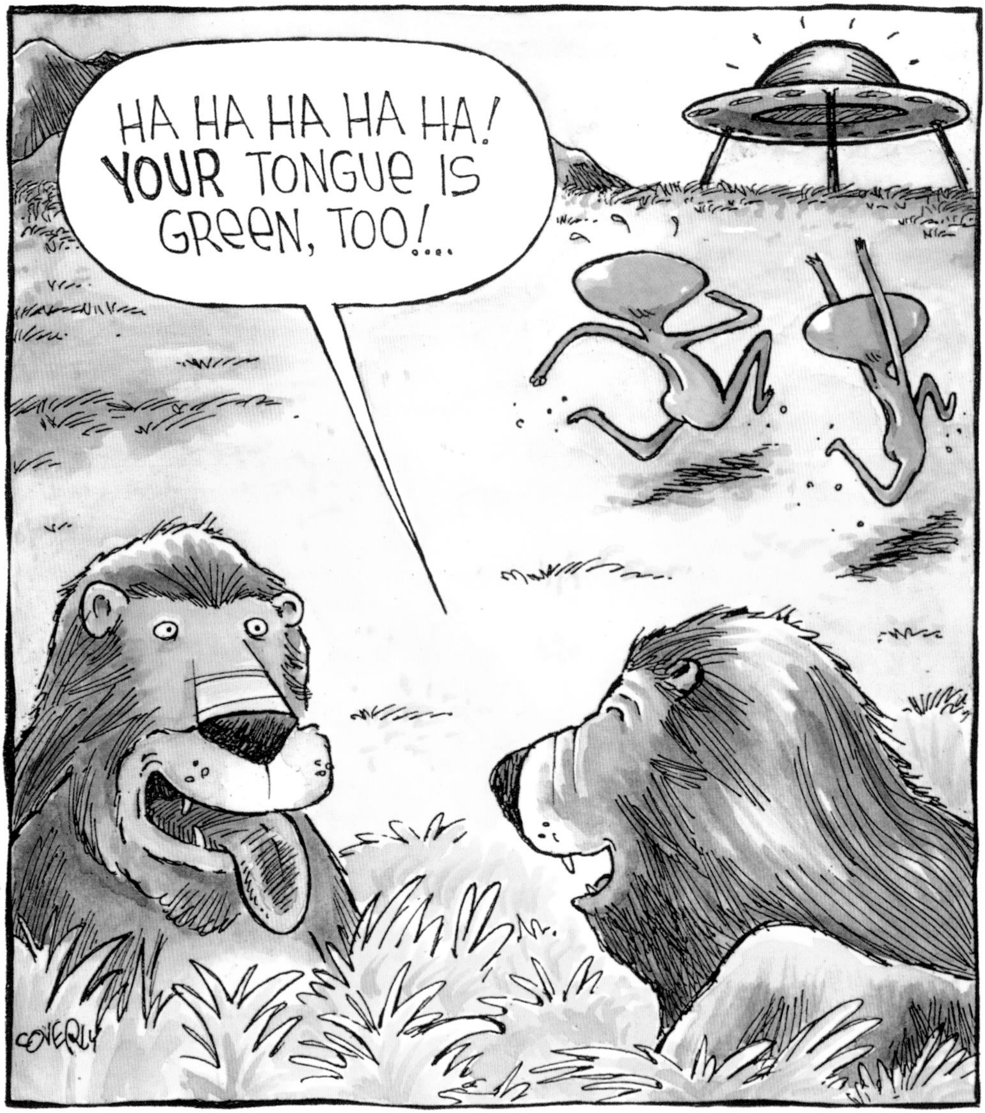
HA HA HA HA HA! YOUR TONGUE IS GREEN, TOO!...
COVERLY

LOST & FOUND
ON SECOND THOUGHT, WHY DON'T YOU JUST COME BACK HERE AND GET IT YOURSELF...
2-22
WWW.CREATORS.COM
©2000 CREATORS SYNDICATE, INC.

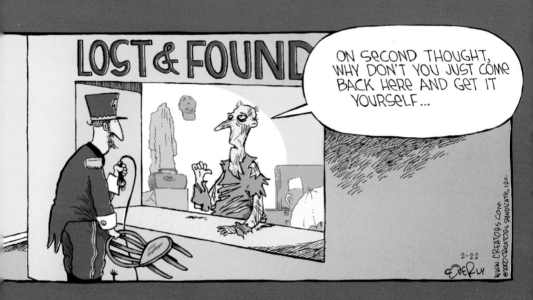

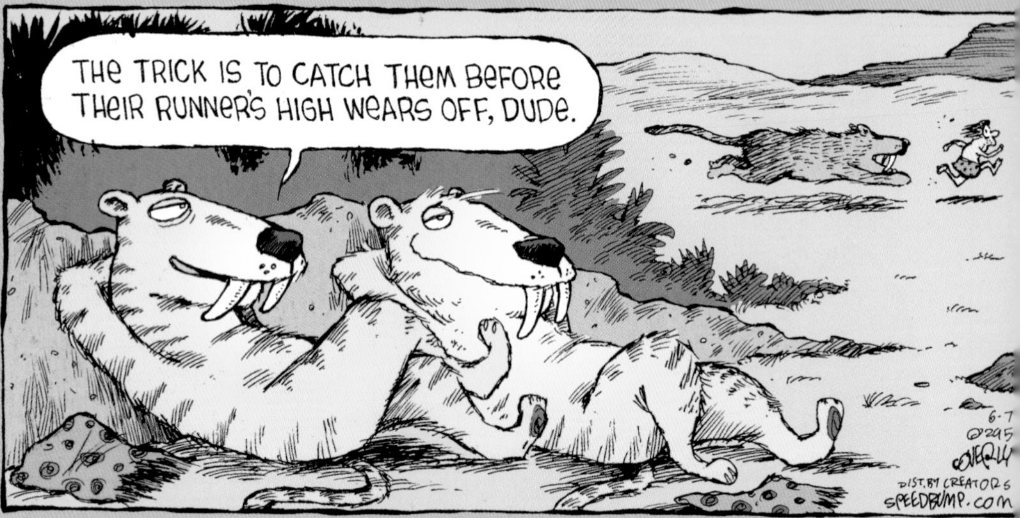
THE TRICK IS TO CATCH THEM BEFORE THEIR RUNNER'S HIGH WEARS OFF, DUDE.
6-7
©2015
COVERLY
DIST. BY CREATORS
SPEEDBUMP.COM

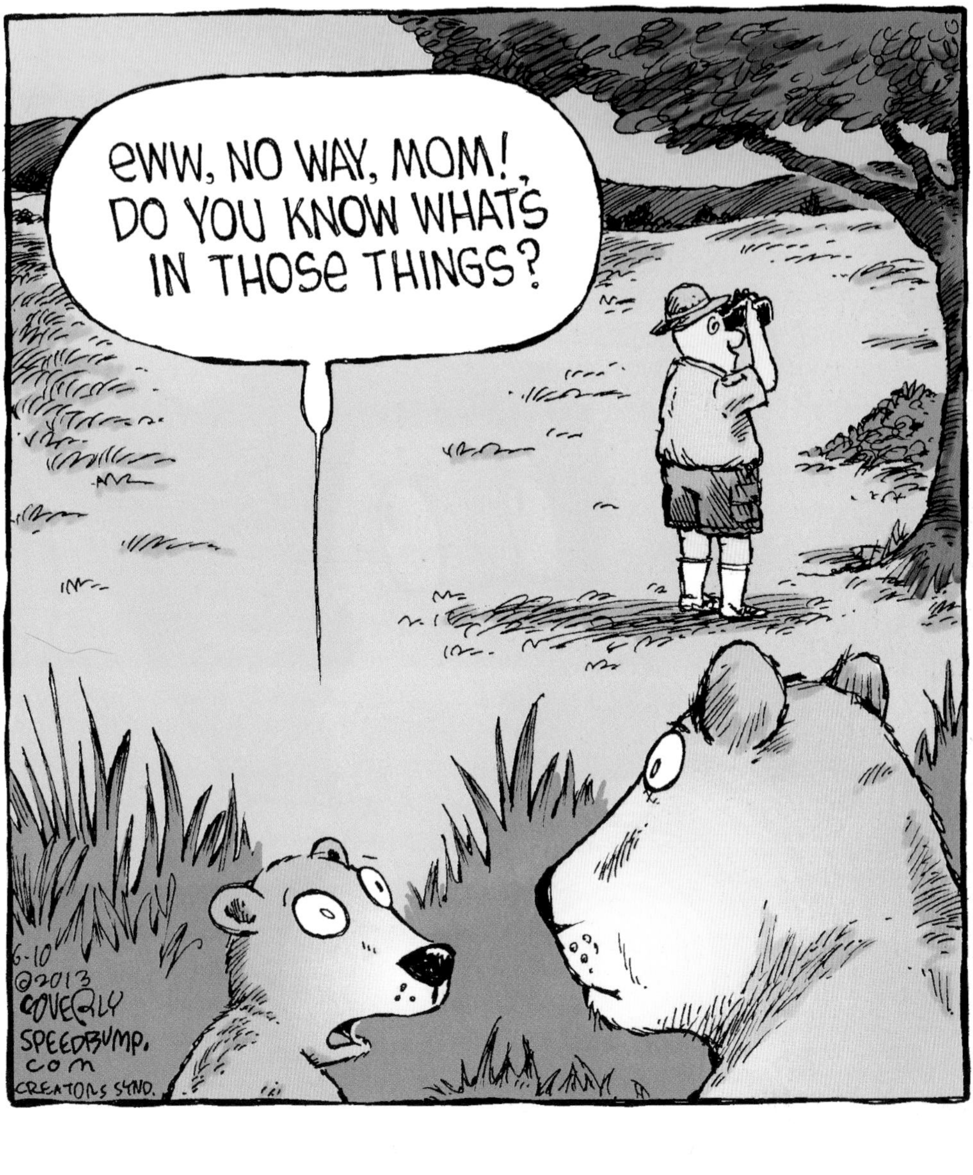
eww, NO WAY, MOM! DO YOU KNOW WHAT'S IN THOSE THINGS?
6-10 ©2013 COVERLY SPEEDBUMP.com CREATORS SYND.

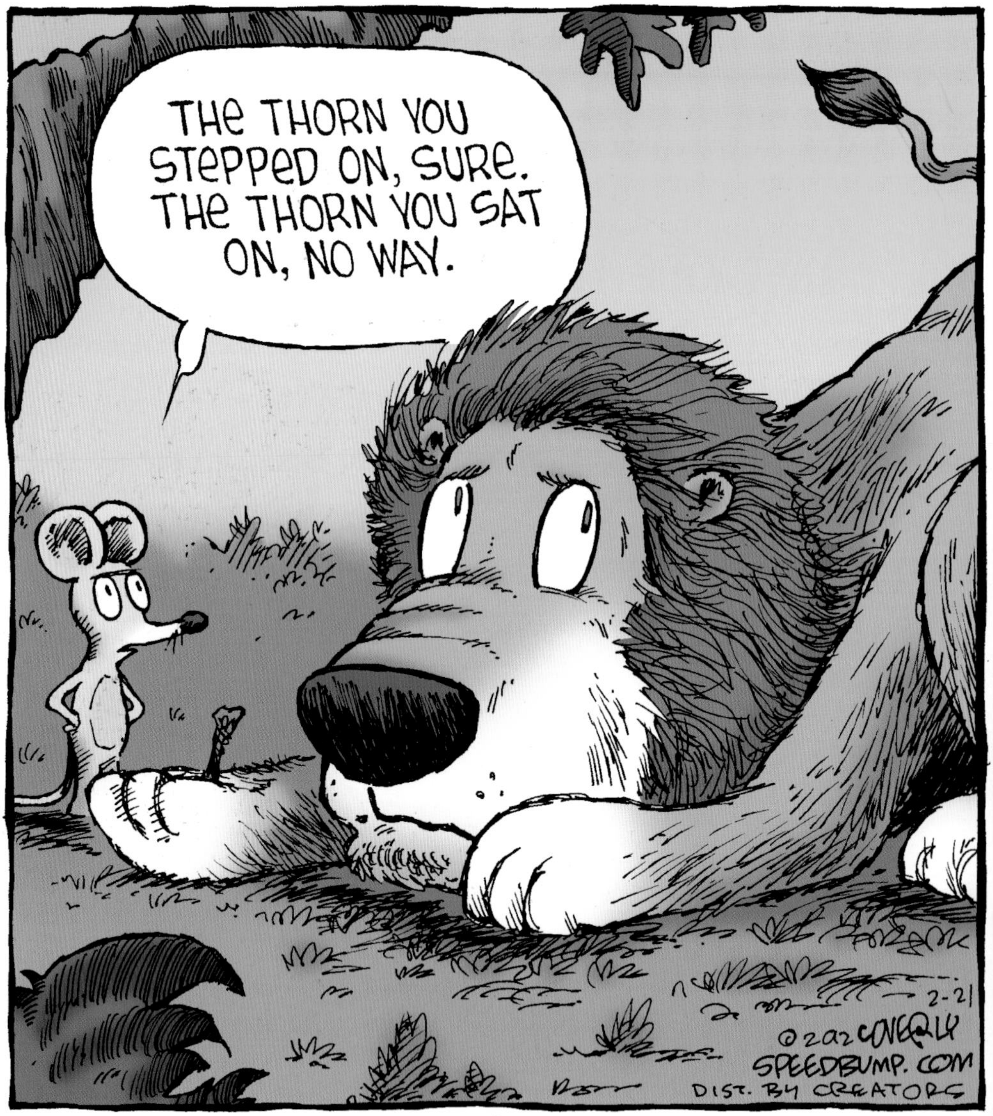
THE THORN YOU STEPPED ON, SURE. THE THORN YOU SAT ON, NO WAY.
2-21
©2021 COVERLY
SPEEDBUMP.COM
DIST. BY CREATORS

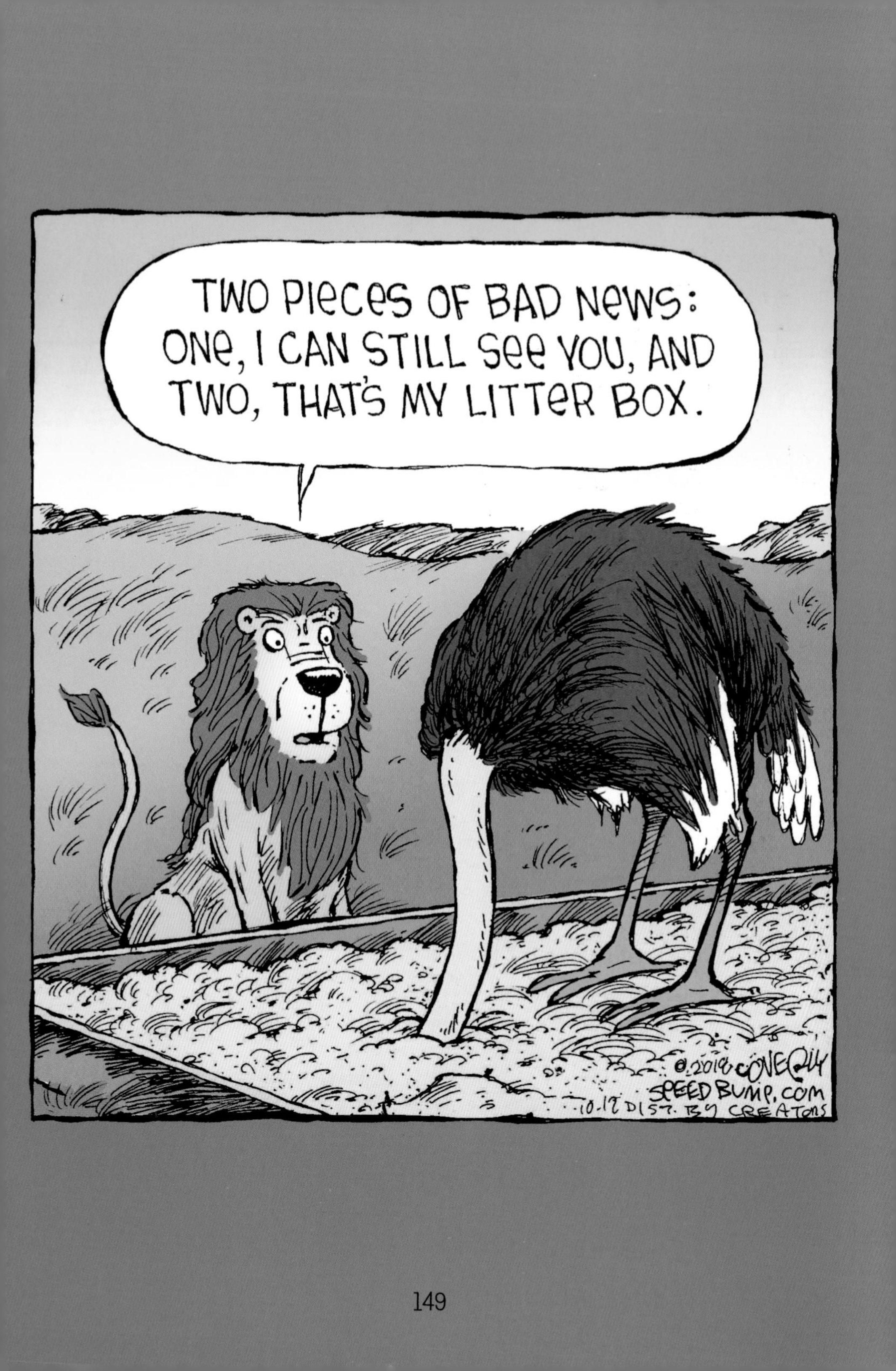
TWO PIECES OF BAD NEWS: ONE, I CAN STILL SEE YOU, AND TWO, THAT'S MY LITTER BOX.
©2018 COVERLY
SPEEDBUMP.COM
10-18 DIST. BY CREATORS

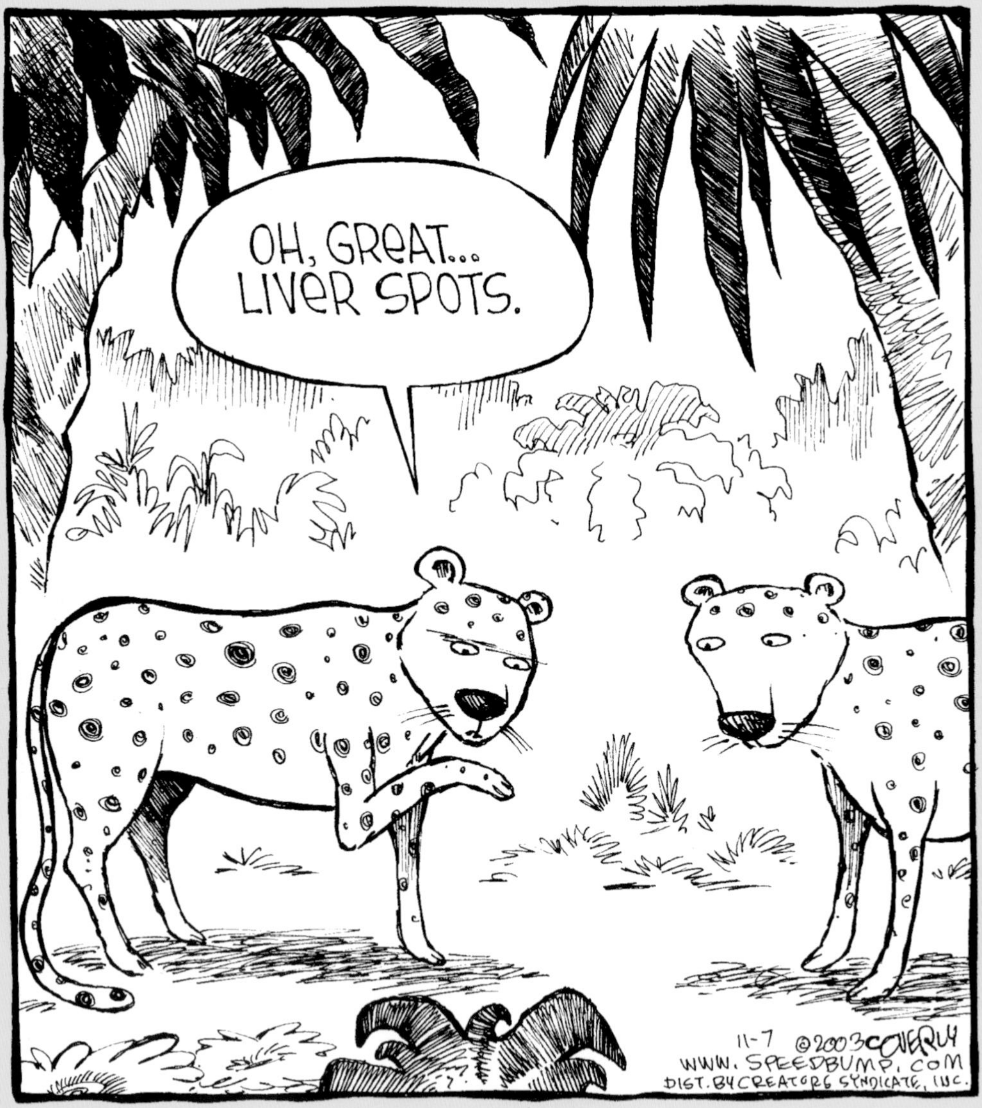
OH, GREAT...
LIVER SPOTS.
11-7 ©2003 COVERLY
WWW.SPEEDBUMP.COM
DIST. BY CREATORS SYNDICATE, INC.

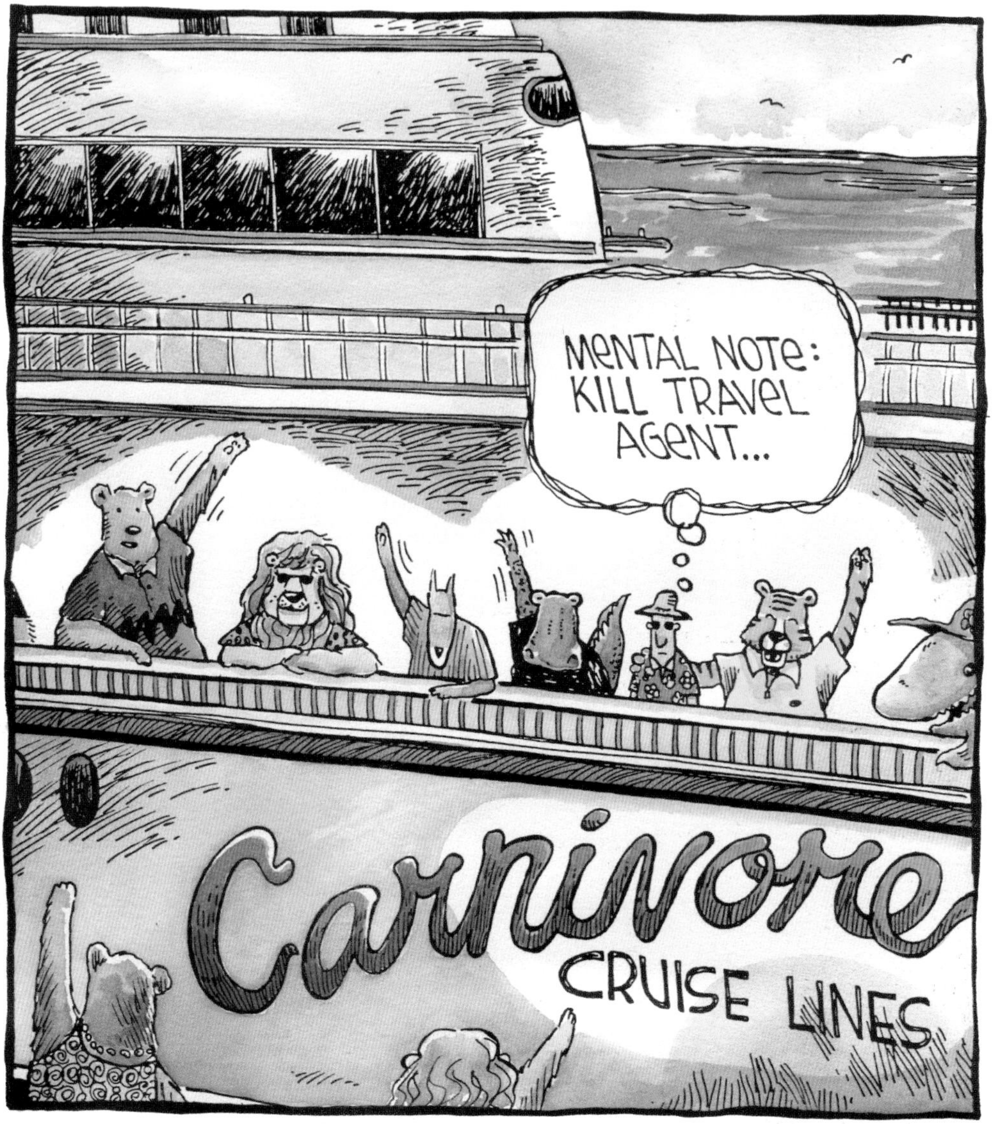
MENTAL NOTE: KILL TRAVEL AGENT...
Carnivore
CRUISE LINES

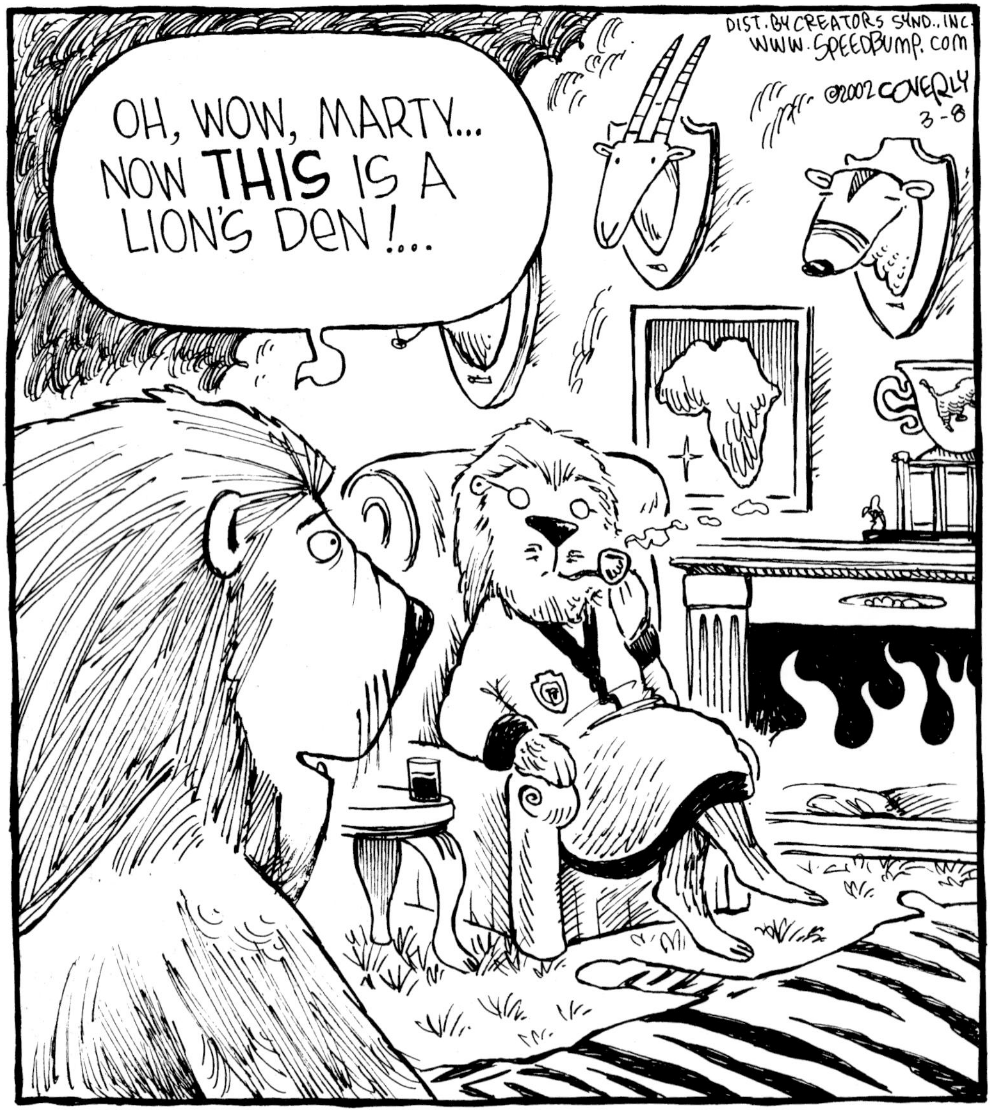
DIST. BY CREATORS SYND., INC.
WWW.SPEEDBUMP.COM
©2002 COVERLY
3-8
OH, WOW, MARTY... NOW THIS IS A LION'S DEN!...

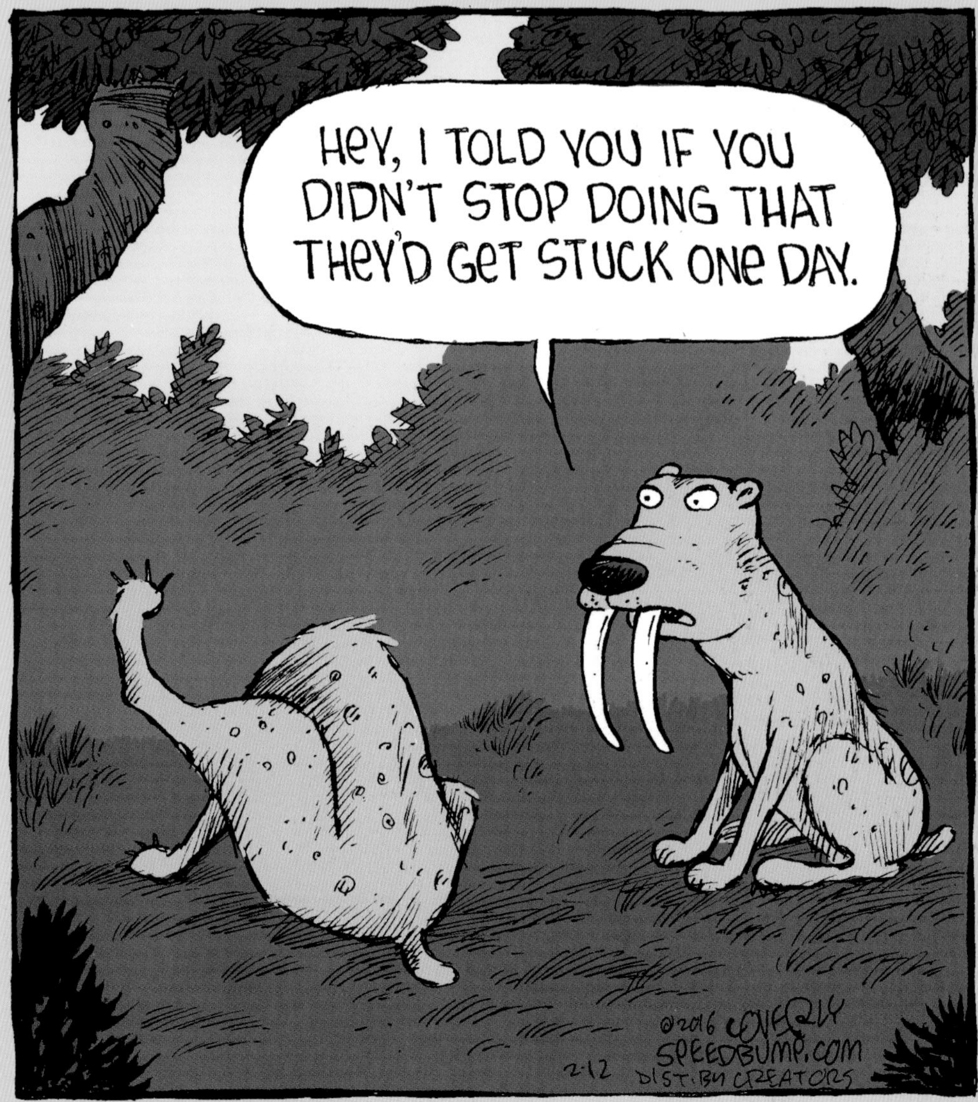
HEY, I TOLD YOU IF YOU DIDN'T STOP DOING THAT THEY'D GET STUCK ONE DAY.
©2016 COVERLY
SPEEDBUMP.COM
2-12
DIST. BY CREATORS

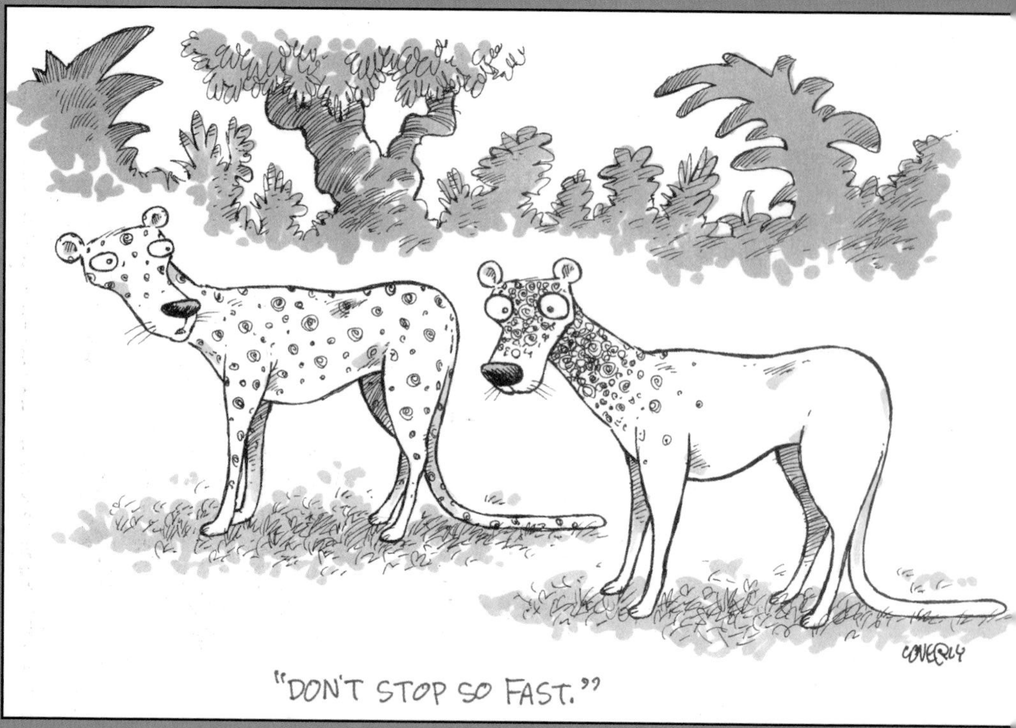
COVERLY

"DON'T STOP SO FAST."

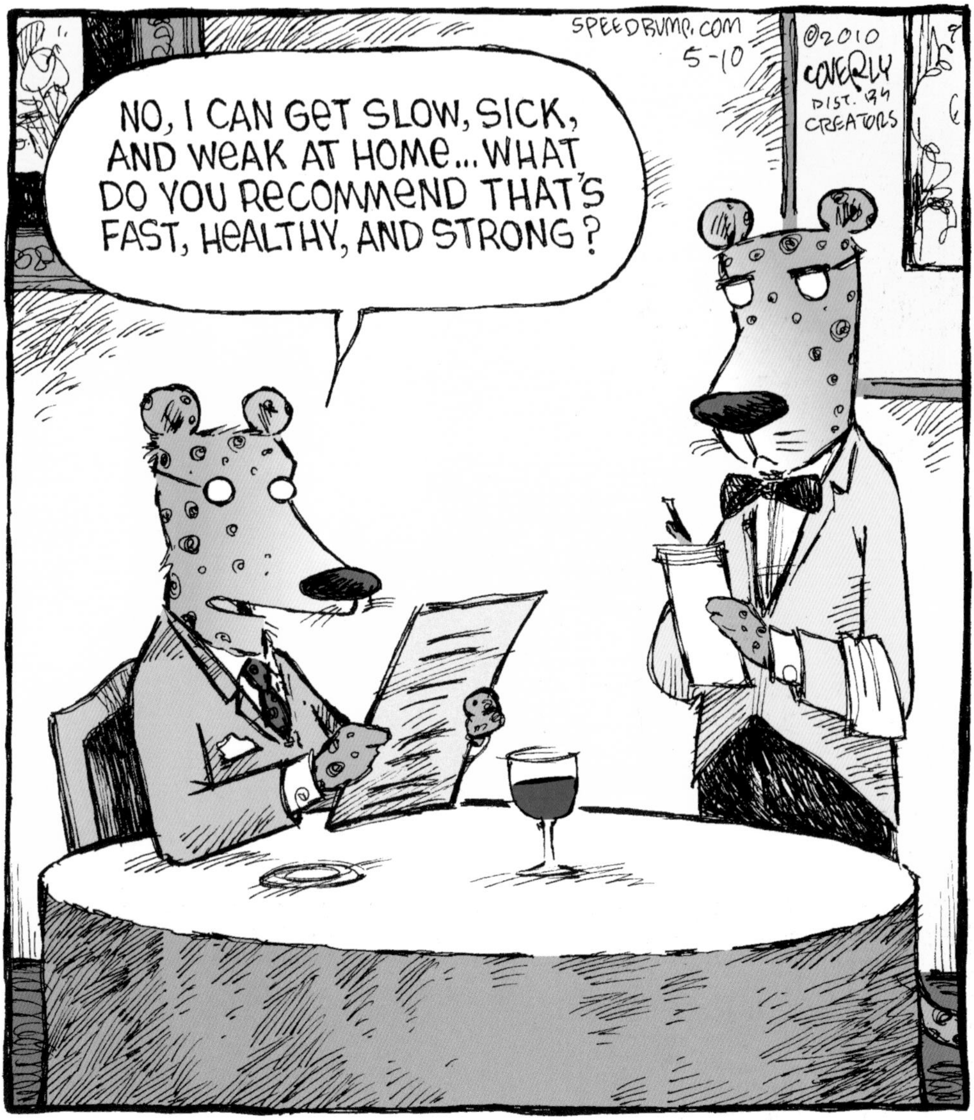
SPEEDBUMP.COM
5-10
©2010
COVERLY
DIST. BY
CREATORS
NO, I CAN GET SLOW, SICK, AND WEAK AT HOME... WHAT DO YOU RECOMMEND THAT'S FAST, HEALTHY, AND STRONG?

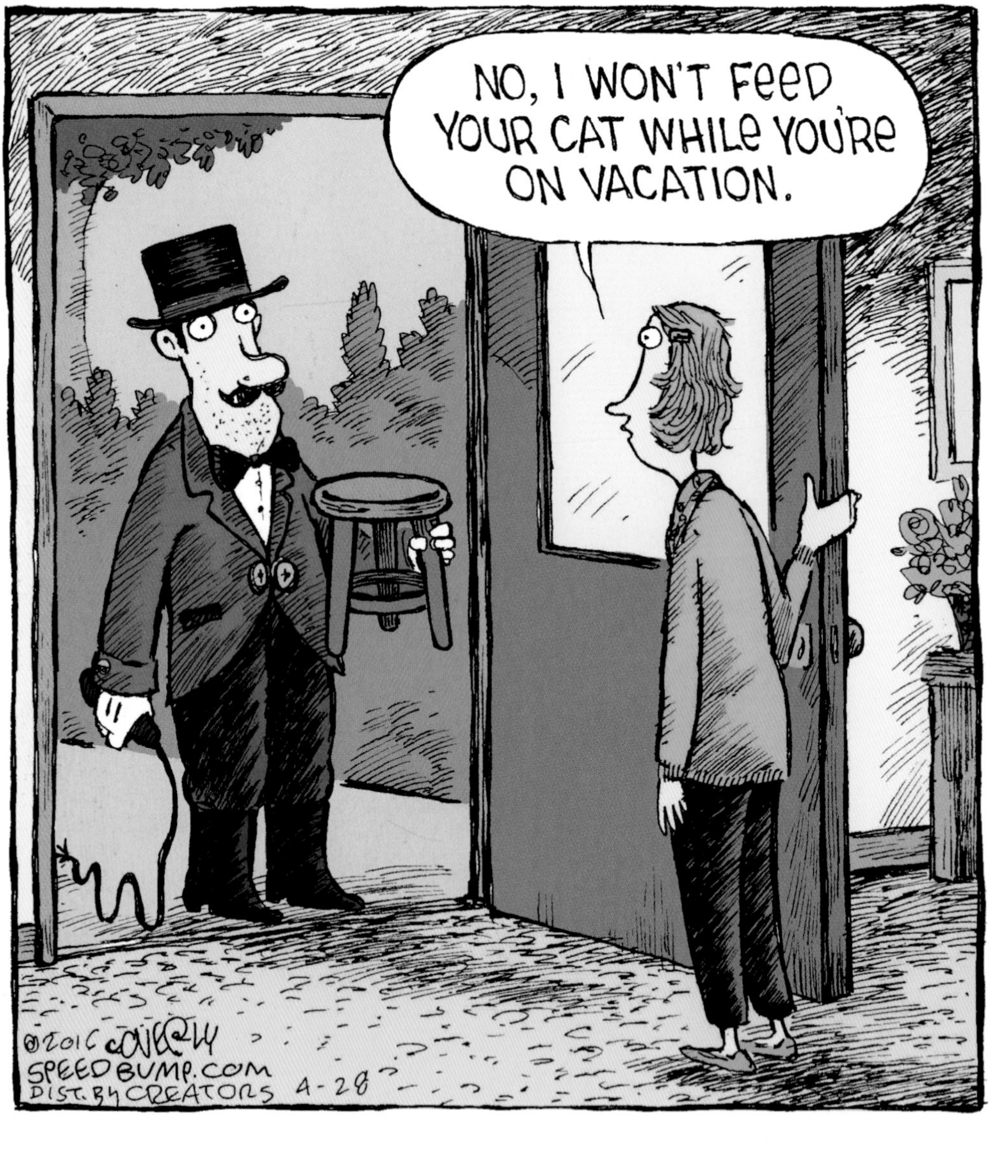
NO, I WON'T FEED YOUR CAT WHILE YOU'RE ON VACATION.
©2016 COVERLY
SPEEDBUMP.COM
DIST. BY CREATORS 4-28

Jay P. Fosgitt

Goonie is an anomaly—a kitty that doesn't scratch the furniture, knock down Christmas trees, or walk on counters or tables. But she loves pretending you're chasing her. She's cuddly in her own way—don't pick her up, don't put her on your lap—she wants to be pressed up against you. She has a tiny, high-pitched meow, unless she really wants your attention. Then she has a bass meow that sounds like funeral wailing. She's aloof and she's a flirt, but only when she wants to be. And above all, she's my little girl.

About Jay P. Fosgitt

Jay P. Fosgitt has drawn comics for Marvel, Image, BOOM!, IDW, Archie, and King Features Syndicate, and drawn children's books for Disney. His own comic creation, *Bodie Troll,* is published by BOOM! Studios, where a second volume is already underway. Jay resides in Michigan with his cat, Goonie.

jayfosgitt.com

CHAPTER 6

REIGNING CATS . . . AND DOGS

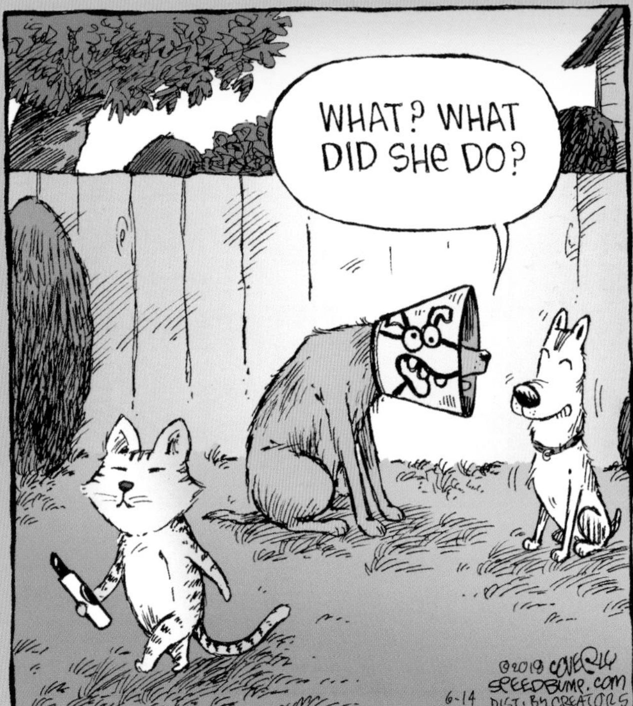
WHAT? WHAT DID SHE DO?
©2019 COVERLY
SPEEDBUMP.com
6-14
DIST. BY CREATORS

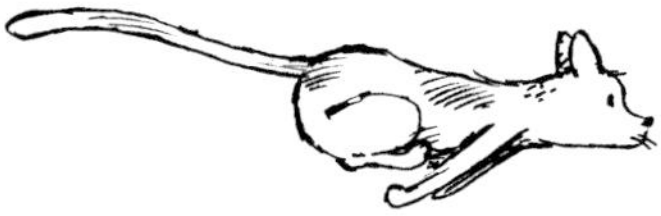

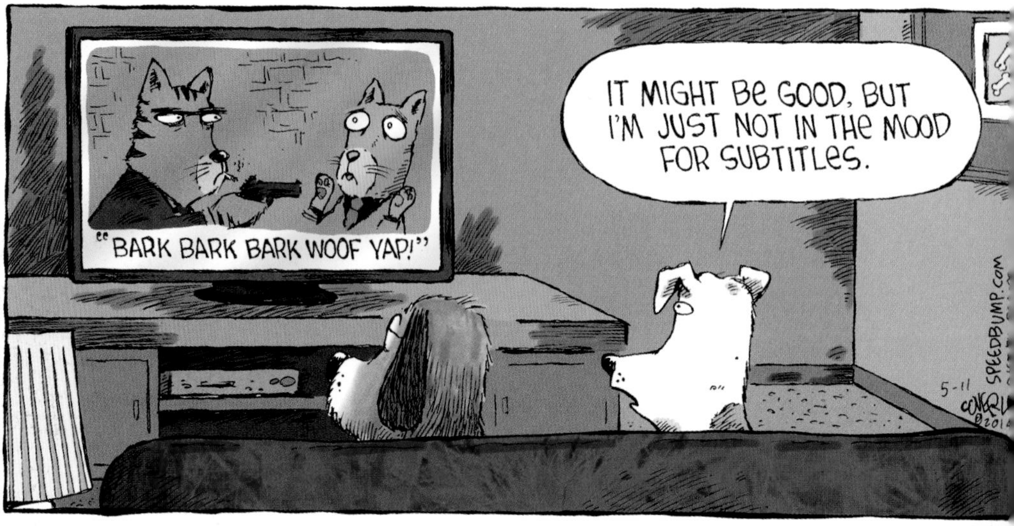
"BARK BARK BARK WOOF YAP!"
IT MIGHT BE GOOD, BUT I'M JUST NOT IN THE MOOD FOR SUBTITLES.
SPEEDBUMP.COM
5-11

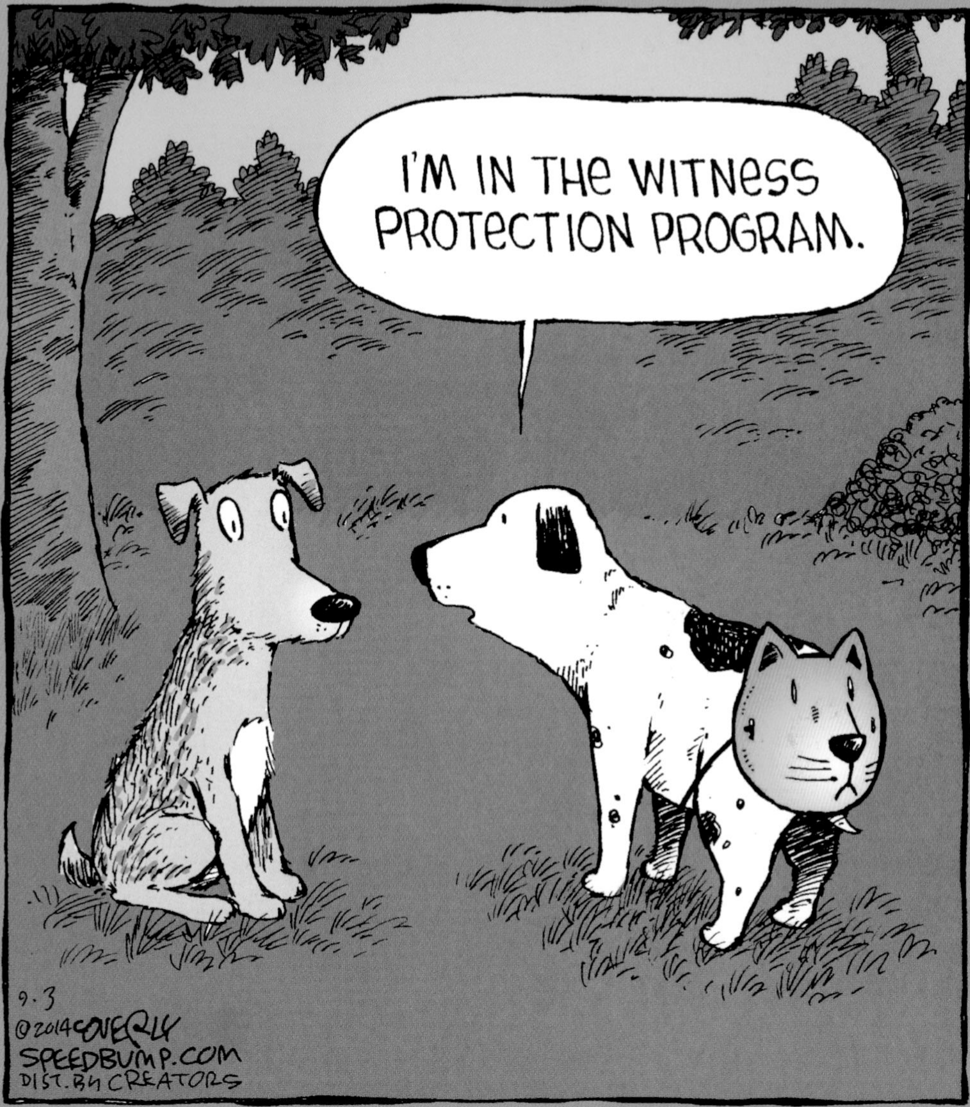
I'M IN THE WITNESS PROTECTION PROGRAM.
9.3
©2014 COVERLY
SPEEDBUMP.COM
DIST. BY CREATORS

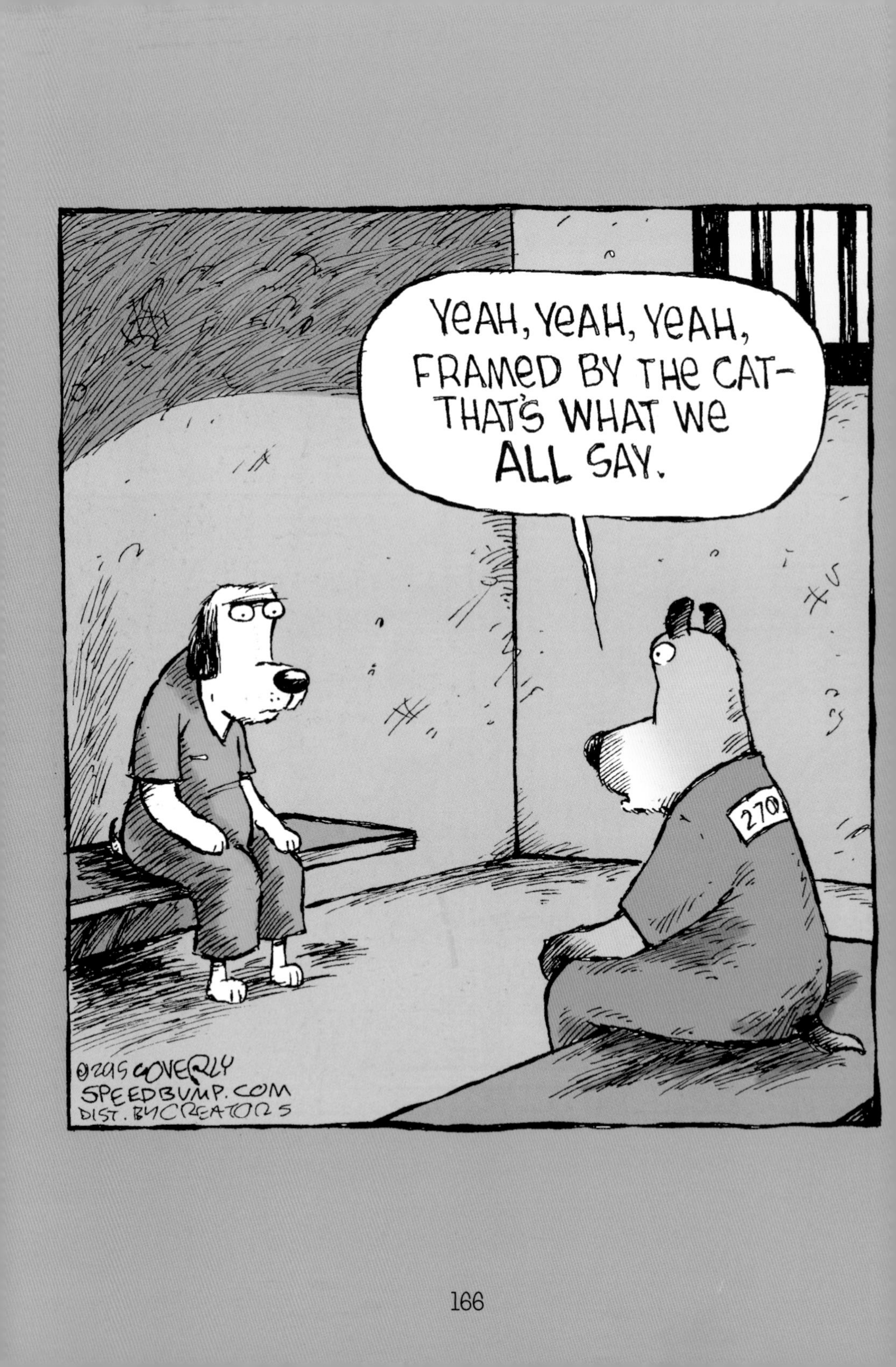
YEAH, YEAH, YEAH, FRAMED BY THE CAT- THAT'S WHAT WE ALL SAY.
270
©2015 COVERLY
SPEEDBUMP.COM
DIST. BY CREATORS

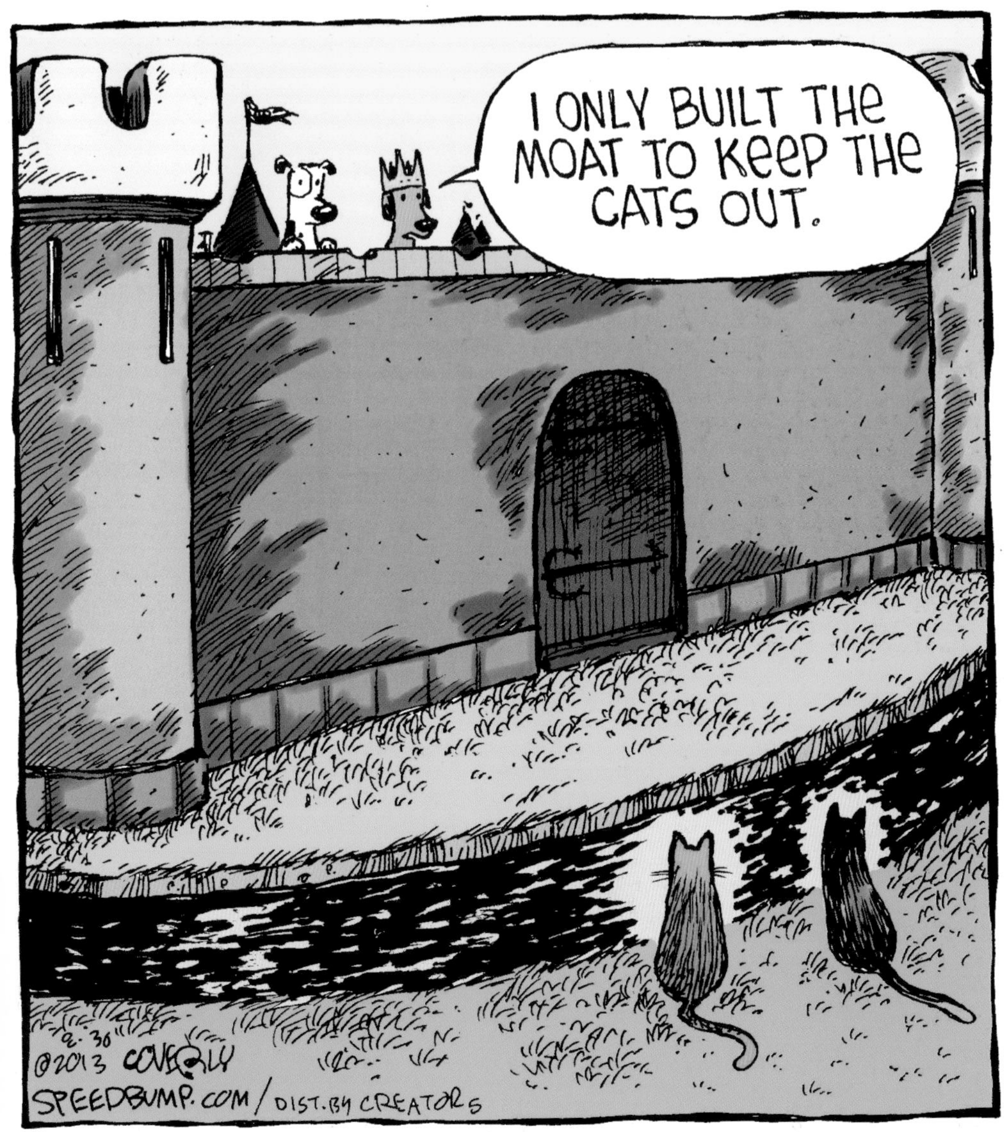
I ONLY BUILT THE MOAT TO KEEP THE CATS OUT.
8-30
©2013 COVERLY
SPEEDBUMP.COM / DIST. BY CREATORS

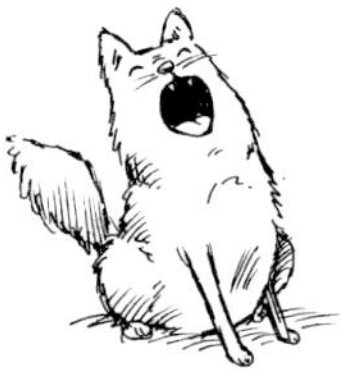

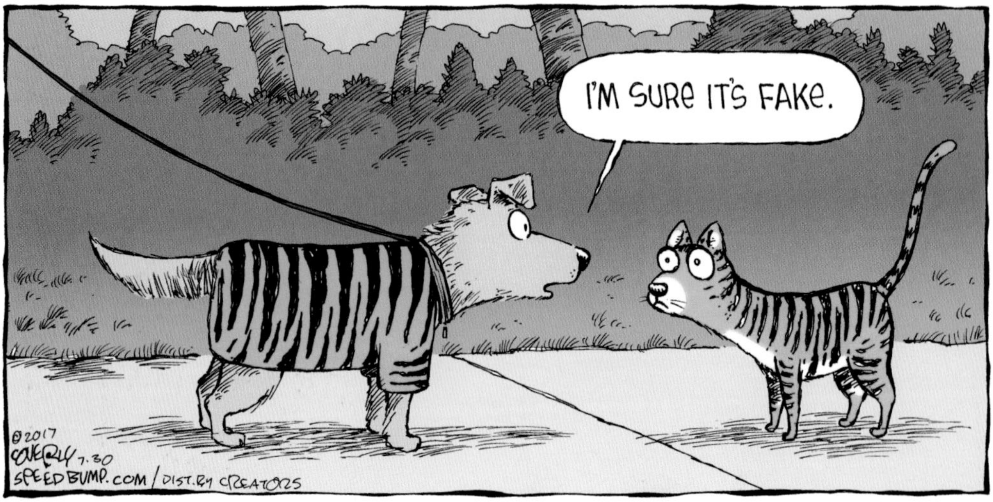
I'M SURE IT'S FAKE.
©2017
EVERLY 7.30
SPEEDBUMP.COM / DIST. BY CREATORS

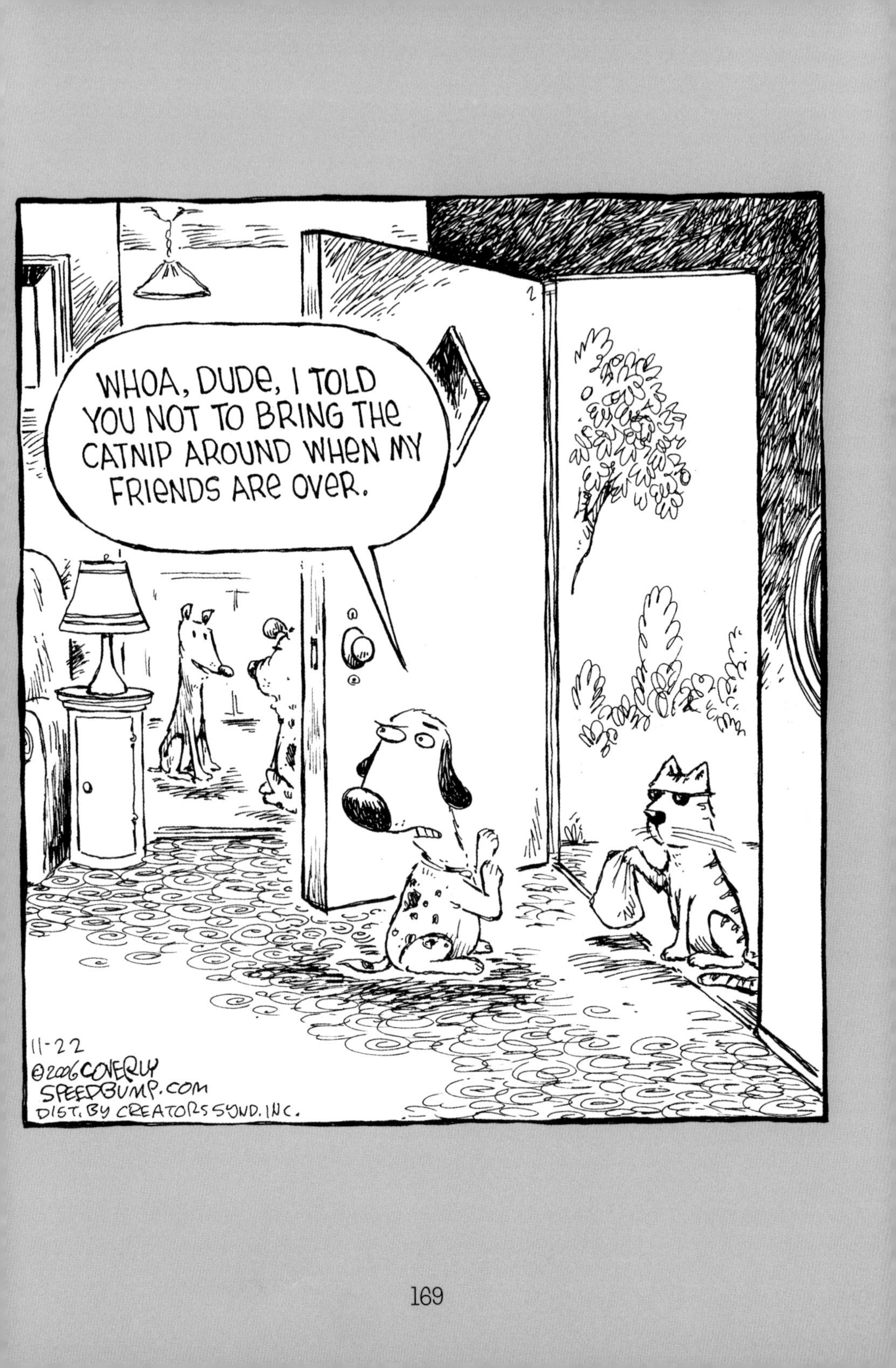
WHOA, DUDE, I TOLD YOU NOT TO BRING THE CATNIP AROUND WHEN MY FRIENDS ARE OVER.
11-22
©2006 COVERLY
SPEEDBUMP.COM
DIST. BY CREATORS SYND. INC.

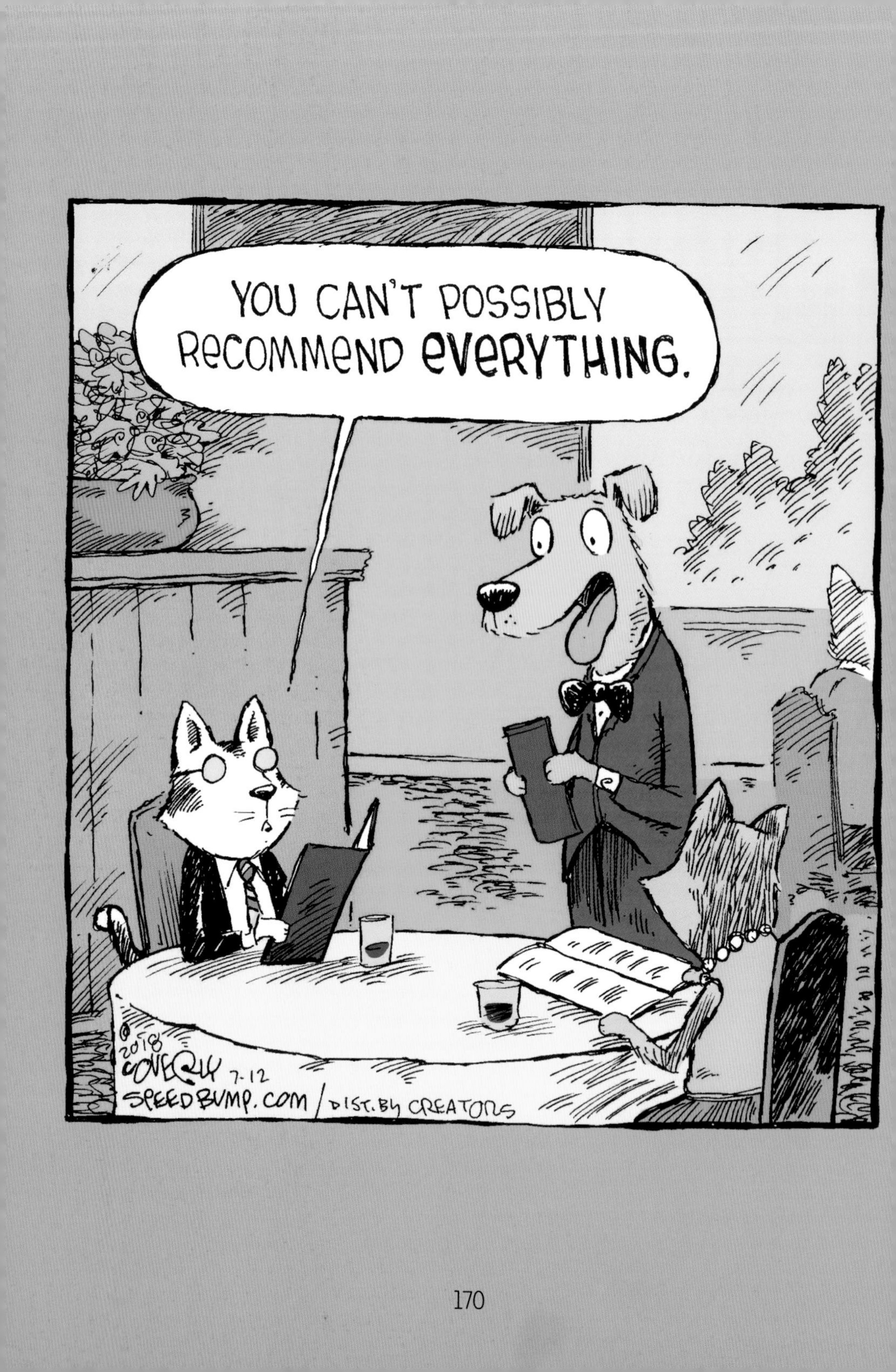
YOU CAN'T POSSIBLY RECOMMEND EVERYTHING.
© 2018 COVERLY 7-12
SPEEDBUMP.COM / DIST. BY CREATORS

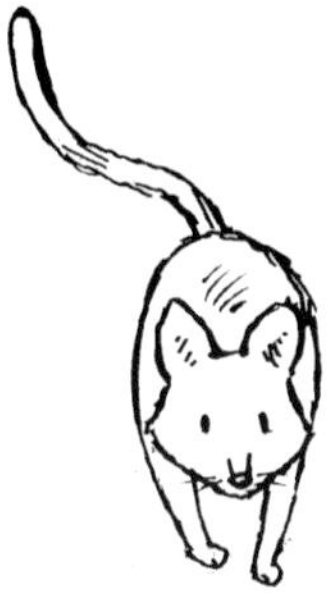

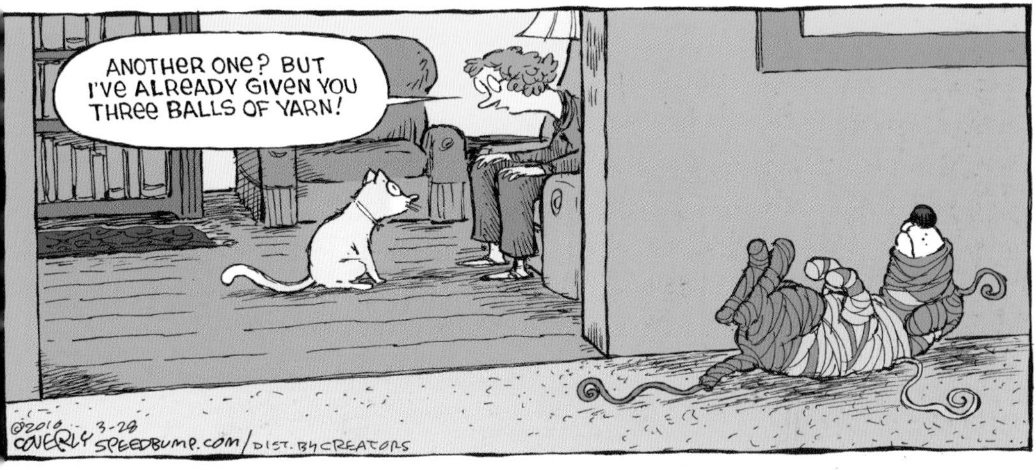
ANOTHER ONE? BUT I'VE ALREADY GIVEN YOU THREE BALLS OF YARN!
©2010 COVERLY 3-28 SPEEDBUMP.COM/DIST. BY CREATORS

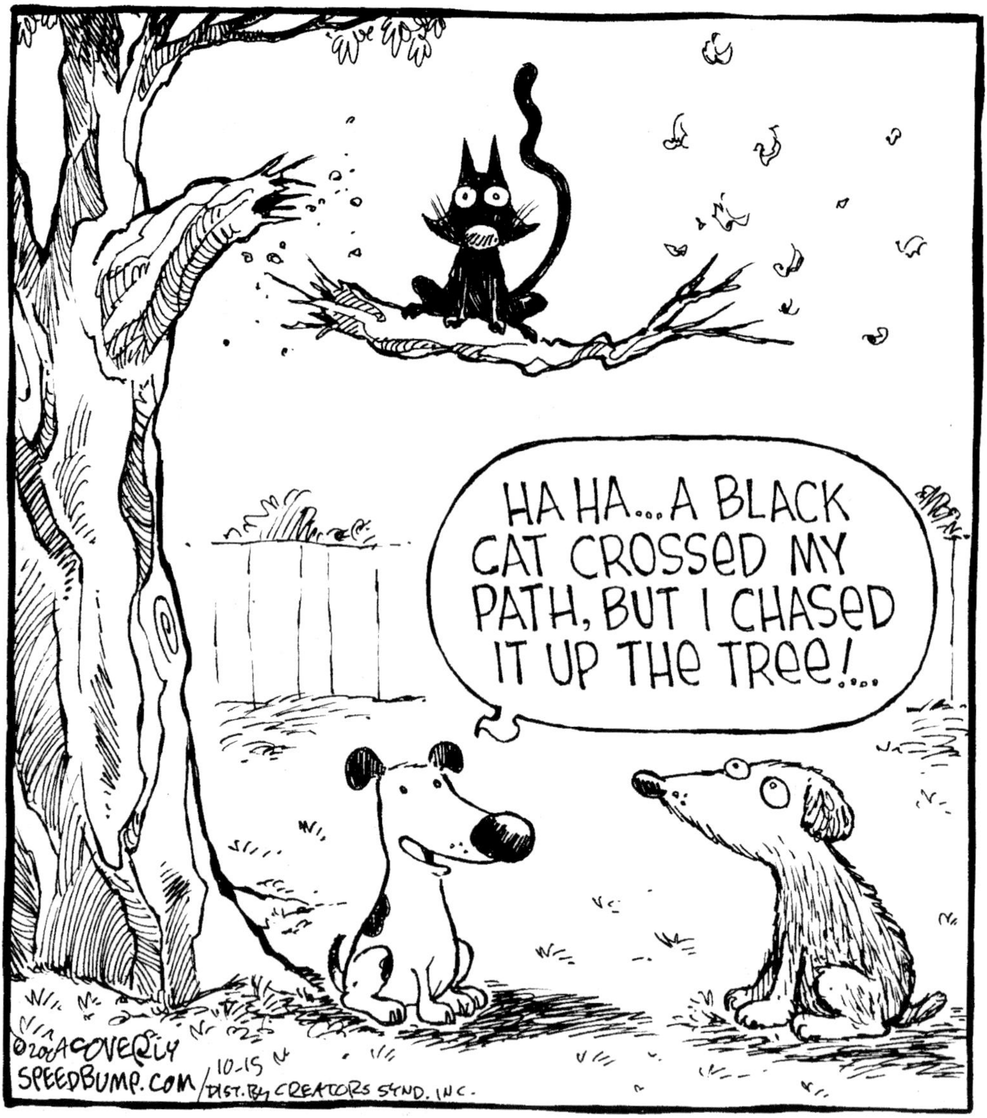
HA HA... A BLACK CAT CROSSED MY PATH, BUT I CHASED IT UP THE TREE!...
©2008 A COVERLY
SPEEDBUMP.COM
10-15
DIST. BY CREATORS SYND. INC.

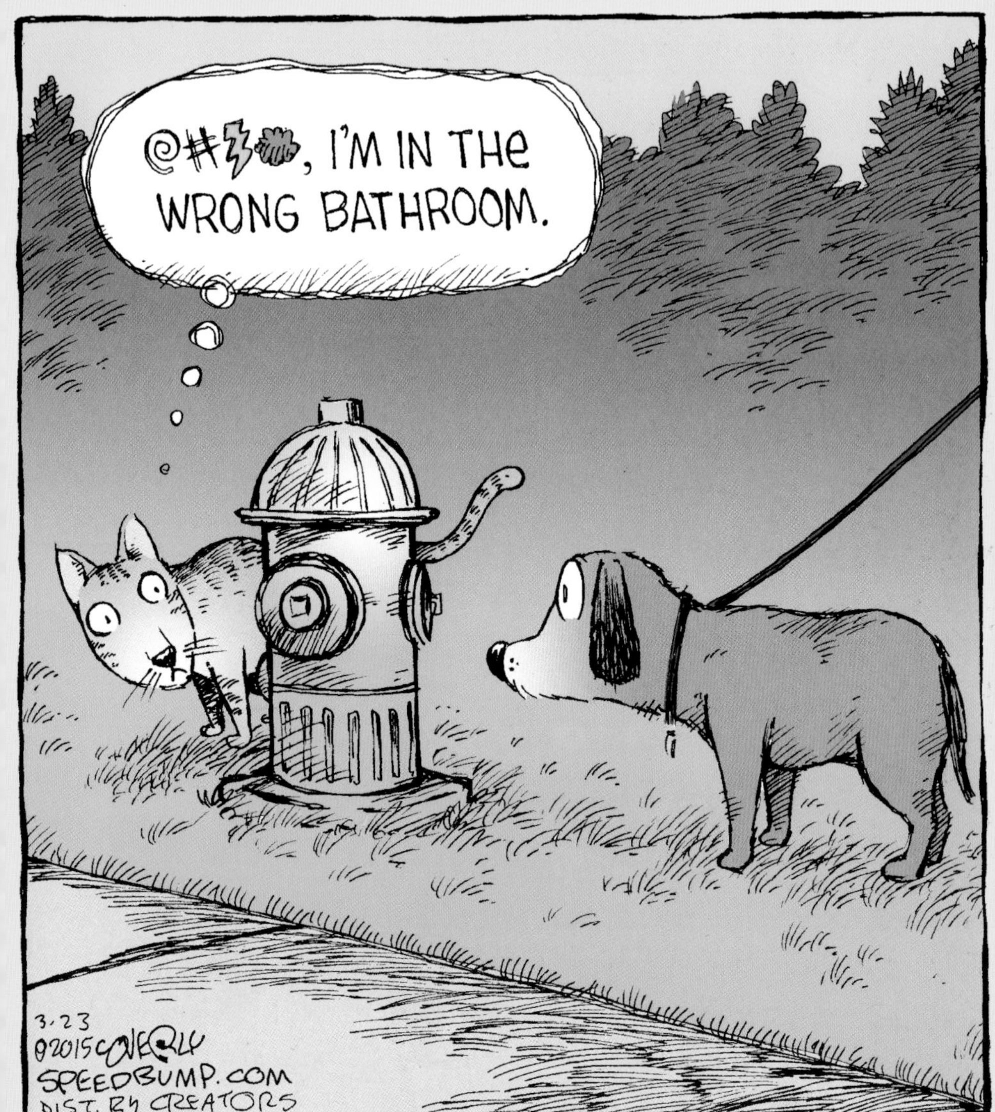
@#%*, I'M IN THE WRONG BATHROOM.
3-23
©2015 COVERLY
SPEEDBUMP.COM
DIST. BY CREATORS

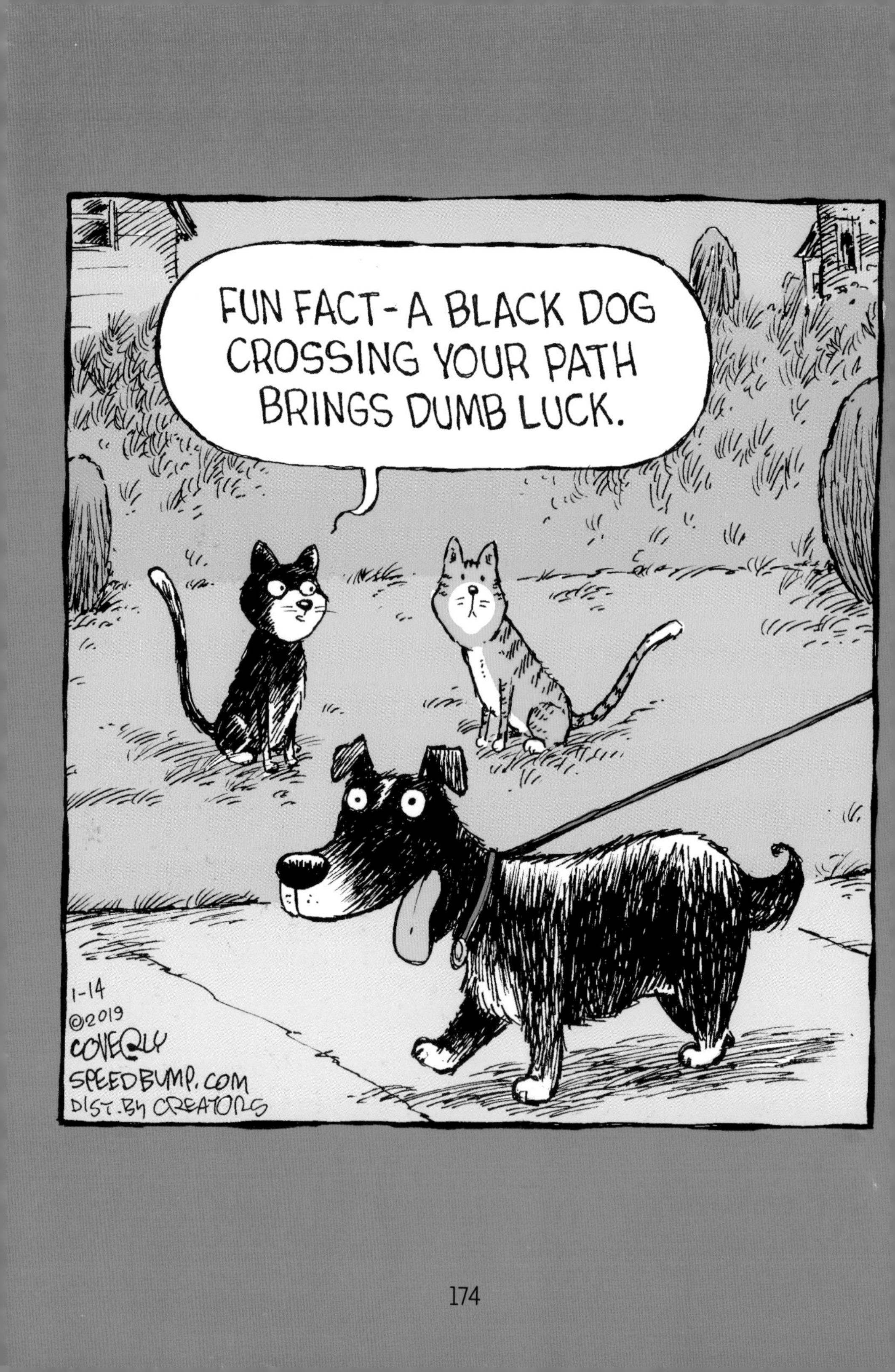
FUN FACT - A BLACK DOG CROSSING YOUR PATH BRINGS DUMB LUCK.
1-14
©2019
COVERLY
SPEEDBUMP.COM
DIST. BY CREATORS

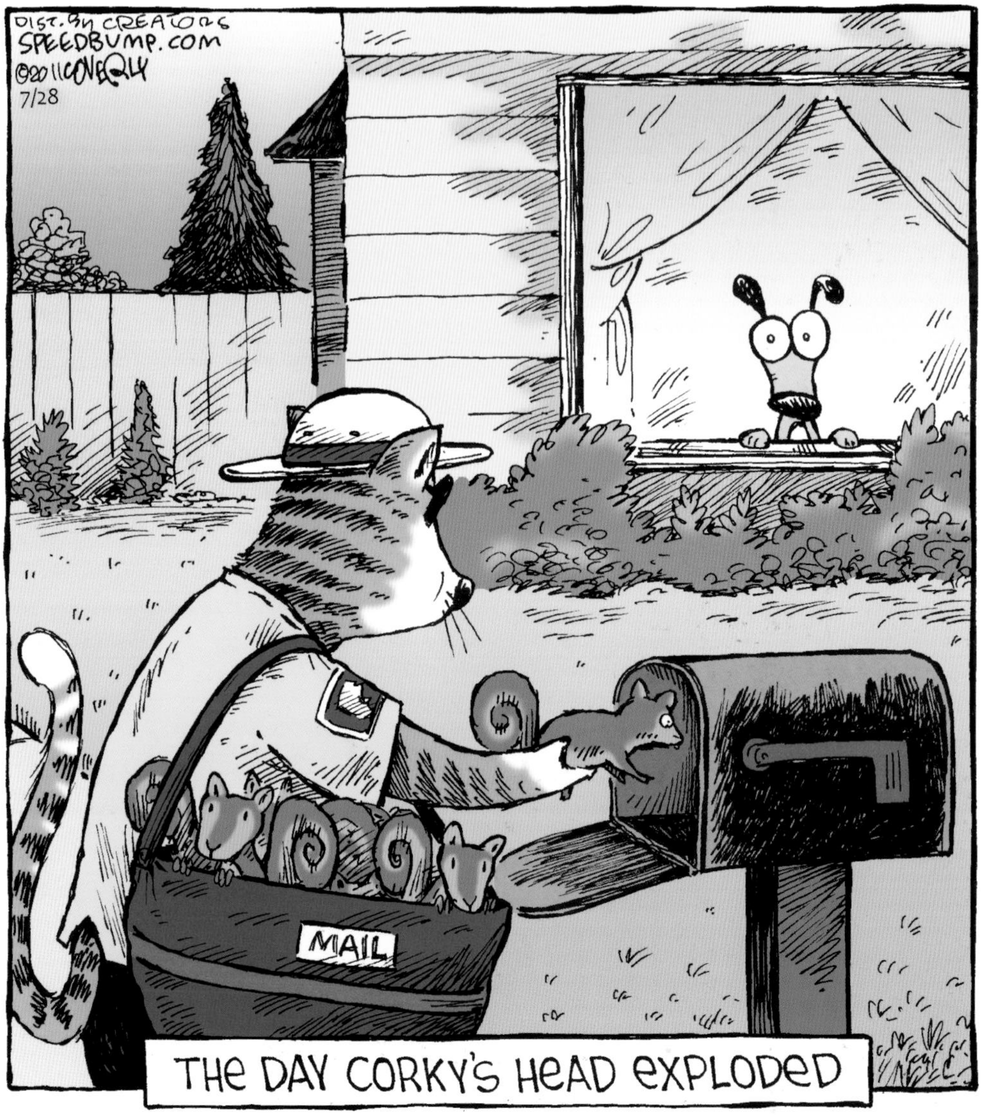
DIST. BY CREATORS
SPEEDBUMP.COM
©2011 COVERLY
7/28
MAIL
THE DAY CORKY'S HEAD EXPLODED

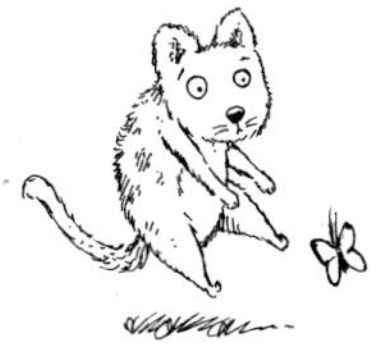

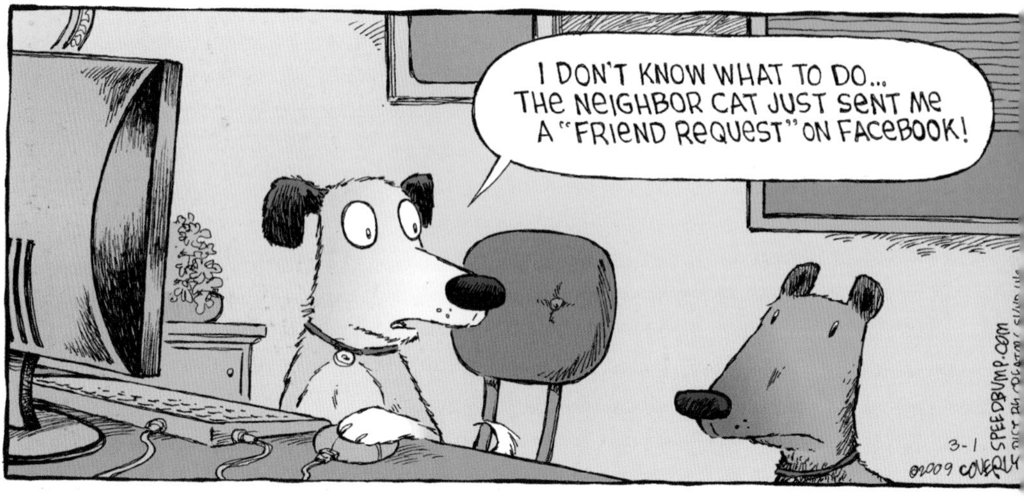
I DON'T KNOW WHAT TO DO...
THE NEIGHBOR CAT JUST SENT ME
A "FRIEND REQUEST" ON FACEBOOK!
3-1
©2009 COVERLY
SPEEDBUMP.COM

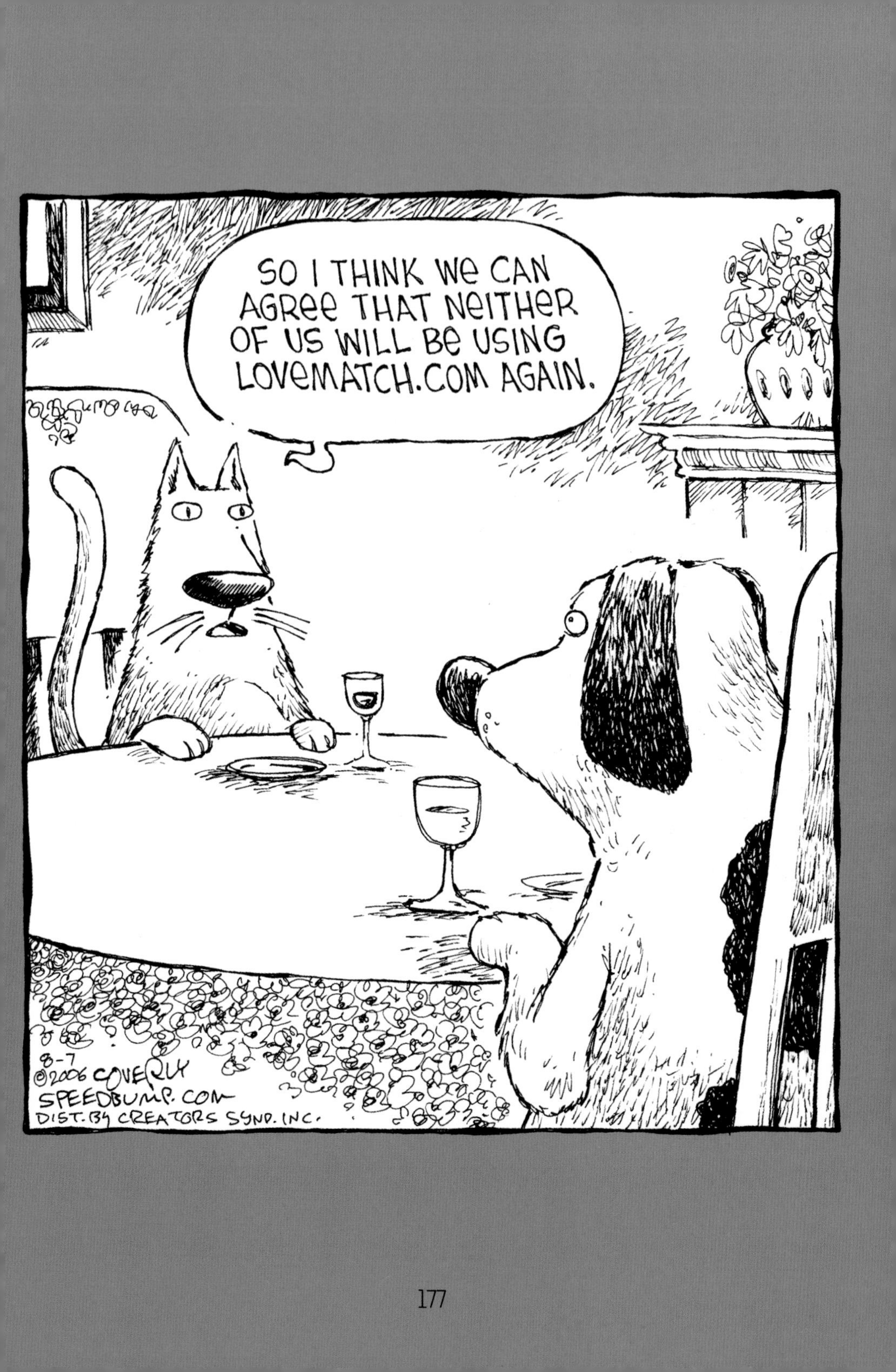
SO I THINK WE CAN AGREE THAT NEITHER OF US WILL BE USING LOVEMATCH.COM AGAIN.
8-7
©2006 COVERLY
SPEEDBUMP.COM
DIST. BY CREATORS SYND. INC.

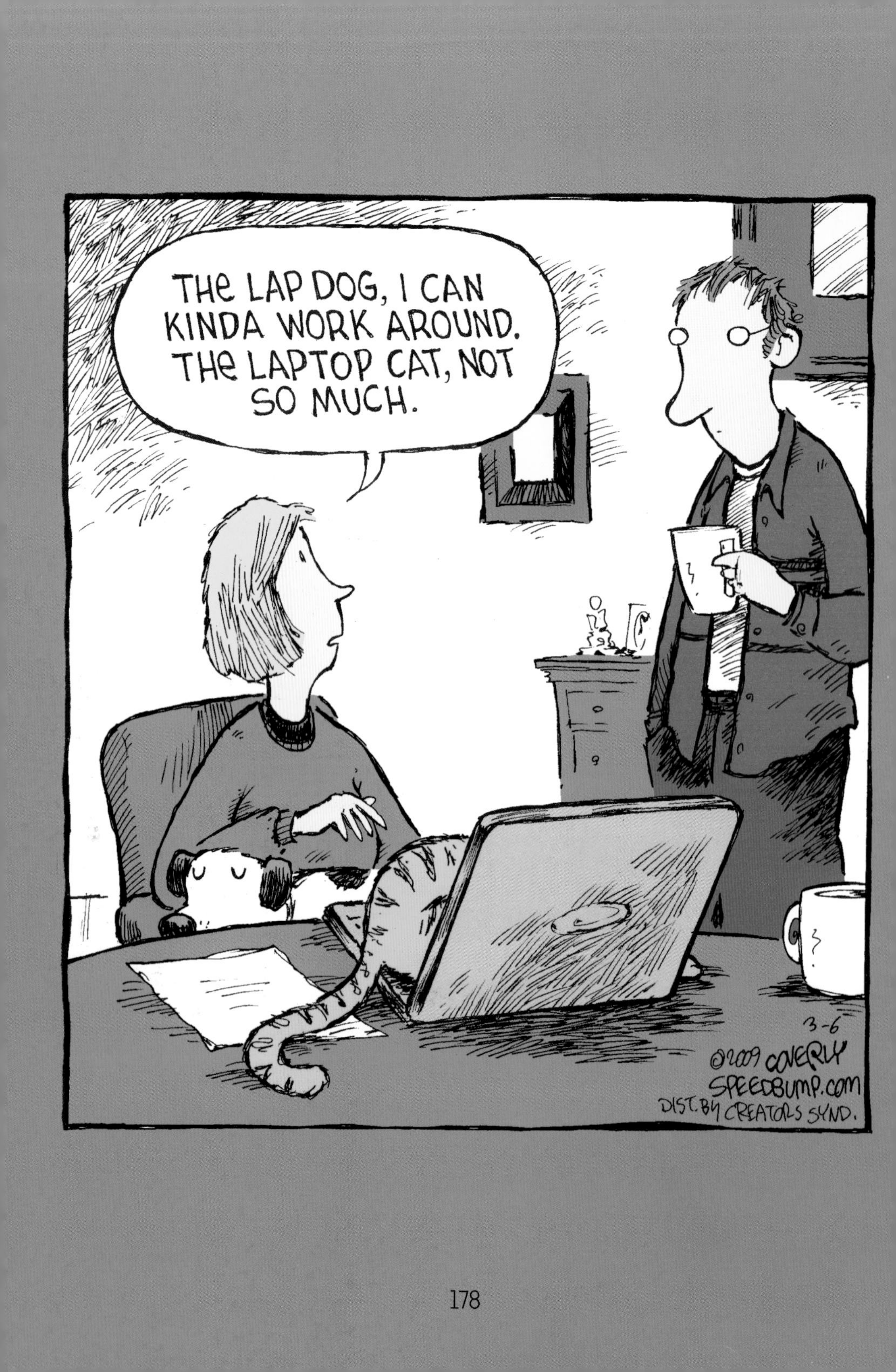
THE LAP DOG, I CAN KINDA WORK AROUND. THE LAPTOP CAT, NOT SO MUCH.
3-6
©2009 COVERLY
SPEEDBUMP.COM
DIST. BY CREATORS SYND.

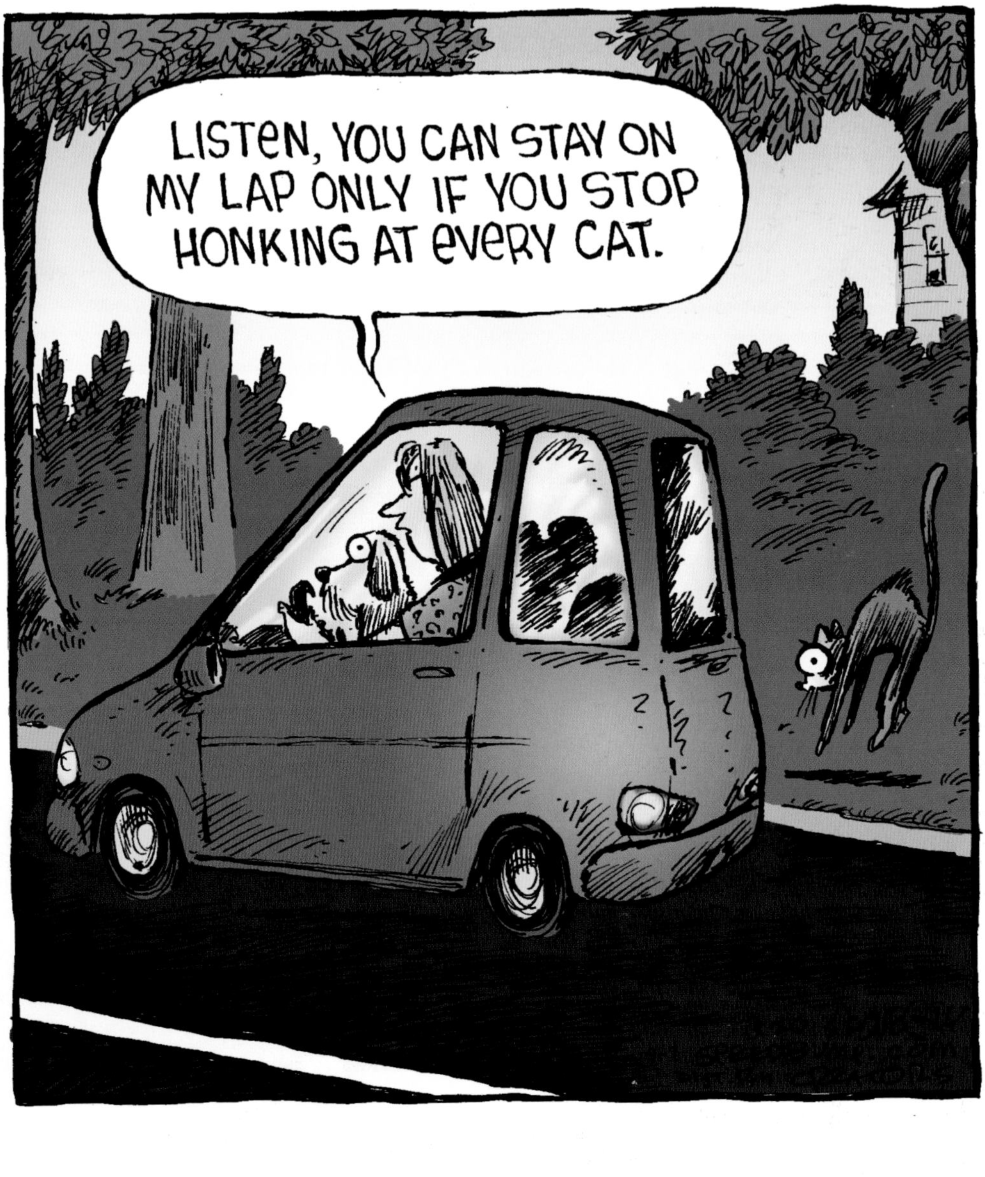
LISTEN, YOU CAN STAY ON MY LAP ONLY IF YOU STOP HONKING AT EVERY CAT.

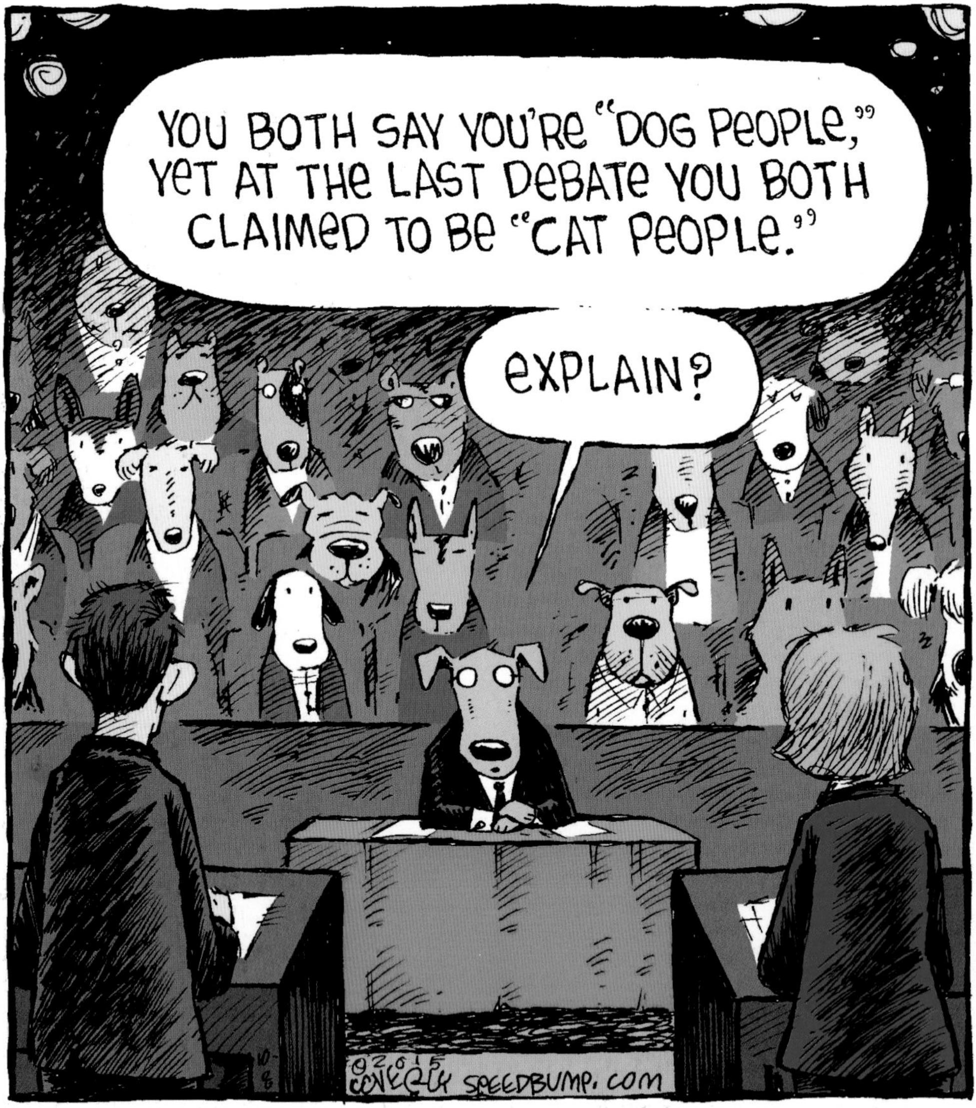

YOU BOTH SAY YOU'RE "DOG PEOPLE," YET AT THE LAST DEBATE YOU BOTH CLAIMED TO BE "CAT PEOPLE."
EXPLAIN?
©2015 COVERLY SPEEDBUMP.COM

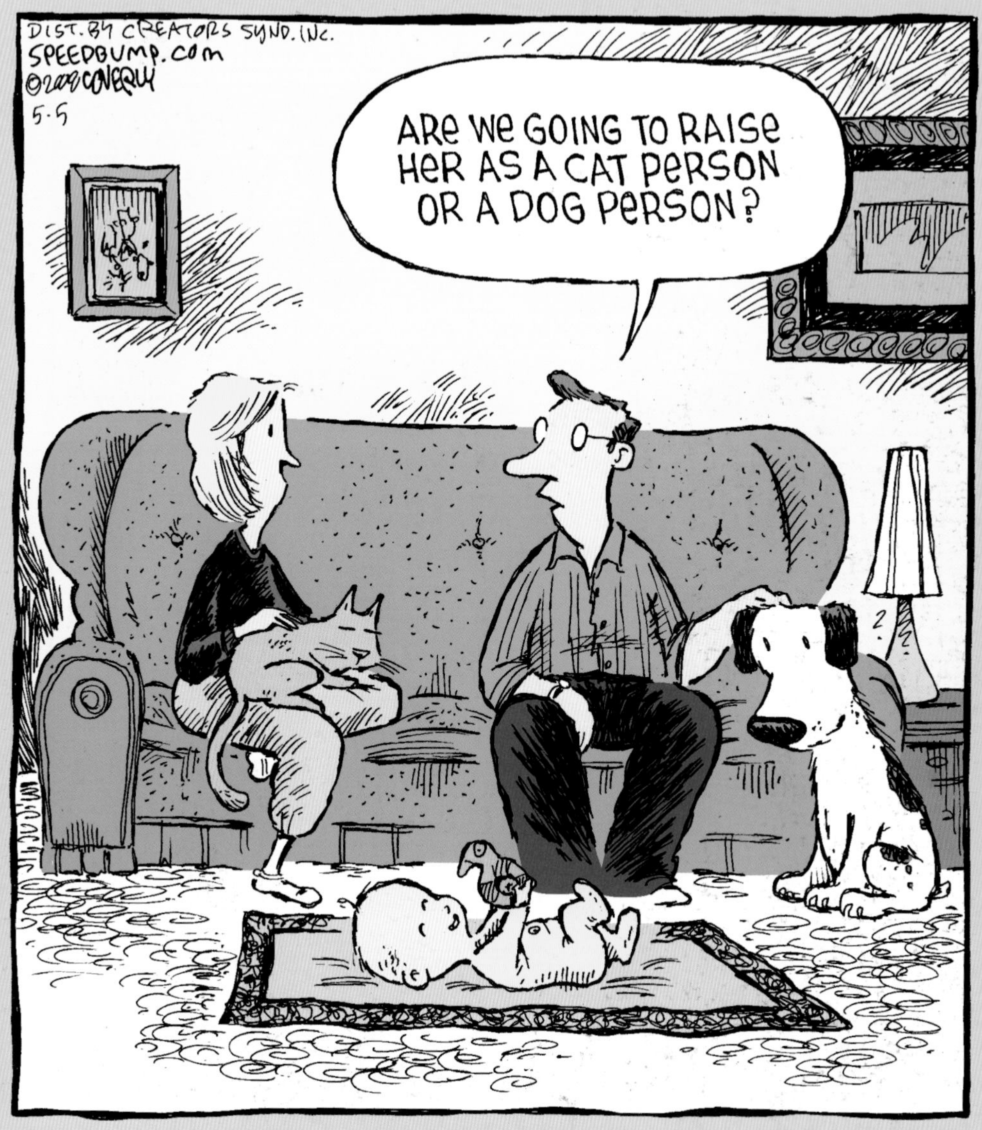
DIST. BY CREATORS SYND. INC.
SPEEDBUMP.COM
©2008 COVERLY
5-5
ARE WE GOING TO RAISE HER AS A CAT PERSON OR A DOG PERSON?

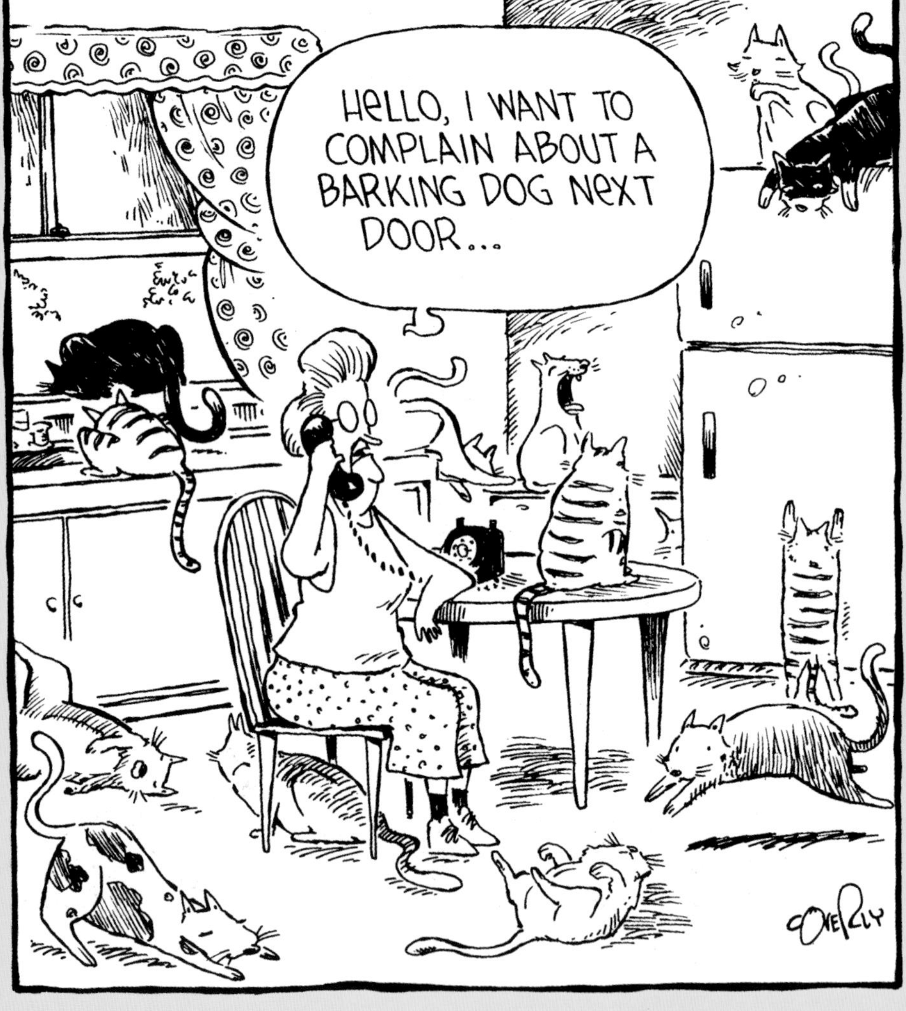
HELLO, I WANT TO COMPLAIN ABOUT A BARKING DOG NEXT DOOR...

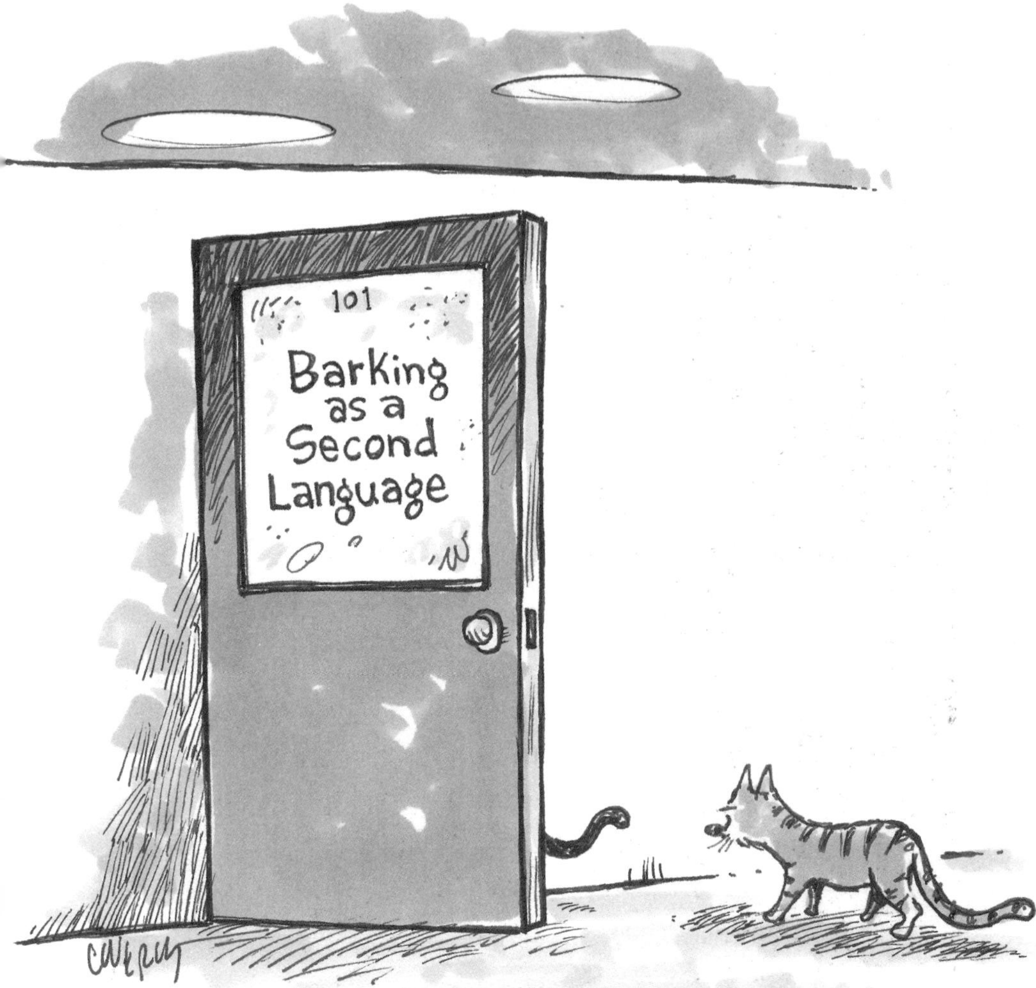
101
Barking as a Second Language

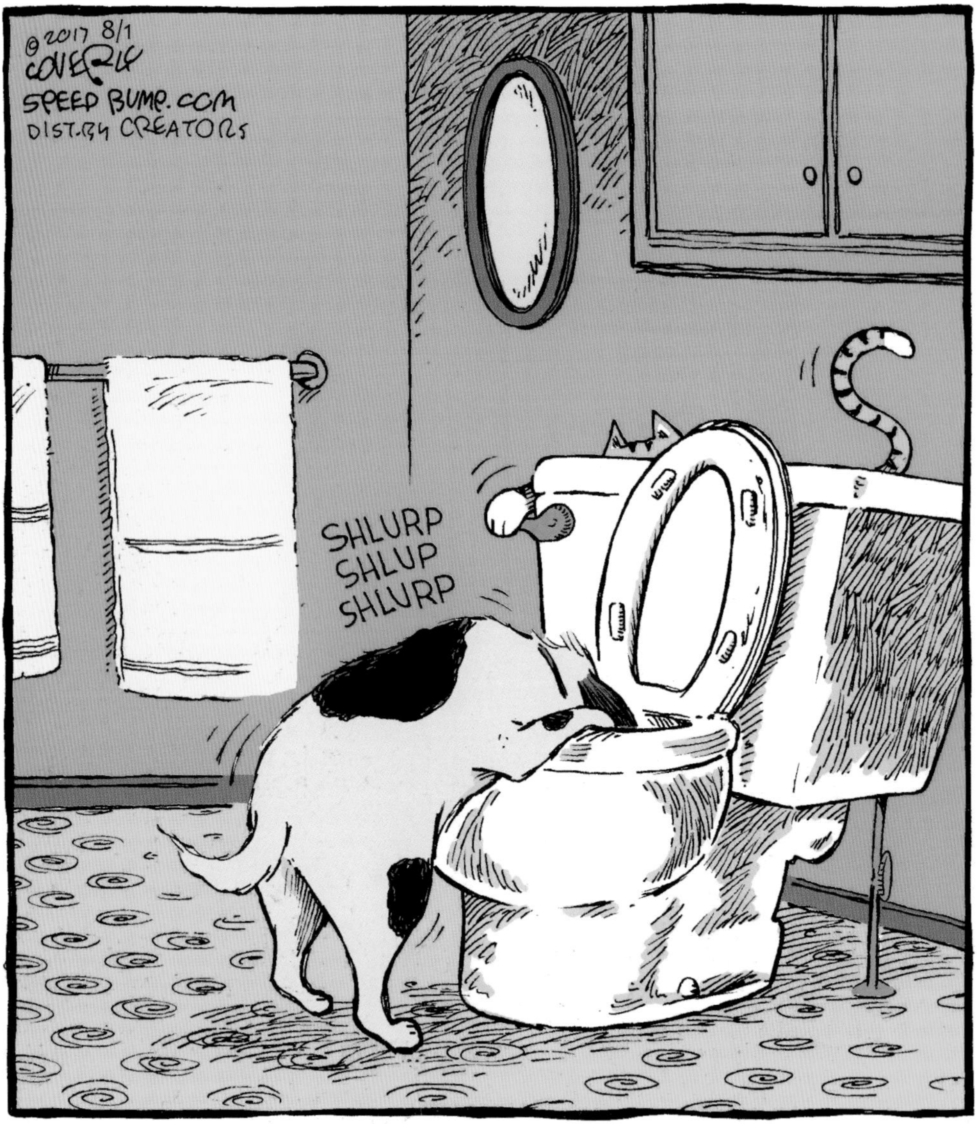
©2017 8/1
COVERLY
SPEEDBUMP.COM
DIST. BY CREATORS
SHLURP
SHLUP
SHLURP

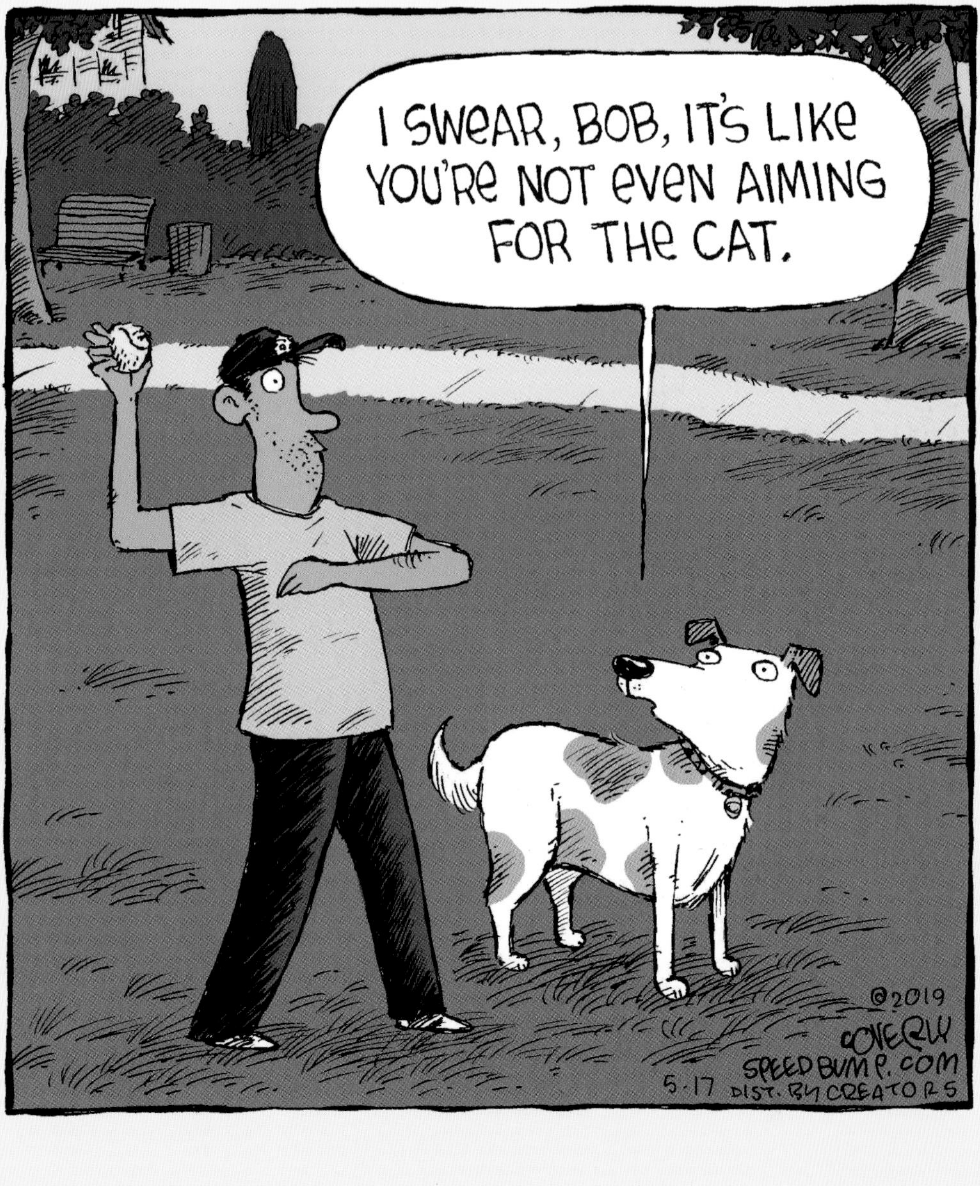
I SWEAR, BOB, IT'S LIKE YOU'RE NOT EVEN AIMING FOR THE CAT.
©2019
COVERLY
SPEEDBUMP.COM
5.17 DIST. BY CREATORS

RICK KIRKMAN

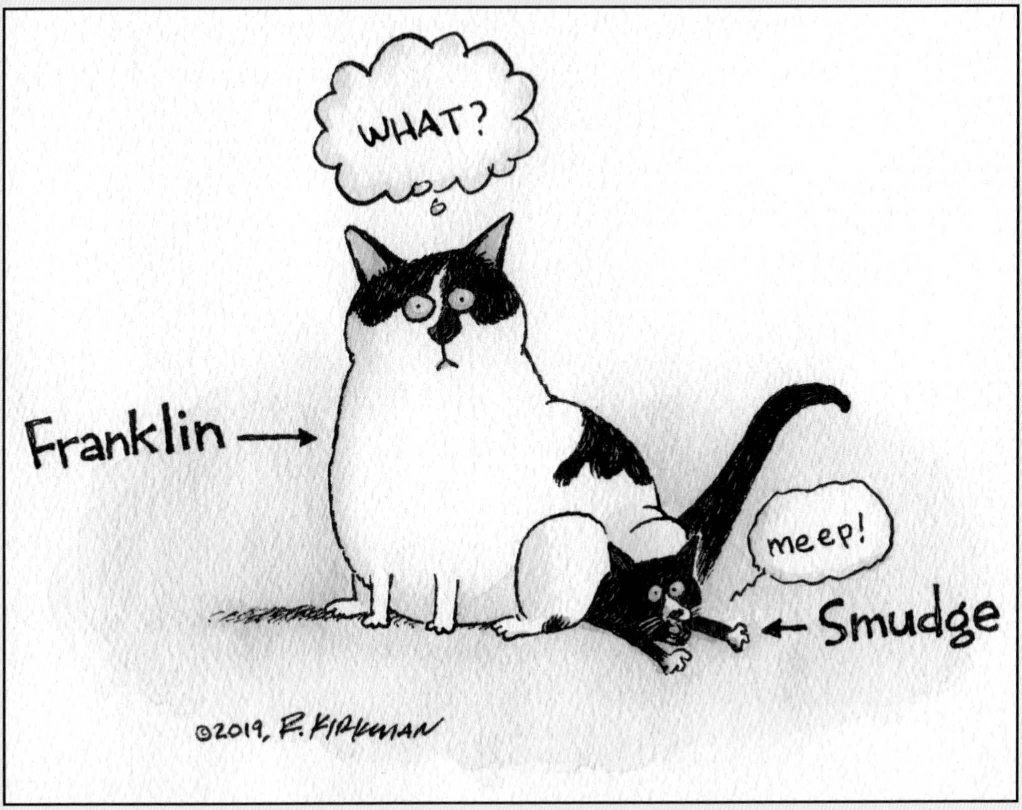
WHAT?
Franklin
meep!
Smudge
©2019, R. KIRKMAN

I was going to write something about these two, but this pretty much tells the story.

About Rick Kirkman

Rick Kirkman was born a poor cartoonist in a log cabin drawn in poor perspective . . . actually, in North Carolina. He was an Air Force brat, attending ten schools in twelve years. He met Jerry Scott in the mid-seventies during Rick's gag cartooning period, and they fantasized about doing a syndicated comic strip together while drawing yellow pages ads. Their collaboration resulted in the creation of the comic strip *Baby Blues*. Jerry writes, Rick draws.

Baby Blues is now syndicated by King Features Syndicate in more than 1200 newspapers. Rick received a Reuben Award for Outstanding Cartoonist of the Year from the National Cartoonists Society in 2012.

Rick lives in the Phoenix area with his family and more cats and dogs than you can shake a stick at. He plays drums and guitar, swims with the dogs, brags about his daughters, and answers Mac tech support questions in his spare time.

babyblues.com

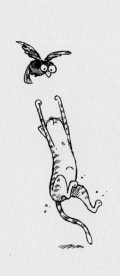

CHAPTER 7
CARTOONS WITHOUT A CAT-EGORY

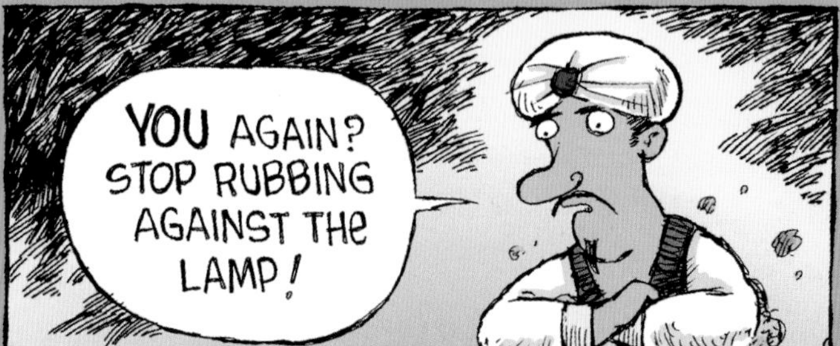
YOU AGAIN? STOP RUBBING AGAINST THE LAMP!
©2015 COVERLY
SPEEDBUMP.COM
12-31 DIST. BY CREATORS

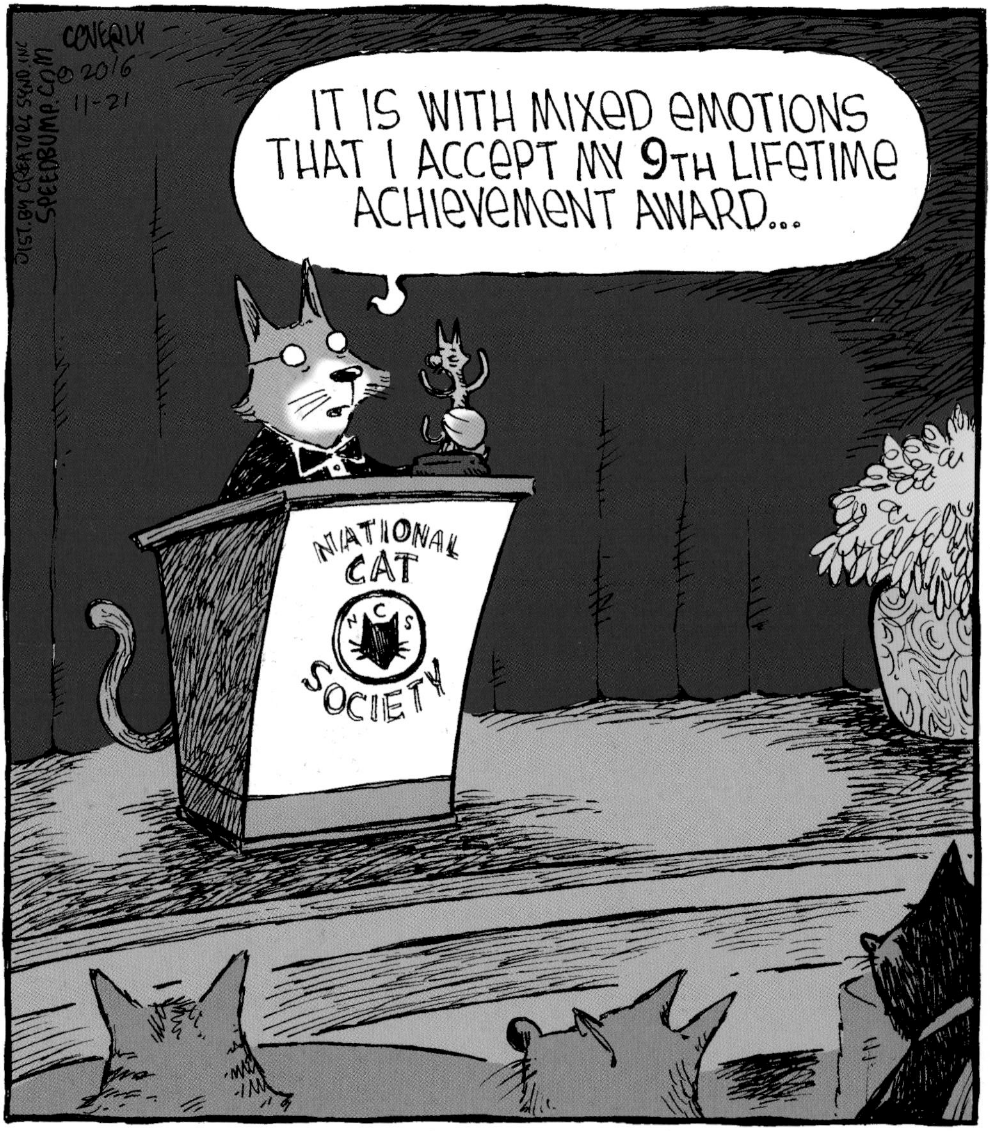
IT IS WITH MIXED EMOTIONS THAT I ACCEPT MY 9TH LIFETIME ACHIEVEMENT AWARD...
NATIONAL CAT SOCIETY
NCS
COVERLY © 2016 11-21
DIST. BY CREATORS SYND. INC
SPEEDBUMP.COM

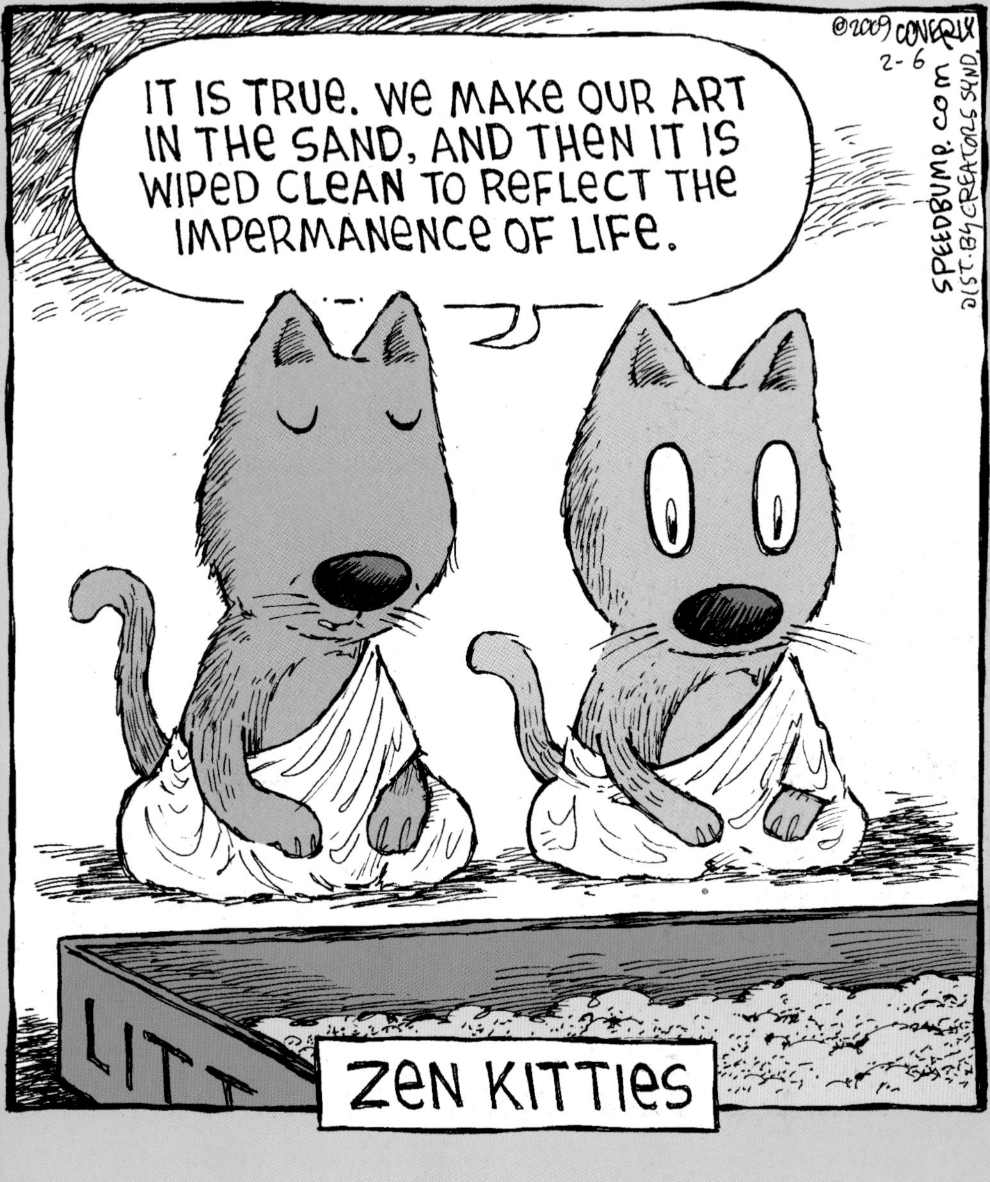
IT IS TRUE. WE MAKE OUR ART IN THE SAND, AND THEN IT IS WIPED CLEAN TO REFLECT THE IMPERMANENCE OF LIFE.
©2009 COVERLY 2-6
SPEEDBUMP.COM
DIST. BY CREATORS SYND.
LITT
ZEN KITTIES

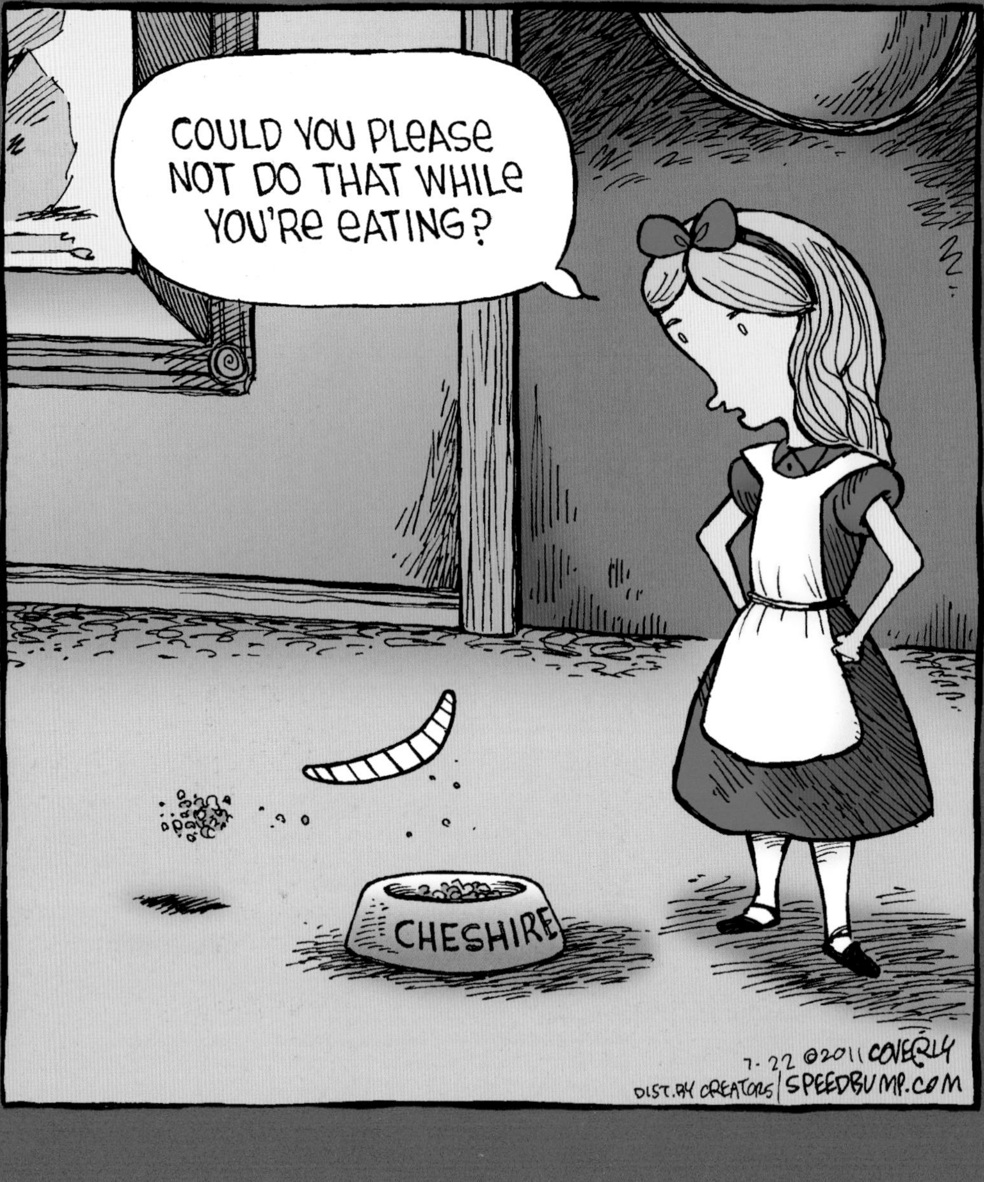
COULD YOU PLEASE NOT DO THAT WHILE YOU'RE EATING?
CHESHIRE
7-22 ©2011 COVERLY
DIST. BY CREATORS | SPEEDBUMP.COM

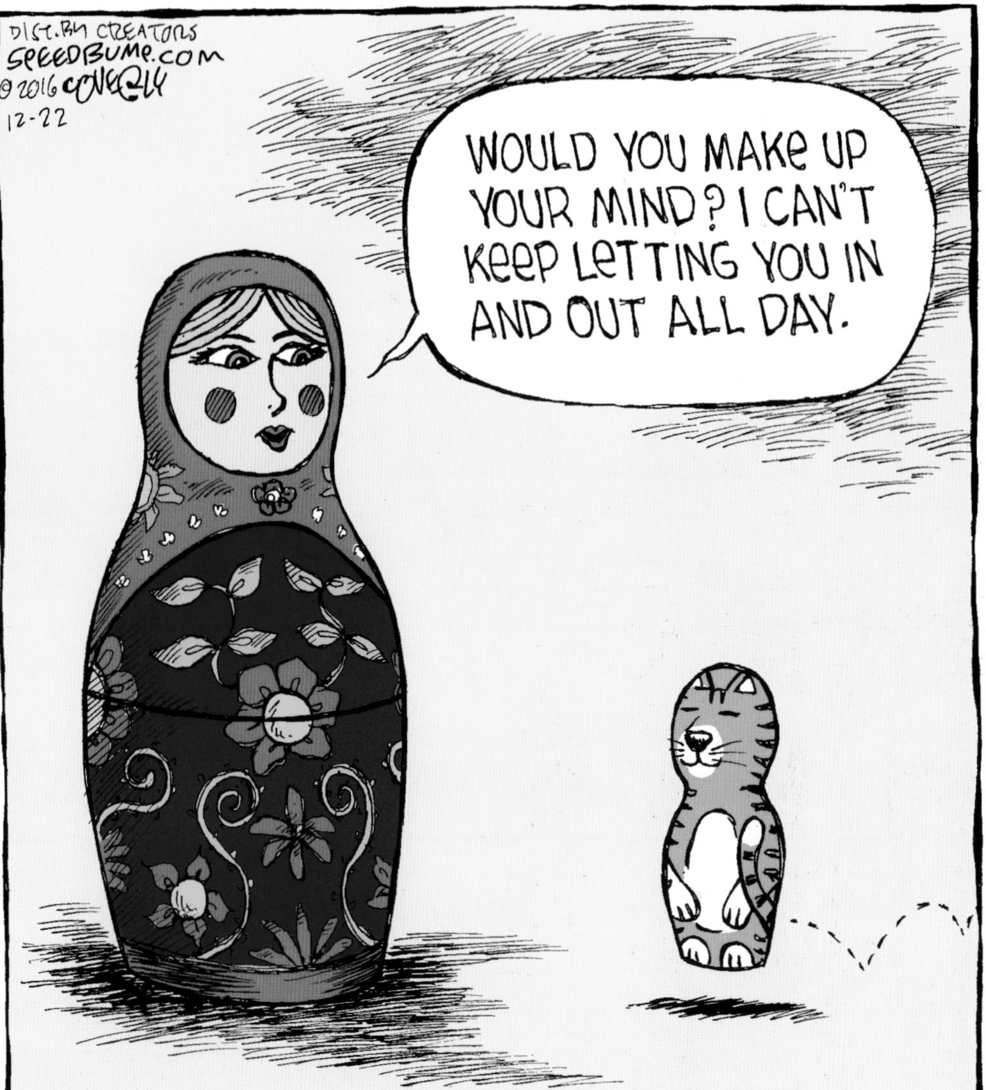
DIST. BY CREATORS
SPEEDBUMP.COM
© 2016 COVERLY
12-22
WOULD YOU MAKE UP YOUR MIND? I CAN'T KEEP LETTING YOU IN AND OUT ALL DAY.

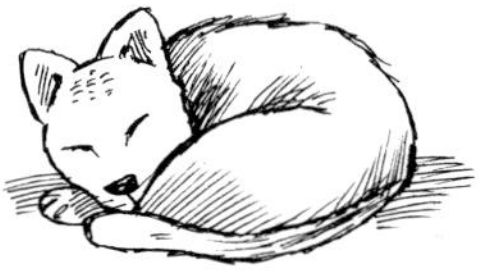

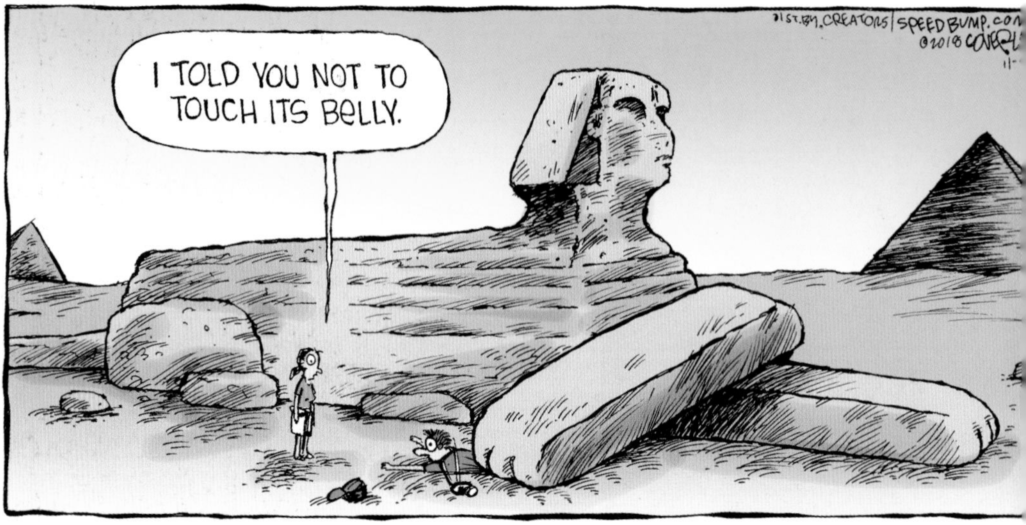
DIST. BY CREATORS
©2018
I TOLD YOU NOT TO TOUCH ITS BeLLY.

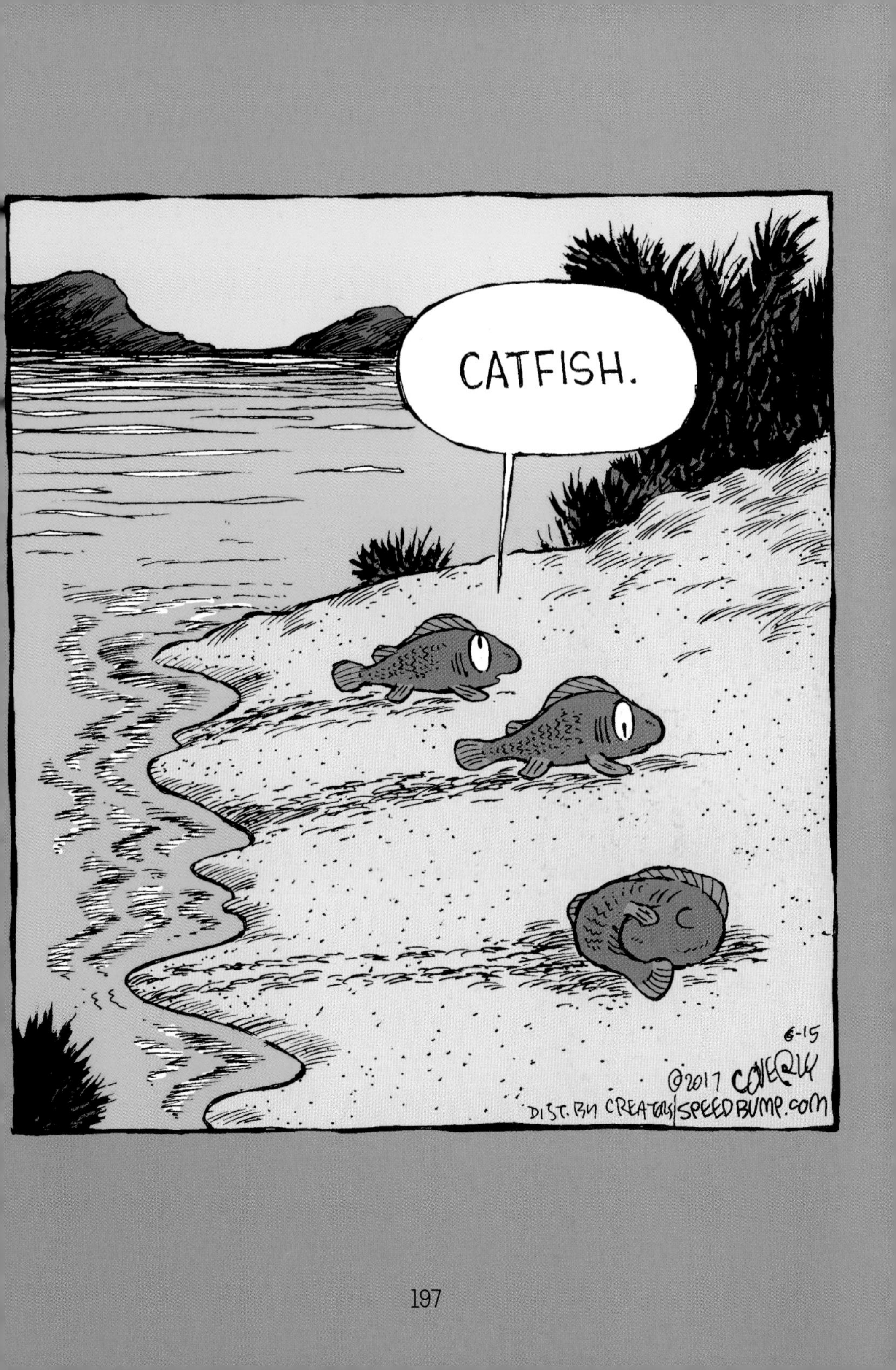
CATFISH.
6-15
©2017 COVERLY
DIST. BY CREATORS | SPEEDBUMP.COM

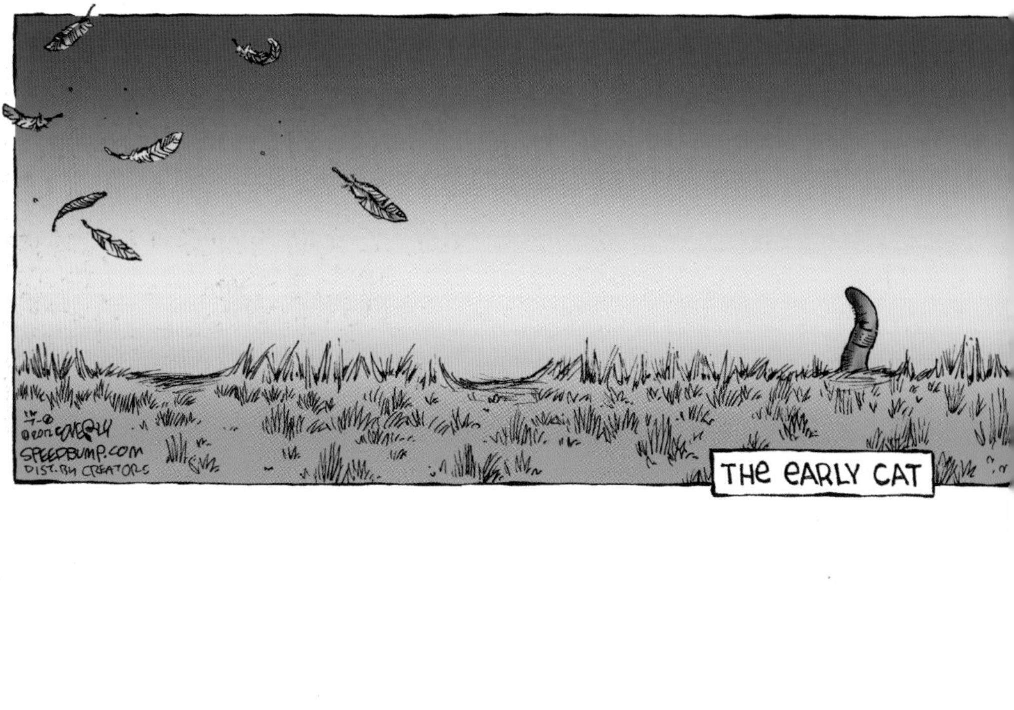
SPEEDBUMP.COM
DIST. BY CREATORS
THE EARLY CAT

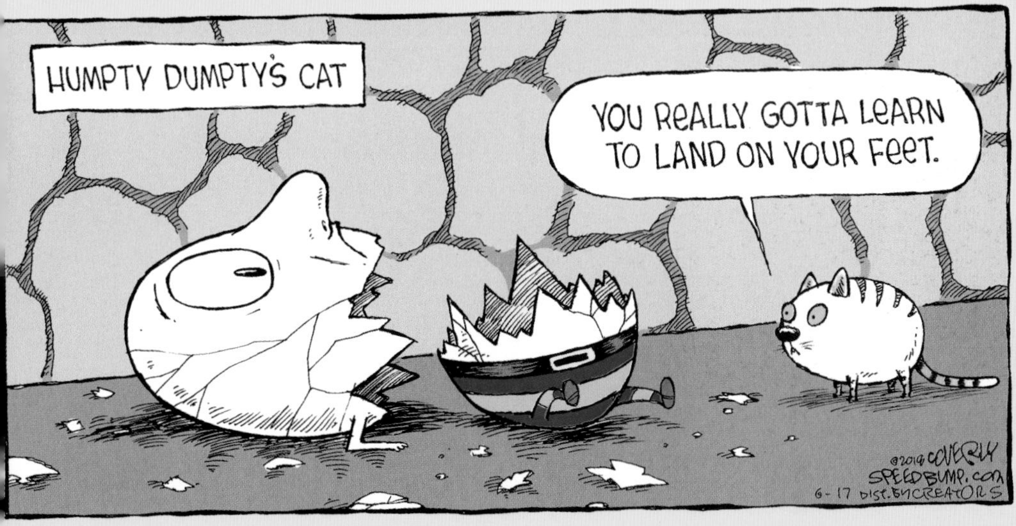
HUMPTY DUMPTY'S CAT
YOU REALLY GOTTA LEARN TO LAND ON YOUR FEET.
©2019 COVERLY
SPEEDBUMP.com
6-17 DIST. BY CREATORS

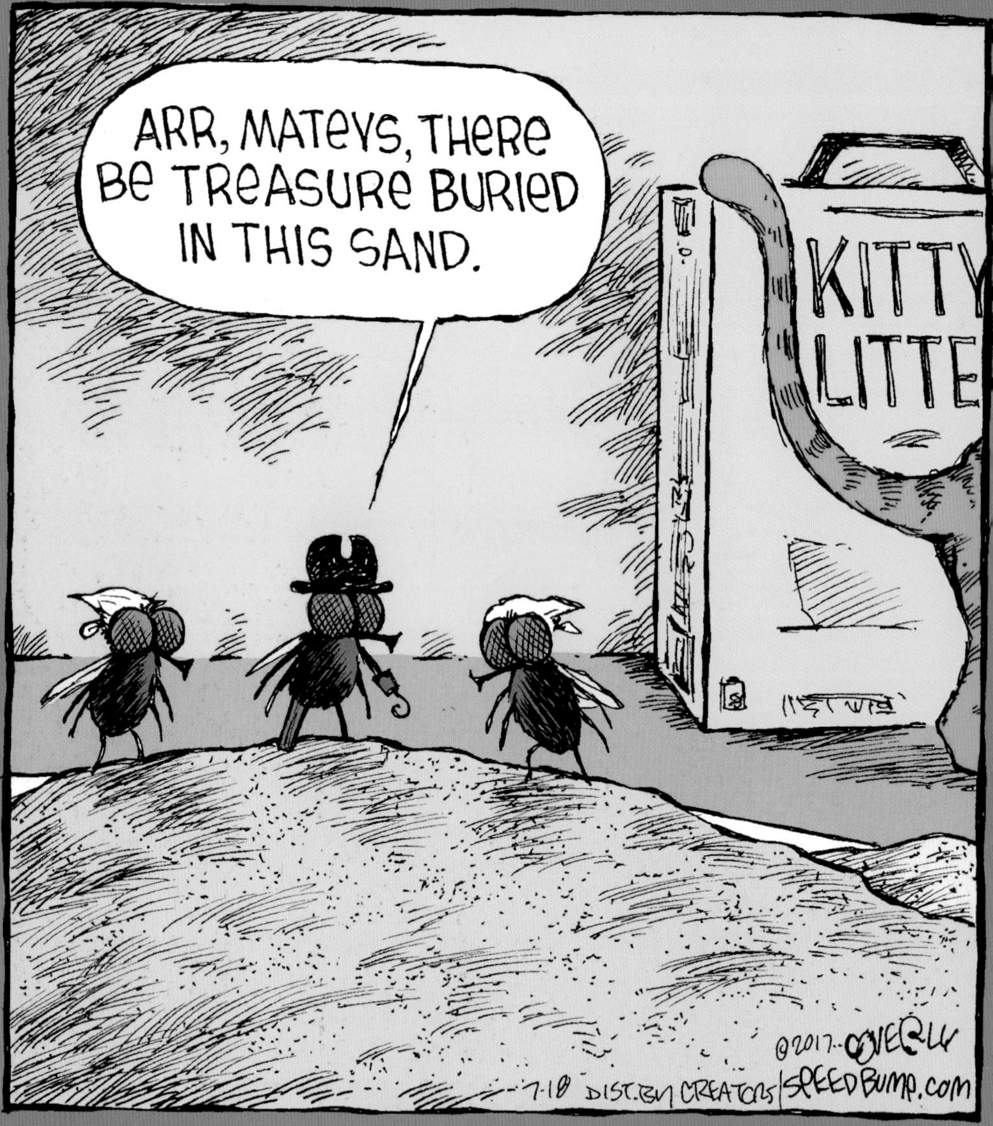
ARR, MATEYS, THERE BE TREASURE BURIED IN THIS SAND.
KITTY LITTE
©2017 DAVE COVERLY
7-18 DIST. BY CREATORS | SPEEDBUMP.COM

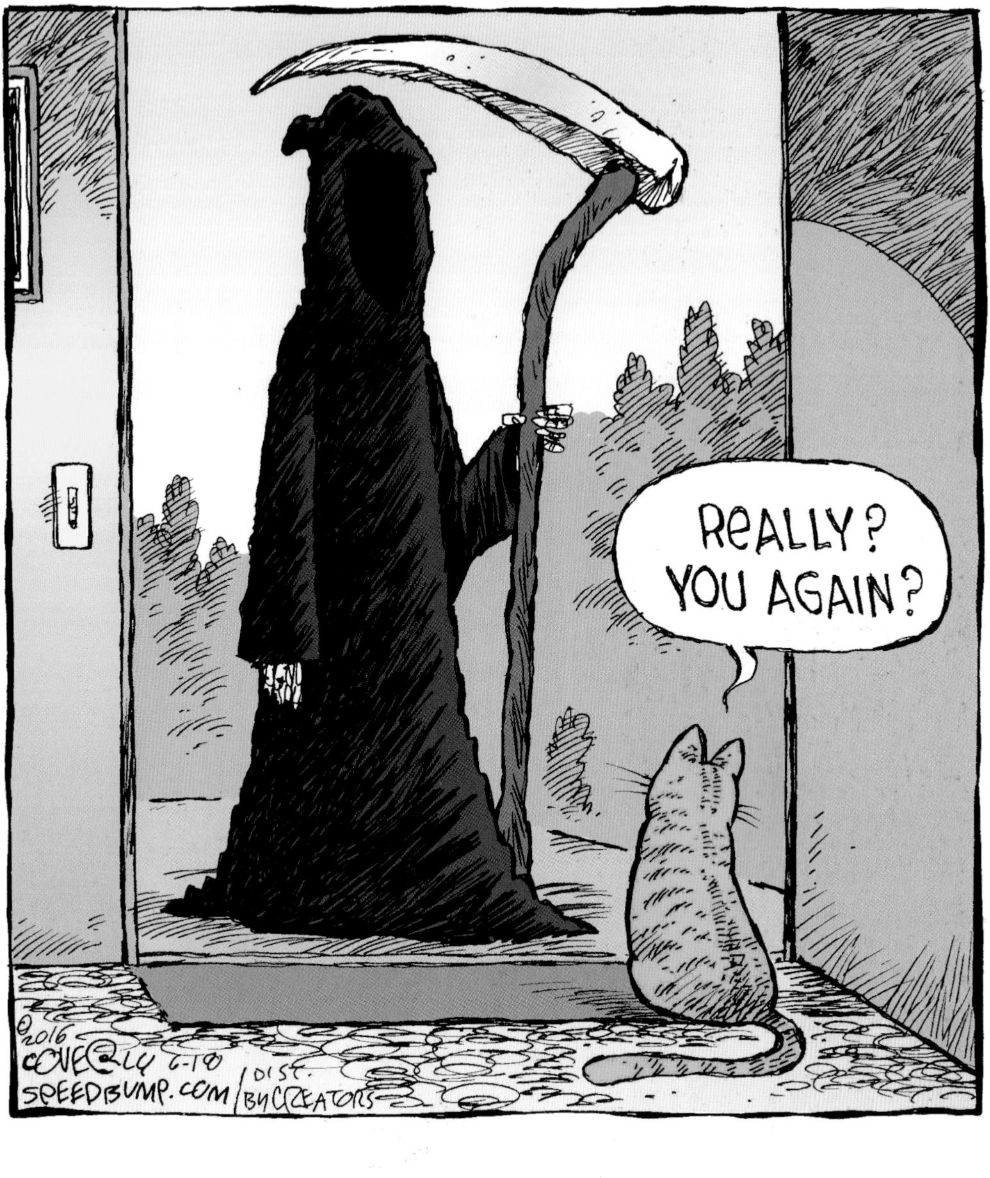
REALLY?
YOU AGAIN?
©2016
COVERLY 6-18
SPEEDBUMP.COM
DIST. BY CREATORS

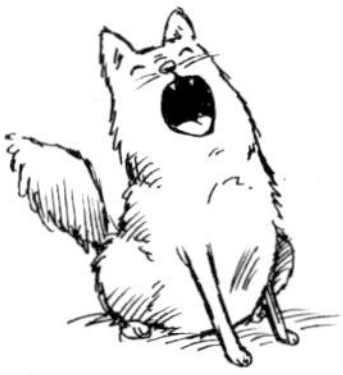

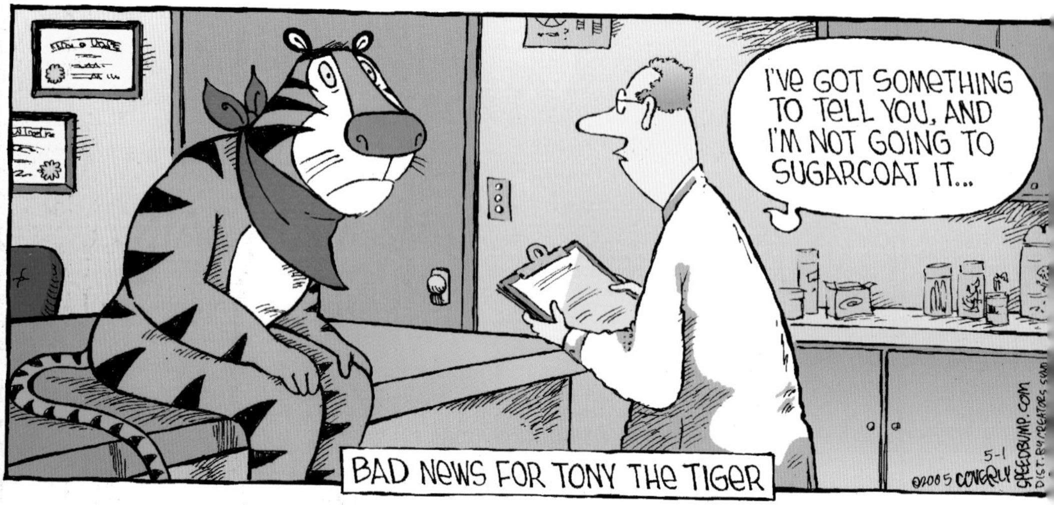
I'VE GOT SOMETHING TO TELL YOU, AND I'M NOT GOING TO SUGARCOAT IT...
BAD NEWS FOR TONY THE TIGER
5-1
©2005 COVERLY
SPEEDBUMP.COM

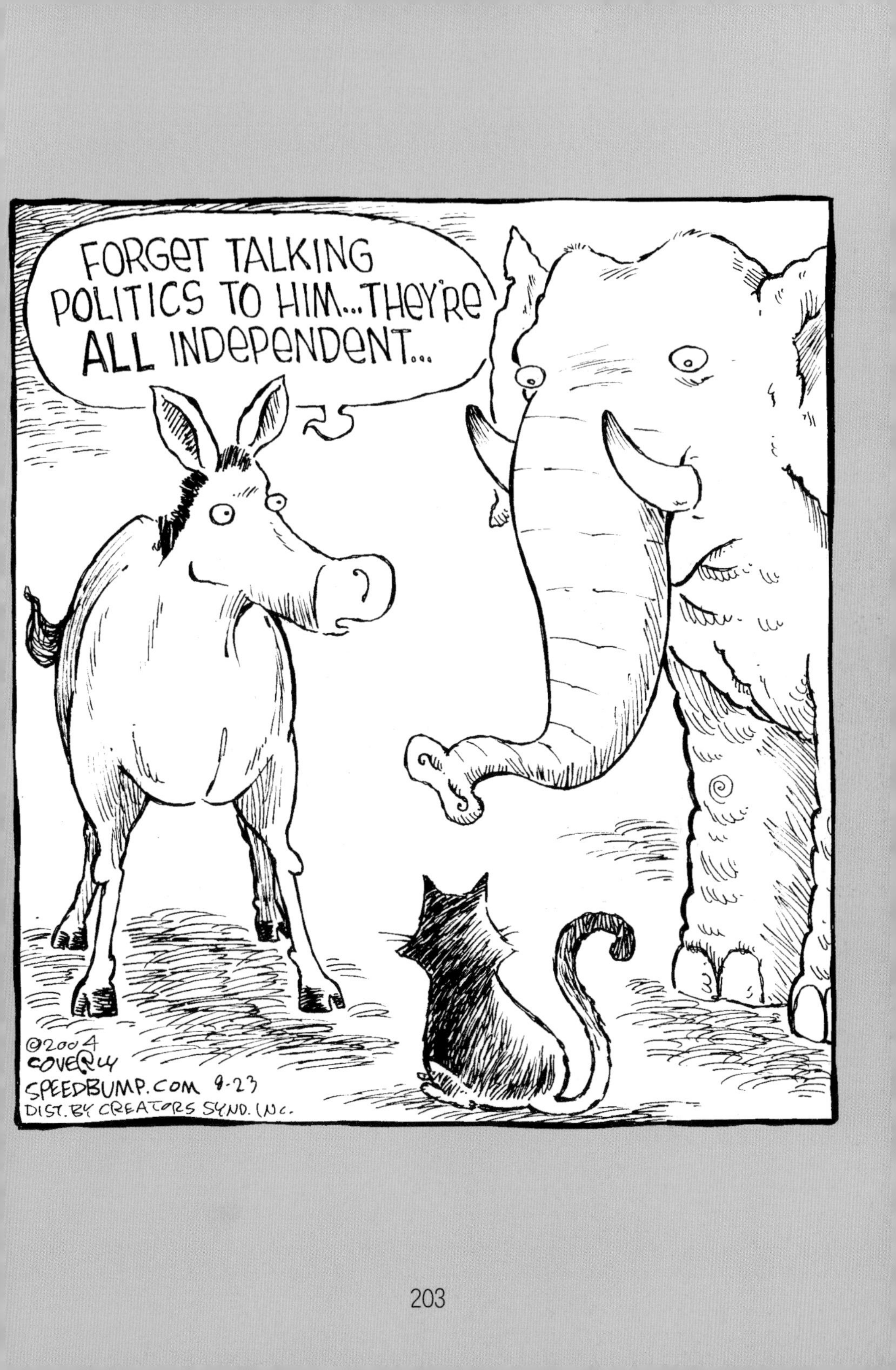
FORGET TALKING POLITICS TO HIM...THEY'RE ALL INDEPENDENT...
©2004
COVERLY
SPEEDBUMP.COM 8-23
DIST. BY CREATORS SYND. INC.

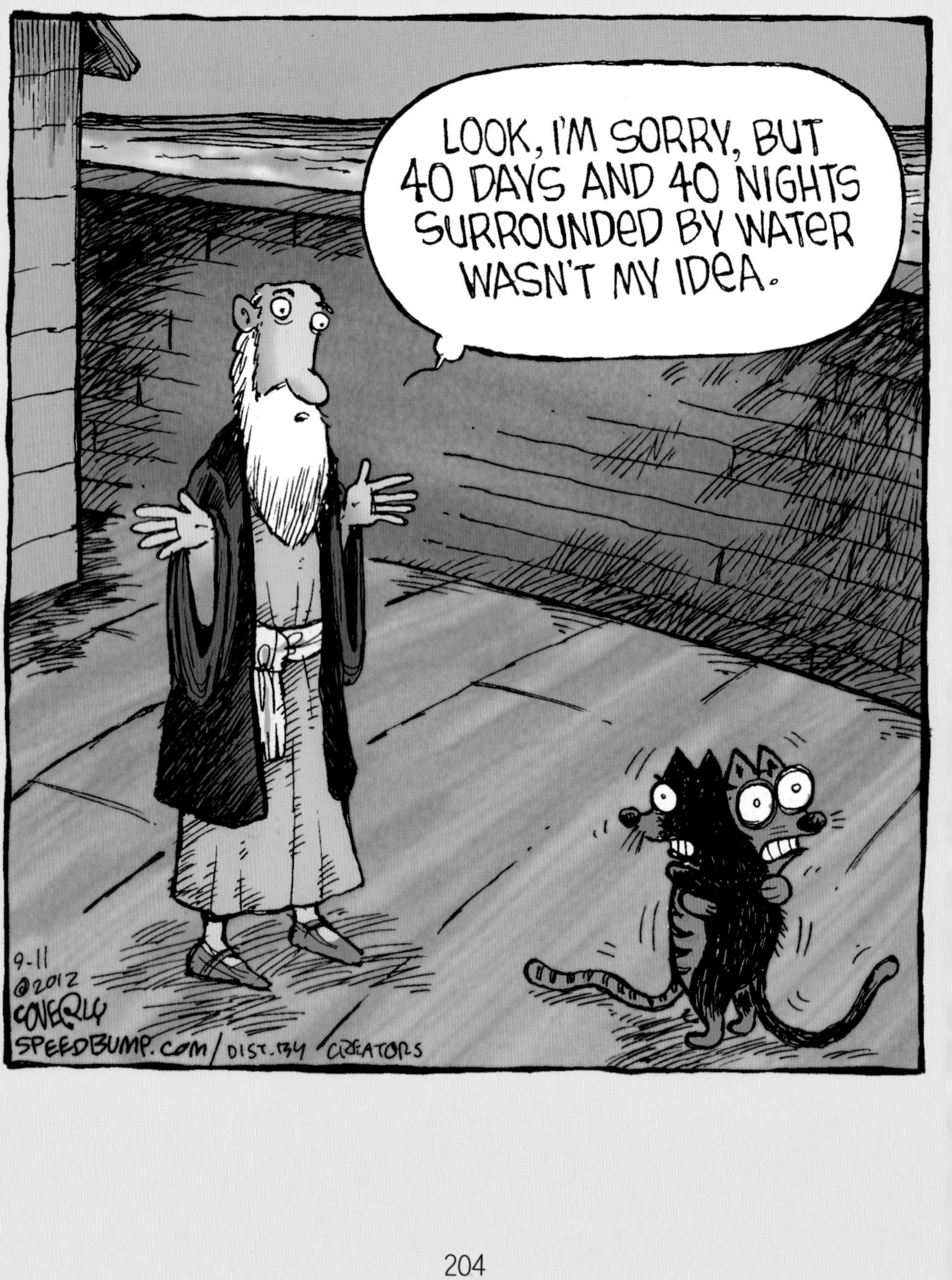
LOOK, I'M SORRY, BUT 40 DAYS AND 40 NIGHTS SURROUNDED BY WATER WASN'T MY IDEA.
9-11
©2012
COVERLY
SPEEDBUMP.COM/DIST. BY CREATORS

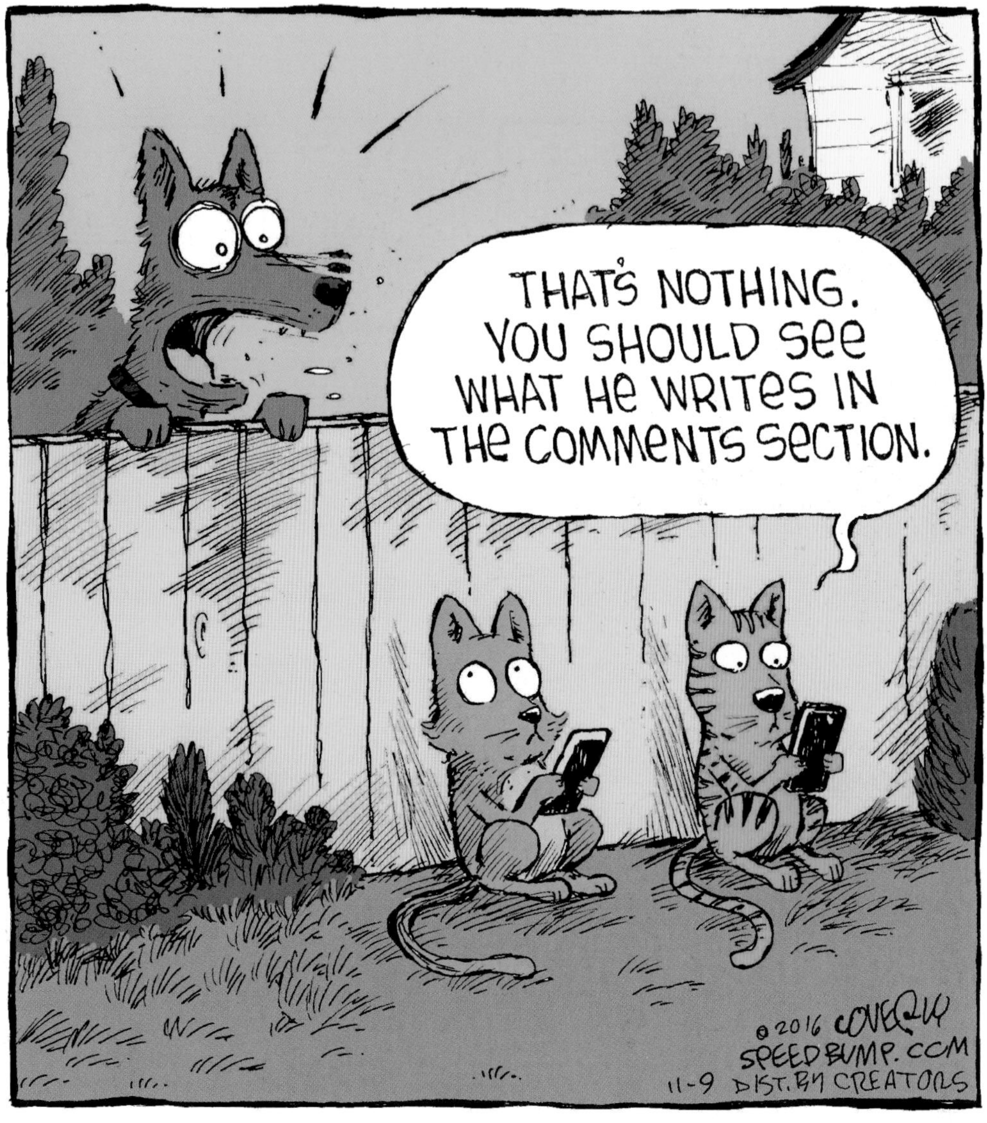
THAT'S NOTHING. YOU SHOULD SEE WHAT HE WRITES IN THE COMMENTS SECTION.
© 2016 COVERLY
SPEEDBUMP.COM
11-9 DIST. BY CREATORS

CAT DOODLES

ALL DOGS GO TO HEAVEN
ALL CATS RUN HEAVEN

can't...reach...

OK, THIS IS NOT WHAT I EXPECTED.
TO KILL A MOCKINGBIRD

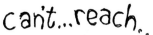

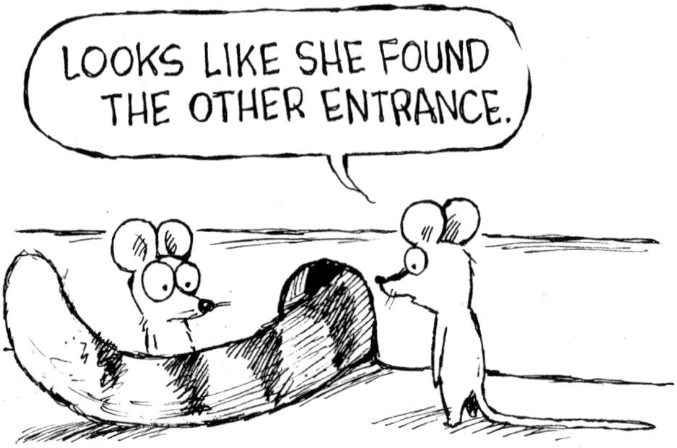
LOOKS LIKE SHE FOUND THE OTHER ENTRANCE.

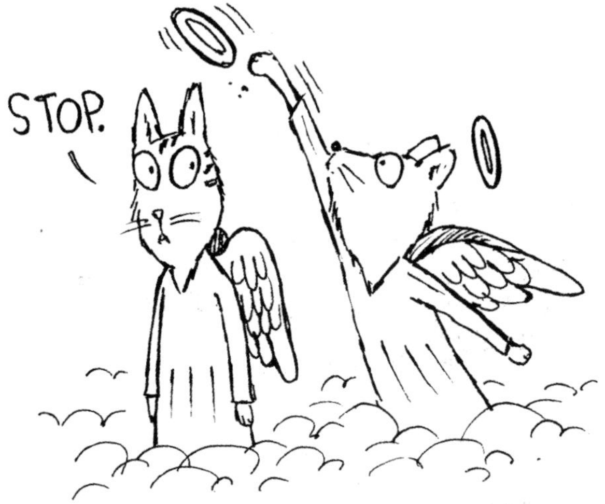
STOP.

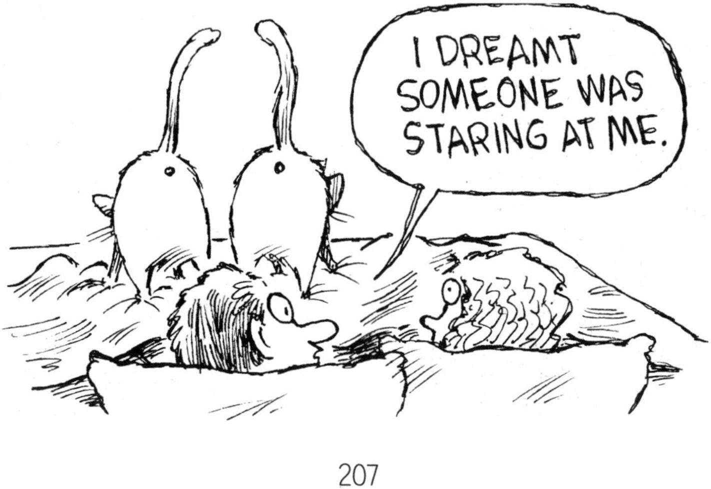
I DREAMT SOMEONE WAS STARING AT ME.

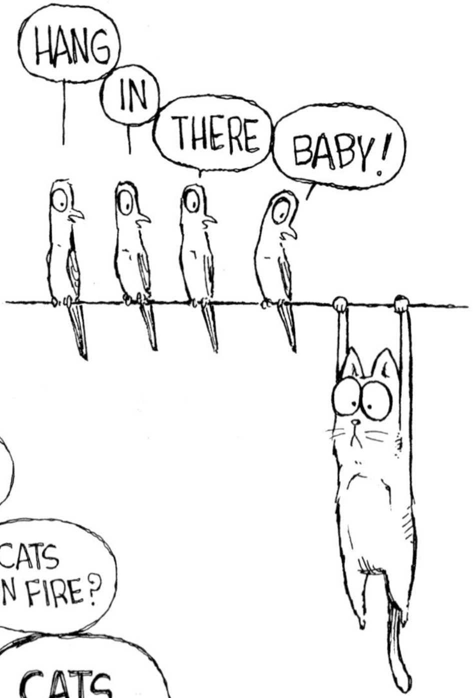
HANG
IN
THERE
BABY!

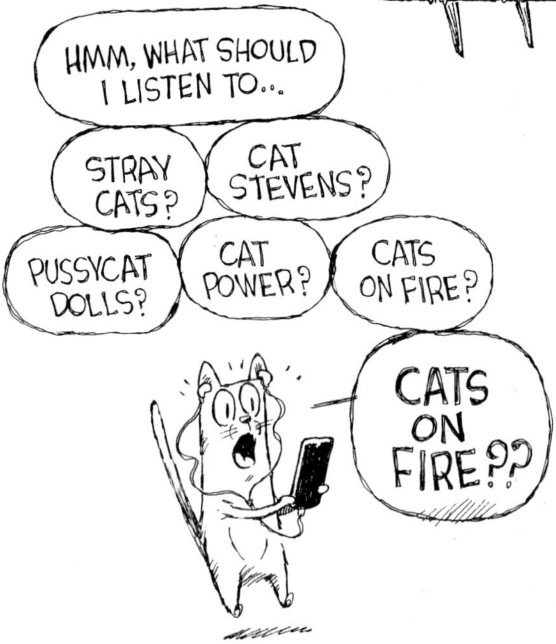
HMM, WHAT SHOULD I LISTEN TO...
STRAY CATS?
CAT STEVENS?
PUSSYCAT DOLLS?
CAT POWER?
CATS ON FIRE?
CATS ON FIRE??

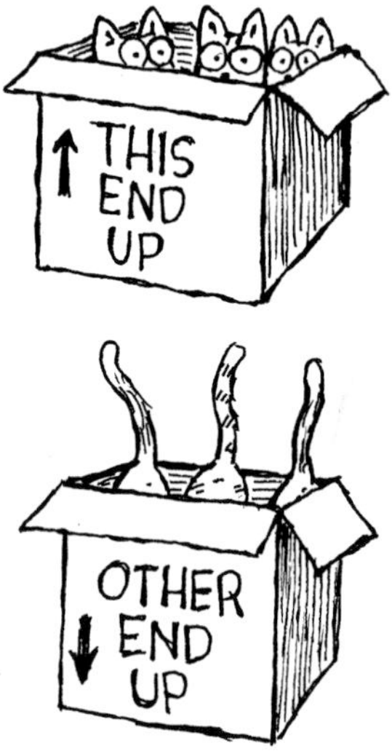
THIS END UP
OTHER END UP

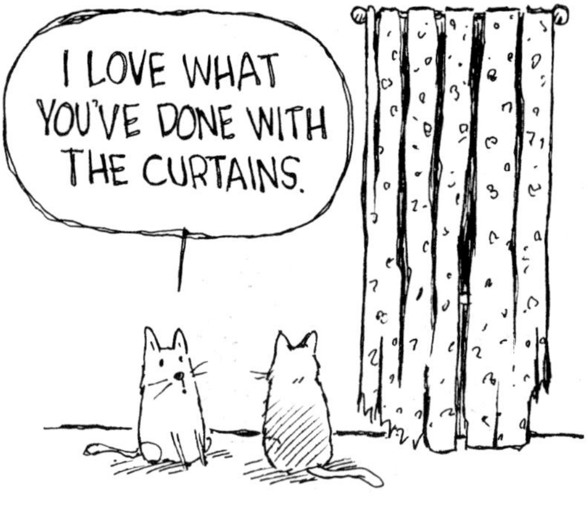
I LOVE WHAT YOU'VE DONE WITH THE CURTAINS.